Simplicity Parenting

By Kim John Payne

Games Children Play

Simplicity Parenting

Beyond Winning
(with Luis Fernando Llosa
and Scott Lancaster)

The Soul of Discipline

Simplicity Parenting

KIM JOHN PAYNE, M.Ed.
with LISA M. ROSS

Ballantine Books Trade Paperbacks
New York

2010 Ballantine Books Trade Paperback Edition

Published in the United States by Ballantine Books,
an imprint of The Random House Publishing Group,
a division of Random House, Inc., New York.

Originally published in hardcover in the United States by
Ballantine Books, an imprint of The Random House Publishing Group,
a division of Random House, Inc., in 2009.

ISBN 978-0-345-50798-3

Printed in the United States of America

www.ballantinebooks.com

18 20 21 19 17

Book design by Mary A. Wirth

To Katharine, the love of my life,
and to Saphira and Johanna, the loves of our lives

— K.J.P.

For Adair and Jack

— L.M.R.

Contents

Introduction

Go confidently in the direction of your dreams.
As you simplify life the laws of the universe will be simpler.

—HENRY DAVID THOREAU

As parents, we're the architects of our family's daily lives. We build a structure for those we love by what we choose to do together, and how we do it. We determine the rhythms of our days; set a pace. There are certainly limits to our control. . . . Ask any parent of a teenager. And it often feels that our lives are controlling us, caught as we are in a mad rush from one responsibility to another. Yet the unique way that we perform this dance of daily activities says a lot about who we are as a family.

You can see what a family holds dear from the pattern of their everyday lives. I've been trained to do so as a counselor and educator, but children need no such fancy training. They pick up the clues naturally. They see the golden overlay on all of our comings and goings, all of our tasks and busyness. This is what they see: With our time and presence we give love. Simple.

And they're quite right; as parents our motivations and intentions are few, our dreams nearly universal. No matter where, no matter how modestly or grandly we live, most of us want what is best for our loved ones. From these few common motivations—love, and the desire to protect and provide for our children—we build families. Every day.

As parents we carry the blueprints, the dreams of what our family could be. The plans change, the whole thing goes way over budget, there are unexpected additions, and the work never ends. Still, through the messiness of construction we see one another with such depth and hope. Our five-year-old boy is still so clearly the baby he once was and sometimes—can you see it?—the young man he will one day be. We draw energy and inspiration from our dreams; our simple, common motivations.

In their development, we can see the extent to which our children feel protected. Surrounded by those they love, they make extraordinary leaps, fantastic moments of revelation and mastery. At our urging or prodding? Never. In flashes they show us who they are . . . revealing their golden, essential selves. And as parents we live for such moments. But we can't schedule them. We can't ask for, or hurry them.

We want our family to be a container of security and peace, where we can be our true selves. We want this most urgently for our children, who are engaged in the slow and tricky business of becoming themselves. Will our love and guidance give them the grace they need to grow? Children are so clearly happiest when they have the time and space to explore their worlds, at play. We may be bouncing between the future and the past, yet our children—the little Zen masters—long to stay suspended, fully engaged, in the moment. Our very best hope is that they'll develop their own voices, their own instincts and resiliency, at their own pace. And despite how many times we forget—sometimes in a single day—we absolutely know that this will take time.

The rest and rejuvenation we want from our homes is getting harder to find. Our work lives have moved in, taking residency in our computers, finding us wherever a phone or pager signal can reach. Children are overbooked as well. While parents may need software programs to keep track of their kids' activities and schedules, developmental psychologist David Elkind notes that children have lost more than twelve hours of free time a week in the past two decades.[1] When "multitasking" is valued as a survival skill, should we be surprised when increasing numbers of our children are being "diagnosed" with "attention difficulties"?

In every aspect of our lives, no matter how trivial, we are confronted with a dizzying array of things (stuff) and choices. The weighing of dozens of brands, features, claims, sizes, and prices, together with the memory scan we do for any warnings or concerns we may have heard; all of this enters into scores of daily decisions. Too much stuff and too many choices. If we're overwhelmed as adults, imagine how our children feel! Whichever came first—too many choices or too much stuff—the end result of both is not happiness. Contrary to everything advertising tells us (but obvious to anyone who has chosen a cellular calling plan), too many choices can be overwhelming. Another form of stress. Not only can it eat away at our time, studies show that having lots of choices can erode our motivation and well-being.

Also finding its way into our homes, lives, and our children's awareness is an avalanche of information, unfiltered and often unbidden. Home used to be a parochial outpost, and the outside world "the big unknown." Parents had trouble conveying all of the information that their children might need to face life "in the real world," beyond the confines of home and neighborhood. Today, "the real world," in all of its graphic reality, is available for view anytime, any place, via the Internet. Our responsibility as gatekeepers is becoming exponentially more difficult even as it's becoming more critical.

You've heard about how a frog dropped into a pot of boiling water will struggle to get out? Nothing surprising there, but it turns out that if you put a frog in a pot of cold water, and slowly heat it to the boiling point, the frog will remain still, without any signs of struggle. Based on the families I've been privileged to work with, the hundreds of parents who've shared with me their concerns, and my own experience as a parent, I believe that the pot we're in today as families is increasingly inhospitable for us all . . . but especially for our children.

Are we building our families on the four pillars of "too much": too much stuff, too many choices, too much information, and too fast? I believe that we are. But I also believe that we don't mean to be. I know for a fact, and I've seen it many times, that parents can bring fresh inspiration and attention to the flow of family life. Without a doubt, as the family's architects we can add a little more space and grace, a little less speed and clutter to our children's daily lives.

My experience with many, many kids and families has helped me figure out ways to reduce the stresses, distractions, and choices—all forms of clutter—in children's lives. I've seen how effective these strategies can be in restoring a child's sense of ease and well-being. This book is about realigning our daily lives with the pace and promise of childhood. Realigning our real lives with the dreams we hold for our families. Its goal is to help you strip away many of the unnecessary, distracting, and overwhelming elements that are scattering our children's attention and burdening their spirits.

To have moments of calm—creative or restful—is a form of deep sustenance for human beings of all ages. Relationships are often built in these pauses, in the incidental moments, when nothing much is going on. This book should give you many ideas on how to reclaim such intervals, how to establish for your children islands of "being" in the torrent of constant doing.

If, as a society, we are embracing speed, it is partially because we are swimming in anxiety. Fed this concern and that worry, we're running as fast as we can to avoid problems and sidestep danger. We address parenting with the same anxious gaze, rushing from this "enrichment opportunity" to that, sensing hidden germs and new hazards, all while doing our level best to provide our children with every advantage now known or soon to be invented. This book is not about hidden dangers, quick fixes, or limited-time opportunities; it is about the long haul. The big picture: a reverence for childhood.

When we act out of reverence, instead of fear, our motivation is stronger, our inspiration boundless. The good news is that there are many things we can do as parents to protect the environment of childhood. To protect the ideal environment for the slow emergence of their identities, resilience, and well-being.

Many of the concepts in this book have their roots in the principles of Waldorf education. One of the most-used forms of independent education worldwide, Waldorf schools emphasize the imagination and the development of the whole child—the heart and hands as well as the head.

The simplification regime outlined in this book is eminently doable, by any family with the inclination and motivation. The steps I outline in this book should be considered as a menu, not a checklist, from which you can choose what is workable and sustainable for your own family. Each family will have its own issues, areas of emphasis, and levels of commitment. There is no "right" order in which to work through the different levels, and no right or wrong time to begin.

The four layers of simplification will serve as a road map as you navigate your own way; each layer will be addressed in detail in the chapters ahead. In Chapter One we'll look at the reasons why simplifying is so critical and effective. We'll also consider how to reclaim the dreams you hold for your family, as these will be your motivation going forward. A short meditation on parental instincts, reminding you (before we get into the practical "work" of simplifying) of what you already know, Chapter Two will help you recognize and address the "overload" in your children in much the way you might do when a little one has a physical fever.

Chapter Three begins at the doorway to your child's bedroom, as we begin to reduce the clutter of too many toys, books, and choices.

Rhythm is another form of simplification, which we'll address in Chapter Four. A more rhythmic daily life establishes beachheads, small islands of calm and predictability in the flow of time. We'll look at how meals and bedtimes can establish the major chords of a day's melody, and consider other possibilities for notes and pauses that a child can count on along the way.

From rhythm we'll look deeper into the pattern of our children's days to consider their schedules. In Chapter Five we'll see how to balance particularly active days with calmer ones, challenging the notion that "free time" means "free to be filled" with lessons, practices, playdates, and appointments. The principle that too much stuff and too many choices is problematic for children can be applied to most aspects of daily life. In Chapter Six we'll consider ways to filter out adult information and concerns from our homes, and our children's awareness. We'll look at parental involvement, and the ties that bind us to our children, ties that must stretch without breaking, as a child circles out and back again, on toward independence. We'll consider ways to simplify our parental involvement and "back out" of hyperparenting, by building a sense of security for our children that they internalize and carry with them as they grow. We'll learn new ways to simplify our involvement, increase our trust, and allow connection rather than anxiety to characterize the relationship we build with our children.

It is never "too late" to bring inspiration and attention to the flow of family life. Parents of young children will find many seeds here to plant toward a family life that continues to protect and nurture as children grow. But every stage in a family's evolution can benefit from a little more space and grace, a little less speed and clutter. Another point to remember, as we begin, is that simplification is often about "doing" less, and trusting more. Trusting that—if they have the time and security—children will explore their worlds in the way, and at the pace, that works best for them.

In my descriptions of how I worked with other families you'll see what might work for your own. No "expert" is required. In reading the stories I share along the way, you'll have moments of recognition and inspiration. My hope is that you will come back to this book and continue to draw ideas and encouragement from it as your children grow.

While your daily life may seem like a radio bandwidth full of static, simplification allows you, with much more regularity and clarity, to tune into your own true signal as a parent. I think you'll find it very gratifying to feel your inner authenticity develop as you bring more awareness and attention to your relationship with your children. And with this process comes more opportunities to see deeply into who your children are becoming.

I sincerely hope this book will inspire you—give you hope, comfort, insights, and ideas—now, and as your children grow.

Simplicity Parenting

ONE

Why Simplify?

We are facing an enormous problem in our lives today. It's so big we can hardly see it, and it's right in front of our face all day, every day. We're all living too big lives, crammed from top to toe with activities, urgencies, and obligations that seem absolute. There's no time to take a breath, no time to look for the source of the problem.

—SARAH SUSANKA, *THE NOT SO BIG LIFE*

James was about eight years old, and entering third grade, when I met his parents. Lovely and very bright people, James's mother was a professor and his father was involved in city government. They were worried about their son having trouble sleeping at night, and his complaints of stomachaches. An eight-year-old boy is fairly well designed to be a picky eater, but James's pickiness was getting extreme. His stomachaches came and went, but they didn't seem food related.

Both parents spoke proudly of how confidently James could speak with adults, but acknowledged that he had trouble connecting with his peers. He avoided things that he felt might be dangerous, and had only very recently learned to ride a bike. "And don't forget the driving thing," his mother mentioned. James's father explained that whenever they drove someplace, James would be the self-appointed policeman in the backseat, letting them know when they were even one or two miles above the speed limit, scanning the road ahead for concerns of any kind. The term "backseat driver" didn't come close to describing his behavior; you can well imagine how relaxing these road trips were.

As I got to know the family, I noticed how much their daily lives were colored by world issues. Both parents were avid news followers. The television was often on and tuned to CNN, whether they were directly focused on it or not. Politically and intellectually oriented, they would discuss issues at great length, particularly environmental concerns. From an early age, James had been listening to these conversations. His parents were proud of his knowledge. They felt that they were raising a little activist, a "citizen of the world," who would grow up informed and concerned.

James's understanding of global warming seemed to rival Al Gore's. That much was apparent. James was also, clearly, becoming a very anxious little fellow. His parents and I worked together on a simplification regime. We made some changes in the home environment and greatly increased the sense of rhythm and predictability in their daily life patterns. But our primary focus was on cutting back James's involvement in his parents' intellectual lives, and his access to information.

How much information was pouring into the house and into James's awareness? Instead of three computers in the house, his parents decided to keep one, in the den off the master bedroom. After much discussion, they actually removed both televisions from the home. They felt that this might be harder on them than it would be on James, and they wanted to test their theory. If there were to be sacrifices, they wanted to bear their share of them. They also realized that the TVs had become mainly sources of background noise in their home. Would they be missed or not? Game Boys and Xboxes were also removed, minimizing the number of screens throughout the house.

I was most impressed, however, by the commitment they made to change some very ingrained habits. Quite bravely, I thought, they aimed to keep their discussion of politics, their jobs, and their concerns to a time after James went to bed. This was hard to do at first, and they had to remind each other frequently to refrain from talking about these things while James was still awake. But the change became second nature. The quality of their nightly talks intensified, and both parents came to really appreciate this time together because it was exclusively theirs.

James's parents noticed changes in him within the first couple of weeks. His level of anxiety went down, and his sleep improved. He started coming up with ideas for projects, and things to do that wouldn't have interested him previously. It was spring, and the weather was outstanding. Was that it? his parents wondered. At first they weren't sure, but the trend continued. He was definitely mucking about more, getting involved in building things, catching lizards, digging holes. Within about three or four weeks' time, James's teacher also reported changes in him. As his play life expanded, his pickiness about food waned. He started interacting with some of the kids in the neighborhood, particularly one with whom a friendship blossomed. I've stayed in contact with this family, and the friend James made when he was going on nine has remained a lifelong buddy. The boys are in their early twenties now, still close and very supportive of each other.

Was all of this directly attributable to the changes James's family made? Was it the lack of TV? Less talk of global warming? Can we point to any one thing that made the real difference? My answer to that would be no, and yes. I don't think there was any one thing, any magic bullet that obliterated James's nervousness and controlling behaviors. But the steps taken to protect James's childhood definitely had an effect on him and his parents, an effect greater than the sum of their parts. James's family environment was altered; both the landscape and the emotional climate of their daily life together changed. His parents brought a new awareness to their parenting, and that continued to serve them. It became the new measure of what did or didn't make sense in their lives. They no longer felt that James had to know everything they knew, or care about everything that concerned them. In acknowledging and protecting that difference, they gave James the freedom to be more deeply and happily his own age.

When you simplify a child's "world," you prepare the way for positive change and growth. This preparatory work is especially important now because our world is characterized by too much stuff. We are building our daily lives, and our families, on the four pillars of too much: too much stuff, too many choices, too much information, and too much speed. With this level of busyness, distractions, time pressure, and clutter (mental and physical), children are robbed of the time and ease they need to explore their worlds and their emerging selves. And since the pressures of "too much" are so universal, we are "adjusting" at a commensurately fast pace. The weirdness of "too much" begins to seem normal. If the water we are swimming in continues to heat up, and we simply adjust as it heats, how will we know to hop out before we boil?

I sincerely believe that our instinct to protect our children will be what motivates us to change. Our impetus out of the proverbial pot will be our desire to protect their childhoods. Even as our own inner voices are silenced by the urgencies and obligations of so much stuff, our instincts as parents still give us pause. We stop short—occasionally or often, depending on how sped up our lives have become—and wonder how this pace is affecting them. Inner alarms are sounded when we confront the huge disconnect between how we believe childhood should be, and how it has become.

Such a moment happened to Canadian journalist Carl Honoré, and was the inspiration for his 2006 book *In Praise of Slowness.* An admitted "speedaholic" himself, Honoré got the idea for his book in just such a moment of great parental alarm. In an airport bookstore while traveling, Honoré saw a series of books called *One Minute Bedtime Stories.* His first impulse was to buy the whole series and have it shipped, immediately, to his house. In that momentary flash he was remembering the many times when he had been reading to his two-year-old son ("Read it again, Daddy!") while thinking about unanswered emails and other things he needed to do. The notion of a one-minute story seemed perfect; wouldn't a few of those each night do the trick? But fortunately, he had a follow-up feeling just as quickly, a sense of alarm and disgust that he—as with so many of us—had reached this point in our mad rush through life. What was this saying, and doing, to our kids?

The Insight

We all have these moments of alarm, don't we? I know that I do. We're confronted with the often simple requests of these small beings (whom we love immeasurably), and yet their pleas seem to be coming from a galaxy far away, from the planet "slow." The two- or three-year-old asking for the same story to be read again and again becomes an eight-year-old who wants to tell you the plot of a movie in such remarkable detail that the retelling will surely take longer than the movie itself. You've figured out a complicated car-pool schedule that requires split-second timing, but saves you a roundtrip or two per week. The whole enterprise grinds to a halt each morning around two laces that will not be tied, or one head of hair that cannot be brushed, or one backpack that is always—but always—missing something.

QUITE SIMPLY:

By simplifying, we protect the environment for childhood's slow, essential unfolding of self.

The genesis for this book came with a professional sense of alarm, though my insight evolved more slowly than Honoré's bookstore revelation. I'm sorry to say it took me well over a decade to fully realize what I had been sensing for a long time. In my late twenties, I completed my training with social services in my home country of Australia, and I volunteered to work with children in Asia at two refugee camps, one in Jakarta, and one in Cambodia, along the Thai-Cambodian border.

In Jakarta the camps were very large, populated by several hundred thousand people who had been dispossessed by political instability. The camps operated like little fiefdoms, with feudal lords and gangs who would "rule" through nasty means, gathering loyalties with promises of protection from other such thug "lords." It was a large, squalid shantytown—or city, really—with shelters made of cardboard and bits of tin or plastic, whatever could be found. Everyone would walk on planks that were laid on the ground, keeping them only slightly above the effluent that would overflow from drainage ditches and open sewers.

Most of the children I lived among and worked with had never known a different home or life apart from the camp. Their lives were characterized by discomfort, illness, fear, and danger. There was little safety or leisure for these children; survival was a family enterprise. As a people and as individuals they had suffered great losses. And sadly, the children were very clearly diagnosable with post-traumatic stress disorder. They were jumpy, nervous, and hypervigilant, wary of anything novel or new. Many had adopted elaborate little rituals around everyday tasks, such as very specific, complicated ways of navigating the maze of the camp, which they imagined would somehow keep them safe. They were distrustful of new relationships, whether with adults or their own peers, and quite a few had hair-trigger tempers.

After leaving Asia I moved to England, where I completed training as a Waldorf teacher. For years and years I worked in school settings and in private practice as a counselor, seeing kids and making diagnoses: ADD, ADHD, OCD, ODD. It came to seem like some sort of a macabre "waltz of the Ds"—an all-too-common dance these days; this fine carving up of our children.

In the early 1990s I was working in a school, and had a private practice west of London. The children I worked with came from a variety of backgrounds, some British, some immigrant, from lower-middle-class to fairly affluent households. Some of the children I saw professionally were overcontrolling in their behavior toward their parents, their environment, and even their play with other children. Sleep and food were common areas of control; they might stop eating all but one or two foods, or not go to sleep until late into the night. Their anger was easily triggered, very often explosive, and parents would be at a loss to explain the reasons for their outbursts. I was also seeing a lot of nervousness in these children. They would startle easily, and have difficulty shaking it off, or relaxing again. They were mistrustful of new situations, whether new material at school, new people in their lives, or any changes in plans or in their regular patterns of activity. I remember one boy who absolutely refused to go on vacation with his parents. He had never been to the beach before, and the prospect seemed to terrify him.

What finally dawned on me was that the treatment plans I was developing for this group of children were identical to those that I had helped develop in Asia. When I looked at my work objectively, I could see no difference between my methods and goals with these children and those I had while treating the children in Jakarta. What I was at last able to grasp was pretty remarkable. I doubted it for as long as I could, until I was certain: These children, these very typical children from an affluent country of the Western world, were showing the signs and symptoms of post-traumatic stress disorder.

I had been trained to associate PTSD with very large wartime events, with life-changing traumas that leave their victims shaken in no small measure. My work over the last twenty years has taken me to many war-torn areas: Africa, Israel, and Northern Ireland, as well as Russia and Hungary during and just after perestroika. I didn't expect to find "war-torn" children in this relatively affluent area in England, but sure enough, that's what I was finding. What struck me first were the similarities in the problematic behaviors adopted by these seemingly disparate groups of children. After so many instances of clinical déjà vu, I couldn't ignore my instincts. Certain of the symptoms and behaviors, I was becoming more and more convinced of the cause. And as I looked more closely at their lives, I realized that for both groups the sanctity of childhood had been breached. Adult life was flooding in unchecked. Privy to their parents' fears, drives, ambitions, and the very fast pace of their lives, the children were busy trying to construct their own boundaries, their own level of safety in behaviors that weren't ultimately helpful. These children were suffering from a different kind of war: the undeclared war on childhood.

QUITE SIMPLY:

Our society—with its pressures of "too much"—
is waging an undeclared war on childhood.

If you looked at the lives of these kids in England, searching for a signature traumatic event, you wouldn't find it. You might expect to see early childhood losses that would cause them to react with such nervousness and distrust, such lack of resiliency and hypervigilance. What I came to realize, however, was that there were enough of the little stresses, a consistent baseline of stress and insecurity, to add up. These little stresses accrue to the point that it makes psychological "sense" for kids to acquire and adopt compensatory behaviors.

The psychological community is in love with acronyms, so I added another—why not?!—to describe what I realized I was seeing: cumulative stress reaction (CSR). It's similar to what the American Psychological Association now, many years later, calls complex post-traumatic stress disorder.

The psychological community is also beginning to recognize that the attributes and behaviors I was seeing—hypervigilance, nervousness, anxiousness, a lack of resiliency, a lack of impulse control, a lack of empathy, and a lack of perspective taking—all worsen when a child accumulates enough little pieces of stress, with enough frequency. Such a consistent pattern of stress can accumulate into a PTSD-type scenario, or CSR.

CSR describes a reaction to a pattern of constant small stresses, a sort of consistent threshold of stress that may build, but rarely dissipates. Please understand that I am not referring here to the level of stress that is a fact of life. I am not suggesting that stress should not exist for children; it does, and it must. Children experience frustrated desires, illnesses, sorrows, and losses. Their lives are not stress free, and childhood is not a series of "rainbow moments," each lovelier than the next. Indeed, imagine the six-year-old who, his dream life full of superheroes and superpowers, discovers in a fall from the backyard cherry tree that he can't fly. His broken left arm is very painful, scary to see, and there is also the frantic trip to the hospital emergency room. Such childhood accidents can be awfully stressful at the time. Yet the next day, and with each retelling as a family story, the episode becomes a classic tale of bravery, of fears calmed by concern, of strength and heroism. (Not the flying variety of heroism—alas—but the kind Ralph Waldo Emerson described: "A hero is no braver than an ordinary man, but he is braver five minutes longer.")

The level of stress described by the term CSR, in its frequency, is very different from the stresses that occur quite regularly and normally in a child's everyday life. In day-to-day life a child's moods and well-being are like a seesaw; stress acts like a weight on one end, but once the stress is gone the overall balance returns. The "gift" of a scraped knee, an argument with a friend, five days flat out with the flu—these can strengthen a child's resilience and their awareness of their own abilities. Such normal stresses are examples of "necessary resistance." We all, including children, need to meet resistance in life in order to learn how to understand it, work through it, and move on. Such stresses may be worrying, but not damaging if we learn we have the skills and the support to deal with them, and move beyond them. Stress that is damaging is either too large, or too constant to move beyond. If our abilities (or a child's abilities) can't match it, then he or she can't understand it, or work through it, and they become stuck in a reoccurring cycle of stress reactions.

CSR is characterized not by the severity of a traumatic event, but rather by the consistency or frequency of small stresses. What was the cumulative effect of these stresses on the children's psyches, and behavior? What I came to understand was that little stresses, collectively, drag on a child's ability to be resilient: mentally, emotionally, and physically. They interfere with concentration, with an emotional baseline of calm, with a sense of security that allows for novelty and change. They interfere with focus, not just for the item or task at hand. These stresses distract from the focus or "task" of childhood: an emerging, developing sense of self.

What has also become increasingly clear to me is that so much of this stress is what we now call daily life. It is the life that surrounds our children, a daily life that is unfortunately not that distinct from those we lead as adults. A daily life submerged in the same media-rich, multitasking, complex, information-overloaded, time-pressured waters as our own.

QUITE SIMPLY:

The pace of our daily lives is increasingly misaligned with the pace of childhood.

This is a fairly depressing notion, really, to think of childhood being under attack. It is also difficult to unravel, or pin down. I don't believe the attack is a result of conscious effort. There doesn't seem to be a "bogeyman" among us, a sinister force at work. No particular being, company, or entity bears responsibility for this. Philip Morris, General Mills, the all-pervading marketers and advertisers, the technophiles promoting cellphones to eight-year-olds—which among these can we blame? All or none, really. I don't think there are any culprits who consciously equate what they're selling or promoting with an assault on childhood.

As a society, however, we've signed on wholeheartedly to the notion that more, bigger, newer, and faster all mean better. We've done so as a sort of survival mechanism. It is a very basic, primitive drive (albeit with its own particularly manic, modern, Western spin). At its most basic level it is understandable, though it no longer serves its original purpose, and we've taken it to the point where it actually threatens, rather than ensures, our survival.

We cram more and more into our homes (even as we're building them bigger) and our lives (even while suffering from busyness and lack of sleep) and our awareness (twenty-four-hour CNN, blogs, BlackBerries, constant online news updates). According to a consumer research group study, the average age at which American kids start using mainstream technology gadgets, such as cellphones, MP3 players, and DVD players, is now 6.7 years.[1] As our worlds accelerate to mach speeds, we not only pull our children along, we also project some of our anxieties about the speed onto them. Is there anything that we don't feel the need to hurry? Anything that we don't feel the need to enrich, improve upon, advance, or compete over? While we haven't figured a way around the nine-month human gestation period, once that baby is born, its childhood seems to be "fair game" for acceleration.

To look at our society's assault on childhood another way, let's take sleep as an analogy. Most of us acknowledge the need for a good chunk of it—seven to eight hours—nightly. Yet many of us would love to be able to function well on significantly less. Some feel that they manage very well on four hours a night. Thomas Roth of the Henry Ford Sleep Disorders Center in Detroit would doubt that, however: "The percentage of the population who need less than five hours of sleep per night, rounded to a whole number," says Roth, "is zero." Robert Stickgold, a Harvard cognitive neuroscientist specializing in sleep research, recounted how a psychiatrist in private practice called to ask whether he knew of any reason not to prescribe modafinil, a new wakefulness-promoting drug, to an undergraduate during exam time. "No—no reason at all not to," Stickgold told the psychiatrist. "Not unless you think sleep does something."[2]

Does sleep do something, besides mark the time between wakefulness? Does childhood do something, other than mark the time until adulthood? We die without sleep, which should render the question moot, but scientists still argue over which processes occur exclusively during sleep. Mental and emotional clarification and improvement of motor skills (a kind of mental "practicing" of movements) take place as we sleep, and some feel sleep helps maintain homeostasis in the brain. The immune system doesn't work properly without sleep, and we know that lack of sleep impairs speech, memory, and innovative, flexible thinking. Rats deprived of sleep die in seventeen to twenty days: Their hair falls out and their metabolisms kick into high gear, burning lots of calories while the rats are just standing still.[3]

Scientists are learning the biological "purpose" of sleep by studying what happens when we're deprived of it. Sleep deprived, people are much less able to retain or use what they learn while awake. They lose resiliency—mental and physical—as their immune system falters. Still we wonder, can we skip it? Can we do without it, or shortchange it in some way, to reclaim the third of our lives that is "lost" to slumber? As a society we seem to be asking the same questions about childhood. What purpose does it serve? Can we speed it up? Can we better prepare our children for adulthood by treating them more like adults?

I worry that we'll understand the "purpose" of childhood by seeing, increasingly, what people are like when they've been rushed through theirs. And I don't think that will be a pretty picture. Childhood has its own mysterious processes, its own pace. When we ask children to "keep up" with a speeded-up world, I believe we are unconsciously doing them harm. We are depriving them of exactly what they need to make their way in an increasingly complex world: well-being and resiliency. And yet I sincerely believe that there are many things we can do as parents to buffer and protect our children's childhoods.

QUITE SIMPLY:

A protected childhood allows for the slow development of identity, well-being, and resiliency.

I was giving a lecture recently and on my way heard a report about global warming. Now James, the dear little fellow I describe earlier, had taught me quite a bit about the subject. But I was thinking as I drove that when problems seem overwhelming, we often rush at them in a state of pure anxiety. Off we go (walking) to the hardware store for recycling bins and fluorescent lightbulbs, stopping first to look at hybrid cars (conveniently, on the way), while picking up trash and making a silent vow that from this day forward organic cotton will be the only fabric to ever touch our children's skin. Why must we do all of this—and more—immediately, if not sooner? To plug up that bloomin' hole in the ozone, of course! Yet our actions would be so much more consistent and ongoing if our motivation were not anxiety, but compassion: a desire to protect the earth.

This reminds me of a man who came to one of my lectures. This guy came under duress, I'm quite certain, at his wife's insistence. Afterward we happened to be standing next to each other, and he turned to me. "Well done!" he said, kindly, about my talk, though I'm not sure he was awake through all of it. "Food for thought, isn't it? I'm a Harvard man myself, and I doubt my Ben will be following my lead unless we get his attention up to snuff! I'll make up a simplification list right away. He has exams next year; do you think that's enough time to get this all turned around?" Now, this man was too well rested to be anxious, but the point is . . . he was missing the point. Acting out of anxiety doesn't usually lead to long-term efforts, or changes, much less large-scale transformations. The point of simplification is not to improve Ben's SAT scores (much as we wish the boy well). Ben's well-being is the goal. Imagine the motivation and inspiration we can bring to our efforts with the larger goal of protecting our beloved children's childhoods? Childhood is also an all-important environment, with its own systems, its own natural processes. And society is poking quite a few holes in the protective filter that should surround childhood to buffer it from adult life and concerns.

The good news is that there are many things we can do as parents to protect the environment of childhood. There are many ways that we can erect filters to stop the speed and stress of adult life from pouring, unchecked, into our kids' homes, heads, and hearts. As my work has become increasingly focused on simplification, I have seen how effective this process can be in restoring a child's sense of ease and well-being. It shifts a family's direction, so that their daily life efforts are in concert, not in opposition, with their dreams.

Before we focus on each layer of simplification in the chapters ahead, I want to give you an overview of the process. I'll take you through a consultation, asking you some of the same questions I've families to consider. In order to act out of hope rather than of reverence for childhood rather than fear of our times, simon begins with dreams. Carl Sandburg once said, "Nothing hapnless first a dream." This is no exception. Your dreams for your family will be your motivation; they'll act as your wings throughout the process.

The Process: Hopes and Dreams

Very often families come to me, whether through a school or private practice setting, because of a child's behavioral issues. The impetus for a call or consultation is similar to a rash; it's usually just an outward sign of something else, a broader or deeper issue. As I mentioned in the introduction, you can see so much, including what a family holds dear, from the pattern of their everyday lives. In order to get a clearer view of a family's issues, I often offer them a choice between several months' worth of family therapy sessions, or a one-day visit from me. Either way, I feel, gives me the same level of insight. Although it amuses me, it doesn't surprise me how often families initially choose months of sessions, Mom and Dad eyeing each other nervously, rather than the visit. Certainly having someone invade your home for an entire day, from wake-up until after the children's bedtimes, is no one's idea of an inviting prospect.

I don't think the observation days are as painful as parents might imagine they will be. When a family chooses this option, I spend the day taking in the family's particular dance of daily activities. I might play with the children, help a bit with the dishes. I often bring a little project with me, something I am making or mending, which keeps my focus from seeming too intense. While my presence is noticeable, I don't sit and stare, clipboard and stopwatch at hand. Essentially I try to stay on the margins, but within the overall mix of daily life. I might also split up my observations to cover part of a school day and part of a weekend day, depending on the particular difficulties or stresses of the family.

Imagine just such an average day for your family, and what it might look like to an observer. What are the difficulties that might arise? What periods of the day are consistently stressful?

A day or two after my home visit, I meet with the parents. We begin these "post-visit" meetings with an interesting, usually very moving discussion about family values. By this I do *not* mean the term co-opted by politicians to convey whatever they may be promoting at the time. I

mean the couple's own vision of their family, how they ima
fore they had children. It is important for them to dream th
before stepping forward, to reclaim the images and hopes
and dear to them. These are the images that guide them through the work ahead. And simplification helps enormously in recovering those dreams.

One of my favorite pictures of my wife is one I took when she was pregnant with our first child, sitting in a rocking chair looking off, deep in thought. It's clear she was thinking about the future. We all had these visions, these dreams of how we wanted our family to be. How did you imagine your children? How did you picture yourselves as parents? You no doubt talked about aspects of your own upbringing . . . those you wanted to emulate, and others that you wanted to avoid at all costs. How did you imagine your home, with children?

As parents we don't often get to live the ideals. Not a spectator sport, parenting is about being in the thick of it. We may be the architects of our family's daily lives, but it's hard to draw blueprints of something that is constantly changing and growing. With kids you don't have much time to dream, and most parents are surprised by how far they've strayed from the dreams they once had for their family. It's true, they had sketchy data at the time. (Which one of you was pushing for the white couch? And wasn't there talk of "Let's just get one toy chest, and keep everything in that"?)

Even if some of the details were unrealistic, your dreams about your family had truth to them. They had meaning, and still do. They show what you valued most when you began this huge undertaking, this family-building. What inspired you then can inspire you still. It has to; families need fresh infusions of hope and imagination. It's strange how we look for meaning everywhere, as though it will be "new," not something that we already know, and constantly have to remember, renew, and reclaim as our own.

QUITE SIMPLY:

Like any work of art, families need inspiration, fresh infusions of hope, and imagination.

Do you remember mentally "grafting" what you loved and admired most in each other onto your future children? Do you remember how you imagined the family group, with shifting heights and shapes as the kids grew? You imagined a life together, with meals shared, games played, school days and chores, sorrows mended, stories told, little triumphs and celebrations. You imagined the milestones of birthdays and holidays, first steps, first words, first days of school. But you also had mental pictures of less eventful moments, the stuff of everyday life: bedtime reading, tying shoes, sharing laughs, pink construction paper valentines, ball games in the almost-darkness of dusk.

You pictured a refuge; your own loving, perhaps quirky, no doubt noisy, funny, supportive, shelter of like-featured but independent souls, with space to accommodate and smells that meant home, and maybe a sweet-natured dog or cat ("Once the kids are old enough to take responsibility for its care!") lying by the hearth ("Not on the white couch!"). You dreamed of the comfort of a family where each member could be their authentic self, well known and well loved.

But did you ever, in your wildest dreams, imagine this much stuff all over the rug and crammed into every inch of space in the house?! No way. That was one of those "overlooked details" in your "family life" dreams. For a lot of the parents I've worked with, the misalignment between what they imagined—what they dreamed—and what their family has become is enormous. And the disconnect is not just in the details—the white couch or the toys everywhere—it is fundamental. "I never thought I would become a sort of taxi on steroids," I remember one mother saying, close to tears. "Sometimes I feel like I am relating more to their coaches, their flute and dance teachers, tutors and therapists, than to them." She felt she had become the vehicle (literally and figuratively) for her kids' lives, lives that had very little to do with her anymore, or with the family as a whole.

A father takes me aside after a lecture. After exchanging small talk for a few minutes he looks down at the carpet, and then into my eyes. "Do you know what really surprises me?" he asks. "I never thought it would be this hard, this draining. Don't get me wrong, I knew there would be conflicts, and I expected plenty of them, especially when the kids hit adolescence. I remember arguing with my parents a lot as a teenager. But I can't imagine what it will be like when my son's a teenager, when our relationship now seems like it's staggering from one clash to the next. Everything is up for negotiation. Everything is talked about, to death. He is like a miniature lawyer. I never imagined going toe to toe, arguing and negotiating ten times a day, with a seven-year-old."

"We didn't think it would be like this." I have heard that phrase over and over again in meetings. The family structures are variable, but whether I was meeting with a traditional married couple, same-sex partners, single parents—it doesn't matter—the realizations are pretty consistent. Parents talk about their dreams as something they have not only envisioned, but were working toward. They look back, sure that their families were moving in the right direction for some time, before they veered off and became something else. "Things have gotten so crazy." "It didn't use to be this way, so out of control."

QUITE SIMPLY:

Our daily lives can become disconnected from the hopes and dreams we hold for our family.

When we think back to what we imagined our lives would be like, we didn't think we would be fighting for our family's survival. Yet again and again, these are the terms used and the feelings expressed. I see parents caught in a stress bath, a sort of "fight or flight" state that is not momentary; it has become the norm. Making do, flying by the seat of our pants, barely seeing one another, always improvising, revolving doors, crazy schedules, unchecked emotions, strangers in the same house.

My conversations with parents are far-ranging, and very moving. They begin, and come back, full circle, to this question: What do you need to move forward, in a way that reclaims your hopes and dreams for your family? The dreams are still very much alive, that much is clear. But also painfully clear is the distance between those dreams and the present reality.

What imagination can be brought to the life that you make and remake together, as a family? Remember, "Nothing happens unless first a dream." Can you recapture your dream of a family life that is big enough to accommodate all of its members? Can you realign your reality with the hopes you had for your family?

With this in mind, the parents I am visiting and I will turn our attention to the day or so we have just spent together. I ask them if they felt that the day held any "flashpoints" or particular problems. After assuring me that I have, ironically, witnessed "the worst parenting day" of their entire lives, they mention incidents that either come up, or often do. We "unpack" the day, paying particular attention to the issues that caused the most distress to remember. The particulars might be very particular ("And you saw how Joey can't even sit still through a meal!"), but meanwhile, we are also setting some broad perimeters together. You see, by this time we have already talked about their dreams for their family, and now they are beginning to address their worries and concerns. Somewhere between the dreams and the concerns is the answer . . . the place to bring imagination, the place to start simplifying.

Parents can sometimes feel overwhelmed by the problems, unable to see a pattern or starting point. Parts of the day may be problematic, such as meals and bedtimes, and we discuss these, looking at them in the context of daily life. Such explosions are rarely the result of the activity itself; they arise from pressures building up long before. As parents become more involved in simplifying, in increasing rhythm and predictability in the home (Chapter Four), they will learn how to build in "pressure valves," little islands of calm throughout the day.

At this early point, our goal is to take the pulse of the family, to see what is happening. How does this picture differ from our vision of family? What would make it better? This is a process that anyone can do. If you look objectively at the pattern of your days together, what are the flashpoints? The points at which tempers rise, cooperation evaporates, and chaos ensues?

Rather than address the particularly worrisome concerns head-on, it is important first to just acknowledge them. It is important as well to look at the areas of our daily lives and parenting that are well aligned with our best intentions. What makes these areas work? In my meetings with parents I listen to their biggest concerns, and together we back off a step or two. A good massage therapist does not push directly into a sore point; instead they work the muscles to either side, loosening them as they go. Healing work in family therapy needs to be pursued with similar grace, so that the changes engender further motivation, not resentment.

The Process: Getting Started

In terms of areas to change I usually see two categories: what is important, and what is doable. What seems the most important is usually not; what is most doable is the place to begin. If you do enough that is doable, you will get to the important, and your motivation will be fueled by your success.

So often we need to find our way to a goal by identifying and discarding what that vision is not. Family is not disparate relationships between individuals and machines, in separate rooms of a house. Childhood is not a race to accumulate all of the consumer goods and stresses of adulthood in record time. Simplification signals a change and makes room for a transformation. It is a stripping away that invites clarity.

QUITE SIMPLY:
Simplification signals a change,
a realignment of our hopes and our everyday lives.

Reacquainted with their dreams for their families, parents and I talk about how a simplification regime might help them change course, how simplifying might make room for a shift, a realignment of their hopes with their everyday lives. It would be great if simplification involved nothing more than backing a dumpster up to the house and discarding piles of stuff. Unfortunately, there's more to it. Children can be overloaded by more than just the physical things bulging out of their closets. But as you'll see, there are simple "tossing out" or "whittling down" steps at each level. Parents and I discuss the four levels of simplification: the environment, rhythm, schedules, and filtering out the adult world. We touch on all of them, and discuss which aspects of the regime feel the most doable. Sometimes I am surprised; some parents want to dive into the more difficult arenas of schedules and filtering out the adult world right away, while other parents cautiously express a willingness to see "a few less" toys around the house. Often a modest goal is an instinctual first step toward something larger. Somehow parents know where to begin to create the necessary space—in their intentions and their lives—for a transformation. Marie's parents chose to address Marie's home environment first, as I'll recommend you do too. Her story shows that by starting with the doable, we can pave the way for broader changes.

Marie was a bright, energetic five-year-old just beginning kindergarten when I first met her parents. She had had a series of babysitters who came to the home, all of whom had trouble controlling her. Marie was "hard work," if you will: very active, unfocused, and with clear attention difficulties. Just before kindergarten, Marie's parents had put her in a day-care center from which, after a couple of months, she was asked to leave. Marie's parents were very nice people, clearly trying to do their best for their daughter. They were both working professionals who led very busy, hectic lives; it had been difficult even finding the time for us to sit down together. At that initial meeting I could see how concerned and defeated they felt in the face of what they called Marie's already "checkered career."

Together we began to work out a simplification regime for the family. Her parents decided to begin with the physical environment of their home, particularly simplifying Marie's room. If the average American child has 150 toys, Marie had at least double that number. Her room was also packed with books, some on shelves, but many in towering piles. There were a few narrow passageways to and from her bed, carved between mountains of books, clothes, and toys. Periodically, the parents assured me, they would undertake an archeological dig in the room to tidy up, only to see chaos return within hours.

Whether they are in bins, baskets, trunks, closets, piles, or heaps, the child's toys are usually our first focus. To the mountain of toys in their bedroom we add the outlying piles from around the house. The accumulated whole is usually a remarkable sight, and not one the parents have fully taken in before.

With a box of large, black, plastic trash bags at hand, we begin the work of cleaning up the area. I suggest that we put half of the toys in the bag—excellent—and then half again. There are always some toys that parents are anxious to get rid of. They dive into the pile, searching with glee for the plastic exploding disasters—the ones that whir, talk, gyrate, or detonate. Essentially, they're looking for the ones that grandparents or bachelor uncles have given. "Shouldn't we keep these as insurance for grandmother's next visit?" Chances are, I assure them, grandmother has no memory of the toy itself, only the joy of giving. Chances are also good that the child has forgotten the toy too, or the toy has one or more of its pieces missing.

In this way, we make a molehill out of a mountain, leaving for the child a mix of toys that they enjoy most consistently, and for the longest periods of time. Rarely are these favorites complex, or motorized; rarely do they "do" anything. The toys that are too detailed or complicated—too "fixed"—can rob a child of an imaginative experience. Dear nighttime toys can never disappear. Even if they are totally hideous, dear nighttime toys are nonnegotiable. The remaining toys have to include a mixture of active toys: building, digging, construction toys; and more receptive toys, such as dolls and stuffed animals, toys that just receive.

There can also be creative materials, such as paints, crayons, and some modeling substances, such as beeswax or clay. The toys with staying power are usually—not always, but pretty consistently—figures of some sort, either dolls or knights or stuffed animals; building toys; and scenes or dwellings of some sort, into which the child loves to project his or her figures, and thus themselves.

We then turn our attention to books, whittling the pile down to one or two of the current favorites. This can truly shock some parents who take pride in their child's love of reading. "Sarah reads five or six books at once!" they implore. Our purpose here is not to discourage reading, but to allow the child to really concentrate on, and revel in, whatever they are reading (or doing) at any given time. I remember Dylan, a very bright, talkative eight-year-old who once started our conversation with this excited pronouncement: "You know what? I just finished number sixteen in the Magic Tree House Series, I'm on the fourth Time Warp Trio, and I just got the new Captain Underpants." "Well," I said, "which of those did you particularly enjoy?" "Oh, I don't know," he said, clearly thinking my question was beside the point, "they're all pretty much the same."

So, with a few large baskets, we had culled Marie's toys way down. The remaining toys were a mix of favorites, the simpler the better: dolls, building toys, cherished bedtime toys, some kitchen things, balls. Almost half of the toys that did not make the cut were thrown away because they were broken or had missing pieces. The rest we put in storage. The stored toys were a sort of toy "library" that the family could draw from provided they replaced one before taking another. We did the same with books, packing and labeling the majority of them for storage, and leaving five or six of favorites, lined neatly on a shelf by Marie's bed.

We didn't just take away toys, we carefully added some. In one of the baskets we put a stack of brightly colored fabric pieces, some rope, and clothespins. We also made sure Marie had a table her size, a large drawing pad, and a box of big crayons. We gathered, washed, and folded an assortment of dress-up clothes that we put in one empty basket.

You might think Marie's first reaction to this "anti-Christmas" would be shock. Not so. I have seen this again and again. She didn't seem to notice, or care, that a good three-quarters or more of her toys and books had been removed. She was taken with the new space, with the freedom it seemed to afford. For days and days she built "houses" with the cloths and clothespins. She would build them and curl up inside, pulling in pillows and sometimes a book or a doll. Every single day for a couple of weeks she repeated this, and it seemed to be doing something for her that she really needed. She came to trust that she could build another the next day, that these were hers to make and have. So each afternoon, after admiring the day's creation, Marie's mother and Marie would take them down, talking as they folded the cloths, unpinned the pins, and put the materials in their basket, ready for the next day.

This was just the first step in a simplification process that included several levels and unfolded over many months. Yet this first step, the change in Marie's room, signaled a kind of sea change, a new awareness that expanded through the family's house and their days; the space and time of their daily lives. This sea change was not just the result of "tidying up." It was a conscious move, both practical and philosophical, toward a more rhythmic, predictable, child-centered home life. By that I do not mean that the home and everything done in it are oriented toward the child, but I absolutely do mean that the home and everything in it are not exclusively oriented toward adults. A certain pace or volume of "stuff" may be tolerable for adults, while it is intolerable, or problematic, for the kids.

Children are such tactile beings. They live so fully by their senses that if they see something, they will also want to touch it, smell it, possibly eat it, maybe throw it, feel what it feels like on their heads, listen to it, sort it, and probably submerge it in water. This is entirely natural. Strap on their pith helmets; they're exploring the world. But imagine the sensory overload that can happen for a child when every surface, every drawer and closet is filled with stuff? So many choices and so much stimuli rob them of time and attention. Too much stuff deprives kids of leisure, and the ability to explore their worlds deeply.

QUITE SIMPLY:

Too much stuff leads to too little time and too little depth in the way kids see and explore their worlds.

Over the years I've seen remarkable, very moving transformations among the families I've come to know and work with. Very simple principles, gradually incorporated into a home, produce dramatic shifts in a family's emotional climate, in their connection to one another. In this work, I often think about a stream, dammed by a pile of rocks that has accumulated gradually . . . so gradually that the rocks have gone unnoticed, but the imbalance is felt. By reducing mental and physical clutter, simplification increases a family's ability to flow together, to focus and deepen their attention, to realign their lives with their dreams.

The Changes

When I first started my simplification consultation work, the transformations I was seeing were unprecedented in my professional experience. As simplification became the heart of my work I felt out on a limb professionally. I had not arrived at these methods through my training or schooling, not through developmental psychology or school counseling, and not through what I knew about psychoanalysis. The schooling and training I had had were complicated, but the simplification approach I was developing was not tricky. It was very, very simple.

At this professional point—some ten years ago—my family and I were living in the beautiful New England college community of Northampton, Massachusetts. My private counseling practice was expanding rapidly as word about this work was getting out. To this day I have the nickname there of "Dr. Trashbag." Given that, you might think this was a low period in my career! Not so. It was very gratifying to see firsthand how effective simplification could be in restoring a child's sense of ease.

Others were noticing as well. If you know the area, you know there are probably more therapists per square block in Northampton than anywhere else in the country, except perhaps Manhattan. I was receiving referrals not only from the families I worked with, but also from the psychologists and psychiatrists in the area. They were finding that their own treatment methods—whether cognitive behavioral therapy, art therapy, or talk therapy—were much more effective once a simplification regime had taken hold in the home. Simplification prepared the space in a child's daily life for changes to take place. As one psychiatrist put it, his treatment work would then "stick" in a way that it had not previously.

The work we were doing was not so much healing work as preparatory work. A simplification regime can create space in a family's habit life and intentions, a vessel for change to occur. That change or growth can take various forms. It can be the result of therapies that are now "sticking," or more easily absorbed and acted upon, or the natural result of childhood growth and development, unchecked by adult levels of stress, stuff, and speed. Simplification protects the environment for childhood's slow, essential unfolding of self. In either case, the transformations we were seeing were remarkable.

You needn't be a therapist to realize that most kids are quirky, aren't they? Most any parent will give you a quick nod of agreement on that score. I feel sorry for my own dear children, actually, because they say that a therapist's offspring are the quirkiest of all! The truth is we all have our quirks, our personalities and idiosyncrasies. We tend to be more tolerant of them in adults, perhaps because we think of adults as "fully formed" and children as "under construction" and thus more malleable.

QUITE SIMPLY:
All children are quirky.

Why simplify? Over the years, as I've come to see how a child's quirks or tendencies can be exacerbated by cumulative stress, I've seen how children can slide along on the spectrum from quirk to disorder when they experience high levels of stress. If I had a big chalkboard, I would write it as this formula: q + s = d; or: quirk plus stress equals disorder. This is especially worrisome in a society that is often quick to judge, label, and prescribe.

Imagine that wonderfully wistful child who loves to be in nature. He or she has a disposition for dreaminess. Very creative, like miniature philosophers, they can tell you a story that circumnavigates the globe before you see the possibility of a conclusion. This is the child who is great good company on vacation at the beach, but can be unbearable in the morning as the school bus is scheduled to arrive. If you add cumulative stress to this child's life, he or she can just slide along the spectrum to ADHD, inattentive type. Their response to stress is to check out; that is their escape route.

Imagine the child who is, and always has been, a doer. She is the one who is at your right hand as you shop, always eager for a task. Or the boy who will do the vacuuming—doesn't mind it—and always has some new trick or feat to show you. He or she is active in physical play, and is capable of attracting a whole group of kids—in the neighborhood or on the playground—to whatever game they are playing. With a consistent pattern of stress this child can slide right into hyperactivity.

Another child you may recognize is the feisty one. If she thinks a teacher is picking on someone, or even if the biggest kid in school is bullying a friend of hers, this child will stick right up for her friend. She may be sticking up for herself more often than not, but she shows courage. She or he will stand up and be counted. A child like this feels things intensely, and has a strong sense of what is or is not fair. Add stress to his life and watch how quickly the child will be labeled as ODD. (To this day I read that as "odd," but it actually stands for oppositional defiance disorder.)

Imagine the child who has a bird egg collection, or a stamp collection. His favorite things—and granted, he has quite a few of them—are all lined up on display. His room seems a bit chaotic to the outside observer, but he knows exactly where everything is. Or she knows where everything goes, and can be quite perturbed if someone "cleans" her room (it is more like archeology than cleaning). She has a wonderful memory for detail in general, and will be the first to say where your car keys are, or the last time you wore that particular outfit. With stress this child can slide into OCD, or just "stuckness," a pronounced rigidity of behavior. She is the one who, when the teacher explains that the field trip has been cancelled due to an impending snowstorm, will melt down.

This sliding along the spectrum is really quite normal. Just as stress can push children in one direction, the reverse is also true. When you really simplify a child's life on a number of levels, back they come. We can see parallels in our own lives. Remember when you were in college, and studying for finals? Or picture yourself (unless you are a perfectly calm, inveterate traveler), the evening before a long plane trip. If you have certain "tendencies" normally, then in stressful situations such as these you "become" those tendencies absolutely. A certain fussiness that you tend toward becomes almost frightfully manifested as you line your clothes up to pack, sorted by size, texture, and hue, darkest to lightest. Or imagine the third-grade teacher who has bravely taken on an ambitious class play. By performance time, she has the phone number of a counselor her friend recommended written on her hand because every single child is displaying, in full plumage, every latent tendency they have.

This happens all the time, this sliding along the behavioral spectrum in response to stress. It's normal and healthy. By dealing with normal stresses, children (and adults) develop ways to cope. They benefit from coping with difficult situations, as they build a sense of competency and self-trust. The very active child, the industrious little soul who becomes a whirling dervish in anticipation of the school play, can also slide back to a calmer state. Sometimes they need help in this, but the expansion and contraction is a normal process and cycle. It is one we all experience.

QUITE SIMPLY:
Stress can push children along the behavioral spectrum. When you simplify a child's life on a number of levels, back they come.

As parents we must not become "harmony addicted." It's tempting to hope that every day might be a sort of "rainbow experience" for our children. Wouldn't that be nice? If only we could suspend them in a sort of happiness bubble. But they need conflict. As Helen Keller noted, "Character cannot be developed in ease and quiet." Children need to find ways to cope with difficult situations; they need to learn that they can. The feisty girl who has such strong feelings and a drive to make herself heard needs to experience that tendency. She may also need to be helped back to her more centered ways of seeing and dealing with the world. The movement itself is a healthy part of life, of building and developing character.

When we overprotect, when we become so neurotic about the perfection of our children's every experience and waking moment, we don't protect them from sliding along the behavioral spectrum. We push them along it.

Building character and emotional resiliency is a lot like developing a healthy immune system. We know that our children need to be exposed to a variety of bugs and viruses in life. Not only is it impossible to avoid, but this exposure is necessary in order to build up their own protective immunological front. We are not going to host our child's fifth birthday party in a hospital intensive care unit, despite the immune-building possibilities. Yet we are often tempted by the other end of the parenting spectrum, looking to shield or vaccinate them from all manner of normal life experiences. By overprotecting them we may make their lives safer (that is, fever free) in the short run, but in the long run we would be leaving them vulnerable, less able to cope with the world around them.

Overparenting creates a lot of tension. Our anxiousness about our children makes them, in turn, anxious. Little ones "graze" on our emotions. They feed on the tone we set, the emotional climate we create. They pick up on the ways in which we are nervous and hypervigilant about their safety, and it makes them nervous; so these feelings cycle. Parental anxiety can also slide children along the spectrum. American journalist Ellen Goodman said something that I find both moving and elemental. I carry a tattered copy of it in my wallet: "The central struggle of parenthood is to let our hopes for our children outweigh our fears."

QUITE SIMPLY:
"The central struggle of parenthood is to let our hopes for our children outweigh our fears."

For the past five or so years I have been involved with my colleague Bonnie River in a research project looking into the efficacy of simplification as a drug-free approach to ADD, or attention deficit disorder.[4] I actually take issue with this label, because I feel that there is no deficit of attention in children diagnosed with ADD. There is an excess of attention, really. These kids can be very attentive, but they have difficulties prioritizing that attention. Their level of attentiveness is not always in accordance with the situation at hand. The acronym that I think more appropriately describes the syndrome is API: attention priority issue.

Our study looked at fifty-five children from thirty-two Waldorf schools in America and Canada. These are children who clearly had attention difficulties, or API. In approaching the schools we asked for their most challenging children, the kids who might just as likely be hanging from the rafters as seated at desks. These were the kids who can hijack a class by monopolizing the teacher's attention. For these kids we devised a simplification regime much like the one outlined in this book, but with particular emphasis on simplifying environment (including dietary changes), screen media, and schedules.

We also simplified information by asking the parents to look at the amount of information their child was absorbing and to cut it in half. This cold-turkey reduction did not just include outside information sources, such as ESPN or *Highlights* magazine; it included dinner table conversation. The distinction is important because we tend to get bogged down in qualifying "good information" or "bad information." We also tend to think of problems as "coming from outside." The premise we wanted to convey with this approach was one of quantity, not "quality." When you look at the information kids absorb on a regular basis there are certainly differences in quality and appropriateness. But we wanted parents to work toward an overall simplification, to dramatically reduce the quantity of information their kids were taking in from all sources.

What we found is that 68 percent of the children whose parents and teachers adhered to the protocol went from clinically dysfunctional to clinically functional in four months. How is this possible, with no drugs involved? We did the study again. Once again we had strict screenings and testing both before and after the protocol. We got the same figures, exactly. Sixty-eight percent of the children went from clinically above the 92nd percentile on the Barclay scale (the commonly accepted psychological testing scale for hyperactivity and inattentiveness) to below the 72nd percentile, or functional, in that amount of time. Now, many of these kids would still be considered "rascals." In the overall school or social community they might still be considered on the margins, or "fringe dwellers." But they had clearly taken a step in from the outside. They had entered the general flow of family and school, play and regular life, some of the time. They had more than their toes wet; they were in the social and academic stream. And if they were still far from the fast track to valedictorian and prom king status, that's all right. If they were still more on the fringe than in the center, that's okay, considering how far they had come.

How could this have happened? How could we get these results with no drugs involved? We've fully embraced the pharmacological approach to behavioral issues in America; there are now more than seven million children taking Ritalin. No other country prescribes psychoactive medications to children the way we do; Americans consume 80 percent of the world's Ritalin.[5] Our reliance on pharmaceuticals is alarming by any standard. It seems, though, partly an outgrowth of popular views of the brain as our "control tower," hardwired and fixed. With this conceptual model, the way to change behavior must be a form of rewiring. Such drugs as Ritalin and Adderall are promoted as rewiring in pill form. Another accepted analogy for the brain is a specific chemical formula, a kind of personal hormonal cocktail. If there is a deficit of serotonin in your brain's mix, then, unfortunately, you may have ADD.

And if you see ADD as entirely a function of brain chemistry, and you see that chemical ratio as fixed, then only chemical intervention makes sense.

Our study counters the view that the brain's "hormonal cocktail" is entirely predetermined and fixed. The impressive and clinically significant behavioral improvements we saw suggest that a child is affected by more than just the chemical levels in their brain, and the tendencies those levels influence. We all have hormonal tendencies. The anxious child has an abundance of cortisone that the body can't fully assimilate; the very active child has tendencies derived from adrenaline. Individual children (and adults) have individual internal landscapes and drivers. What our study shows is that these chemical landscapes and drivers (hormones and tendencies) can be affected by changes in a child's environment, and their lives. Behavioral tendencies can be soothed or relaxed by creating calm

QUITE SIMPLY:

Behavioral tendencies can be soothed or relaxed by creating calm.

In our study of children with serious symptoms of ADHD we found that when we simplified their lives they returned to a reachable and teachable state. They emerged from "amygdala hijack," a term Daniel Goleman coined in his book *Emotional Intelligence.* The amygdala is a very ancient part of our brain that determines whether we respond to a threat with either a "fight" or a "flight" to safety. This was a very handy function when dinosaurs roamed the earth. The amygdala also has a memory function, but one just attuned to trauma. So, in addition to fight/flight, the amygdala determines "Am I going to eat you, or are you going to eat me?" And more specifically, "Have you taken a bite out of me in the past?" In response to a perceived threat the amygdala then "hijacks," or bypasses, the thinking and feeling centers of the brain with a reaction that may be inappropriate to the real situation.

When a child emerges from amygdala hijack, and their behavior is no longer governed by a short-circuited response to stress or perceived danger, it changes. We saw positive changes—both an increase in attentive and a decrease in hypermotoric (too much movement) behavior—

in our study. These improvements, and the move from clinically dysfunctional ratings to functional ratings, can also be achieved through drugs like Ritalin or Adderall. But the one thing that was achieved by our methods that is not measurably achieved through drugs is this: The children in our study also experienced a 36.8 percent increase in academic and cognitive ability. Such indicators are flat with the psychotropic drugs; with Ritalin use you do not see any noticeable trough or peak in academic performance.

Good news on the homework front? Yes, but the message here extends well beyond the practical or everyday; it is wonderfully hopeful news on a basic human level. The results suggest that by paying attention to our children's environments, we can improve their ability to pay attention themselves. The "methods" used in our study were not enacted in a laboratory setting. They did not include any drugs or medications. These were lifestyle changes made by parents, teachers, and the children themselves: methods available to anyone. The "protocol" was simplification: a building up of their vitality, or etheric forces, and a quieting down of their stimulation. This study indicates that simplification can be helpful to children on a number of fronts.

I am not denying the efficacy of, or categorically decrying the use of, prescription drugs for behavioral issues. Quite clearly some children have been helped enormously by Ritalin and other drugs. I believe that these drugs have their place in a "toolbox" of methods and interventions to help children maintain a reachable and teachable state. However, I do believe they've been grossly overused and overprescribed. A mother approached me recently at a teacher workshop that I was leading. She asked to speak with me at the end of the meeting, and I could tell her concerns were more personal than professional. As we sat in two small school desks facing each other, in a now empty room, she began to cry.

Just a few days previously her son Thomas had started a regimen of Ritalin, on the recommendation of a psychologist. Thomas had had problems in school for some time and was on the verge of being expelled for his unruly, disruptive behavior. Without knowing her son, I couldn't address her situation very deeply or personally. But I have certainly seen many like it. And I could see that she was acting carefully and conscientiously, out of love, not frustration.

I told her that I think of these drugs largely as scaffolding. When a building needs work you erect scaffolding to reach the chimney or roof, to add masonry or flashing, whatever might be necessary. When the work is over, you take the scaffolding away. A lot of this medication for kids has become scaffolding, rusted in place. I think of it not as structural, not a solid addition or even buttressing. I see these drugs, most of the time, as temporary measures. Your child is about to be kicked out of school? You can modify their behavior, "pull them back" into an acceptable framework with these medicines. You can buy some time with drugs. But I don't believe they are a long-range substitute for the "work" of simplifying a child's daily life and environment. Or the "work" of understanding how a particular child learns, and making adjustments accordingly. And I think this "work" is best done, if possible, before rather than after pharmaceutical intervention.

Remarkable research is being done in a field of neurology that looks at the flexibility, or malleability, of the human brain: neuroplasticity. It has long been known that young children have enormously resilient brains. Infants can sustain massive brain injuries, losing an entire cerebral hemisphere, and still experience nearly normal development into adulthood. It was thought that this "plasticity" disappears as children reach adulthood, and their neural pathways become "fixed," but it now seems that even as we age we retain some neuroplasticity. Neurologists studying meditation and prayer are discovering new things about the structure and function of the brain and how it can be changed. In her book *Train Your Mind, Change Your Brain,* journalist Sharon Begley has written about this research, and how the thousand-years-old practices of Tibetan Buddhism are informing the cutting-edge science of neuroplasticity today.[6]

Begley describes how neurologists have been astounded by the measurable, replicable effects of meditation practice on the mind and brain. Their brain scan evidence showed that the neural activity of highly trained monks was "off the charts" (in relation to standard measures, and in relation to the neural activity of more novice monks), even when they were not meditating. The areas of the brain where such emotional complexities as maternal love and empathy are believed to be centered (caudate and right insula), and feelings of joy and happiness (left prefrontal cortex), were actually anatomically enlarged, structurally altered by virtue of the monks' lives and their meditation practices.

These results send a strong message of hope, with wide implications. It suggests that the brain has its own capacities for reorganization and repair, which could be harnessed to benefit stroke victims as well as a wide range of people with learning disabilities, senility, or depression. By recognizing neuroplasticity as a real and powerful force, we can wrest ourselves back from genetic and chemical predeterminism, from the notion that we are nothing more than a fixed pattern of genes and neural chemistry. One of the world's best-known neurologists, Oliver Sacks, the author of *The Man Who Mistook His Wife for a Hat,* among other terrific books, said in one of his lectures, "With neurology, if you go far enough with it, and you keep going, you end up getting weird. If you go a little further, you end up in the spirit."

If the brain is not the originator, the absolute control tower of our personalities, feelings, and behavior, could the brain be part of a much larger system that includes the mind, body, and spirit? The brain plasticity research, and even our own pilot study into ADD, suggest that our minds not only affect the other parts of the system but also are affected by them. For centuries Tibetan monks have followed a spiritual practice centered on meditation, which in turn has affected their immune systems and the very structure of their brains. In our study, we built up the children's physical and etheric vitality while quieting down the stimulation they were taking in. For a good percentage of these kids, this afforded them the ease to be more responsive and less reactive in their behavior and their schoolwork. Kids are not monks who can meditate for hours a day, but they do the equivalent when they are involved in play, in deep, uninterrupted play.

Some people may take issue with the term *spirit.* (You'll notice I let Oliver Sacks say it first.) Yet there is another way to look at this, one I think most parents will respond to wholeheartedly. As parents we know, without question, that who our children are is more than the sum of their genes or behavioral tendencies. Yes, she has her maternal grandmother's rich auburn hair, and those blue eyes are definitely her dad's. Her facial features are quite clearly her mother, in miniature, but her sharp, analytical tendencies are exactly like her father's. And so the genetic cards are dealt. Yet most any parent can relate to the mysterious, singular nature of each child, the thing we refer to when we say that, from birth, from the moment we first met our son or daughter, "they were who they were."

Aristotle used the term *telos* to describe this, a thing or person's essence, their intrinsic intent. Part of an acorn's telos, or destiny, is to become an oak. An acorn carries its telos within, from the beginning. Beyond our genetic gifts to them, beyond what they absorb from us and their environment, children seem to arrive with something of their very own, a telos, or intrinsic nature. That essential nature, apparent from the beginning, also points to their future, as an acorn suggests an oak. Our children come to us with a deep destiny—here again, some may say spirit—that needs to be heard. It must be honored.

QUITE SIMPLY:
Our children come to us with a deep destiny that needs to be honored.

As a society, and sometimes as parents, look at how myopic we are becoming. If we focus exclusively on the chemical makeup of a child's brain, we miss the larger contexts of who they are, and what influences them (their lives, families, their environments). If we focus exclusively on their tendencies, we miss the child; we can miss their destiny, or telos. By seeing only tendencies, syndromes, and labels, we risk not seeing our children's intrinsic intent, their deep biographical gesture in the world.

What we "see," what we bring our attention and presence to, is at the heart of who we are. And for our children, it is at the heart of who they are becoming. Why simplify? Because by simplifying our children's lives we can remove some of the stresses of too-much and too-fast that obstruct their focus and interfere with an emotional baseline of calm and security. A little grace is needed, after all, for them to develop into the people they're meant to be, especially in a world that is constantly bombarding them (and us) with the distractions of so many things, so much information, speed, and urgency. These stresses distract from the focus or "task" of childhood: an emerging, developing sense of self.

As parents we also define ourselves by what we bring our attention and presence to. This is easy to forget when daily life feels more like triage. By eliminating some of the clutter in our lives we can concentrate on what we really value, not just what we're buried under, or deluged with. With simplification we can bring an infusion of inspiration to our daily lives; set a tone that honors our families' needs before the world's demands. Allow our hopes for our children to outweigh our fears. Realign our lives with our dreams for our family, and our hopes for what childhood could and should be.

Yet simplification is not just about taking things away. It is about making room, creating space in your life, your intentions, and your heart. With less physical and mental clutter, your attention expands, and your awareness deepens.

Again and again parents have told me how a simplification regime gave them a greater sense of ease and allowed them to see beyond what their children tended to do or not do, to who they were. We see it in flashes, of course—our children's telos—but seeing it within the push and pull of everyday life takes patience. It isn't always easy to recognize the oak in the shape of an acorn. After all, our parenting may be affected by too much clutter and stress, just as our children's behavior is. We can become trapped in our own amygdala hijack, a sort of emergency response to parenting, characterized more by fear than by understanding. But with fewer distractions we can develop a wider perspective, the broader view of our own best parental instincts. This is the view that takes in your child, in their wholeness. It honors their pace, and their needs, their gift for soaking in their experiential "now."

Why simplify? The primary reason is that it will provide your child with greater ease and well-being. Islands of being, in the mad torrent of constant doing. With fewer distractions their attention expands, their focus can deepen, and they have more mental and physical space to explore the world in the manner their destiny demands.

As a parent your attention will also expand with a little less mental clutter in your life. And your awareness of your child will deepen. Beyond all of the benefits of simplification that I've outlined, there is another. It is one of those slow creepers, an unexpected joyful suffusion, something most parents would not have thought possible. The most elemental and powerful reason to simplify is this: As your awareness of your children widens and deepens, so too will your love.

You may be wondering how you can possibly make changes in your family's daily lives when you're already so busy. It's one thing to embrace the ideas in this book but quite another to implement them. Where do you start? How can you marshal your best intentions and put them into action?

I've found that the simplest path to real and lasting change is through the imagination. "Nothing happens unless first a dream. . . ." When you create a mental image of your hopes, you chart a course. You create a picture that you can then step into. Like a lasso thrown around a star, your imagination navigates the surest path to your goal.

Here, and at the end of each chapter, I invite you to relive some of the ideas and images we've covered and to imagine how they might work in your own home.

Imagine your home . . .

- as a place where time moves a little slower.
- becoming less cluttered and more visually relaxing.
- with space, and time, for childhood—and with time for one another every day.
- as a place where play and exploration are allowed, and honored.
- having more ease as you begin to limit distractions and to say no to the stress of too much, too fast, too soon.
- as a sense of calm and security take hold.
- becoming a place where those we love know it, by virtue of our attention, protection, and appreciation.

TWO

Soul Fever

Let's begin at a comfortable starting place for any process: by remembering and appreciating what we already know. We know our children, that's for sure. We know them as no one else possibly could. We know their best, shining selves, and every degree removed from that. The edge of their "too little sleep" selves, the delight of their "overcome with silliness" selves, and the sometimes dangerous intersection of those two. We know the cadence of their voices, their smells, the meaning behind their expressions, the things that engage them. We almost always know what they want to say, but can't.

The depth of our knowledge of these small beings is phenomenal. It's certainly more than just what an accumulation of days, moods, or experiences would show us. More than what we've learned from others on the subject (of kids), or what we've experienced directly. More than everything we've done to record the time we've spent together . . . our notes and pictures, our videos and memories. Yes, we know our kids better than everything we could show, or tell you about them. We see them with a sort of X-ray vision, after all. Not exactly a superpower, but as close as we come to one. We see our children with a depth of vision equal to the sum of our attention, our connection, our love for them, and our fervent desire to understand them.

This deep, instinctual knowledge of our kids—like everything else—waxes and wanes. While our love may always be there, our attention can suffer; our connection can sometimes falter, and when this happens, understanding them can seem like a whole lot of work. Our instincts are not always strong. Simplification is about stripping away the distractions and clutter that monopolize our attention and threaten our connection. It's about giving kids the ease to become themselves, and giving us the ease to pay attention. To more fully develop, and to trust, our instincts.

In the chapters ahead, we'll begin the practical steps of simplifying, of peeling away the stresses and excesses that can overwhelm a child's emotional well-being and short-circuit our instincts. But first let's look at how, with attention and connection, we can recognize when a child is overwhelmed. When they are being rushed along by too much stuff, speed, stress, or when they have what I think of as an emotional or "soul fever." Let's look at how, instinctively, we treat an emotional fever in much the same way we do a physical fever: by drawing the child close and suspending their normal routines.

As parents, we develop an instinctual sense of what to do when our children get sick. Our instincts are part childhood memories of what brought us comfort, a bit of science, a large dose of compassion, and some parental adrenaline. After all, it's a rare mom or dad who isn't humbled by their baby's first high fever, or by a long night spent sitting perfectly upright—motionless—holding a little one so congested that they can only breathe in one position. Sometimes routine, sometimes downright stressful, our children's illnesses are never convenient. Yet over time we develop ways to see them through, changing our schedules and rising to the occasion.

We learn how to support them through the chills, coughs, fevers, and rashes we come to expect. Our instincts even carry us (and them) through some of the more unusual symptoms ("So *this* is 'projectile vomiting!' ") they surprise us with ("You have nasty red bumps *where*?!"). We learn that comfort is a large part of healing, an essential ingredient in any recipe for "getting better."

One touch of their forehead, one glance at their dull eyes and we know . . . the signs of physical fever are unmistakable, unavoidable. And so we begin the process of caretaking.

Just as inevitably, our little ones (into adolescence and beyond) will experience what I've come to call "soul fevers." Something is not right; they're upset, overwhelmed, at odds with the world. And most of all, at odds with their truest selves. From the toddler who absolutely can't tolerate your authority when she is so newly intoxicated with her own, to the same child, eleven years later, who longs to fit into a social circle that bullies and berates her. Whether the source of the malady was internal or external, it's now raging within, occupying the child's attention and affecting their behavior. Affecting, also, the emotional climate of the home. You could think of these as "emotional fevers," yet I prefer "soul fever" because there is something so uniquely individual about the way each child manifests their tribulation. Just as one child never seems to run a fever, while her sister's temperature climbs into triple digits for the slightest cold, so each child wrestles their inner trials in their own way.

Often when I'm giving a talk about parenting today, a parent will ask, "How can I tell when my child is overwhelmed?" It is a common question, usually followed by "And what can I do about it?" As for the first question, my short answer is: instincts. Instincts that we may need to develop, or redevelop. Instincts that should be—and can be—as clear and reliable as those we count on to recognize and care for our children when they're ill.

This book is my best attempt to answer "What can we do about it?" It's a question that so many of us ask ourselves. The truth is, what we do, instinctually, to care for our children when they're sick could be boiled down to this: we *simplify*. This is *exactly* what we need to do when they are overwhelmed; stretched thin and stressed out by the effects of having too much stuff, too many choices, and jumping through their days too fast. It is also what we need to do when their fever is emotional rather than physical. Emotional growing pains, or soul fevers, are as natural and inevitable as the common cold, and can be "treated" in remarkably similar ways. Simplification gives children the ease they need to realign with their true selves, their real age, and with their own world rather than the stress and pressures of the adult world.

Let's start here, then, with an example that serves as a metaphor for the whole process of simplification. Let's look at what we tend to do without even thinking about it once we feel our child's fevered brow, or see in them a telltale listlessness. The steps we take, and the attention we bring to caring for our children when they're sick is, essentially, simplification. We'll look at the signs and symptoms of soul fevers as well, and go through the steps we can take to help our children build their emotional immune systems, their resiliency. Just as we notice when they're fighting a physical fever, we can become more attuned to their soul fevers, and when they're simply overwhelmed.

We can learn to recognize when their systems are out of balance. Remembering what we already know (and what it is so easy to forget when *we* are overloaded and overwhelmed), we'll reawaken our caretaking instincts by simplifying.

Noticing

Physical Fever: We begin to care for our child when we notice they're not well. Shivery or hot, slower to respond, not interested in eating, a heavy, vacant look in their eyes . . . from these signs, individually or in combination, we can tell they're "off," "not themselves." Your daughter may seem fine to me—active and bright—but one look in her eyes and *you* know that she has or is getting the cold her brother had last week. Their little bodies are not extensions of our own, but sometimes it feels that way, given how naturally we notice their physical fluctuations.

Soul Fever: Generally, we need to see a few symptoms of disquiet to identify a soul fever. Inner turmoil extends beyond a bad mood or brief snit. It also lasts longer. A child with a soul fever stays "out of sorts," taking more than a step or two toward their quirky tendencies. A child being sullen is usually just that; but if they're sullen then feisty, and tangling with friends they usually adore, we might take a second look. Soul fevers begin with a sort of prickliness, which can take different forms. Kids respond to an inner unease characteristically, depending on their temperament. An introverted child may withdraw physically and emotionally, but still perhaps "snipe," or "take potshots," at others to announce their discomfort. An extroverted child usually manifests their unease more directly, with anger or blaming.

The younger the child, the more obvious they make their unhappy state. They may become hypersensitive, aware of itchy labels, twisted tights, noises that they wouldn't otherwise even notice. Little things bother them. Tantrums become deeper, more intractable. Sleep patterns change. You can often see little changes in their posture: shoulders raised, fists clenched. Most of all, they are much more easily "set off" than usual; their emotional switch has a hair-trigger sensitivity.

You could say that they are acting "out of character," but in truth, their character is amplified, almost caricatured. In middle childhood you might see shifts in friendships, in dress or work habits. For middle school kids and teenagers you might notice your child having difficulty settling into things, whether homework, a hobby, or any activity that would usually hold their attention. Of course challenging rules and boundaries is the teenager's developmental job, but with soul fever you may notice particularly feisty challenges to rules that are firmly in place, accepted, and have never been challenged before.

Let's take an extra moment to consider adolescence, a particularly "feverish" developmental stage. Adolescence is all about polarities, and swinging between them. You can picture fairly typical ends of a spectrum: the teenager who is either a whirlwind of activity, or a motionless, dead weight on the couch. The kid who can suddenly outlast you way into the night can also sleep through their little brother's noon band practice. There is a need to belong in adolescence that's so intense it seems primal, yet a teenage boy or girl can spend more time alone, in their rooms, than they ever did before. A teenager's parents know that they can't make a comment, no matter how innocent, that is absolutely immune to challenge. Most every kid, in adolescence, seems to be heading toward a legal career. Yet among their peers the same child can be the picture of conformity, a wet noodle of agreement and acquiescence.

The movement between these polarities is the norm in adolescence. When a teenager is having difficulty, when they're emotionally out of sorts, they tend to get stuck in one extreme or the other, becoming tenacious and myopic. I remember a student I had, Teresa, who was fourteen years old, and her life was rather topsy-turvy. She had many adults in her life (parents, stepparents, and various parent substitutes), but she had little consistent, commanding, and compassionate adult presence. One day in class Teresa was being quite disruptive, in an entertaining, attention-seeking way. When I asked her to get back to her work, she realized that she definitely had everyone's attention now, and she wanted to escalate the situation. It wasn't my finest moment as a teacher, but I remember asking her, "Must you be so subjective?" to which she shot back "Do you have to use such big words when you're losing the argument?" When I explained what *subjective* meant, using the well-worn cliché of not seeing the forest for the trees, she looked at me with pure disdain. "I'm fourteen, that's my job!" With that she turned and walked out of the room.

Teresa was right; teenagers are very self-absorbed. But she was also stuck. These outbursts—symptoms of the same soul fever—were echoing throughout her life. In no arena—home, school, or friends—was she getting the counterbalance she needed. Nobody was helping her fill the middle ground, showing the value of warmth rather than anger's pure heat. Nobody was modeling compromise, how to build or hold on to relationships. She was being allowed to revel in her own power and independence, repressing her need to belong.

The developmental purpose of adolescence's polarities is a zigzaggedy path toward self-regulation. We now know the brain is still developing during these years, particularly those sections that are critical for judgment and reason. What allows a teenager to move between polarities is the (boring) stability in their lives. A safe and stable context allows teens to swing between polarities without getting stuck in one extreme or another. It gives them a center, a plumb line to use as they learn to regulate their behavior. Luckily for Teresa (who is now a college graduate and in her late twenties, by the way), the adults in her life—family, teachers, and an athletic coach—met while she was in high school to discuss and commit to ways to provide more form and consistency in her life.

The first step then, toward taking care of our child's soul fever, just as with a physical fever, is noticing it. And there will be times when just that—our noticing—will be enough for a child to feel bolstered, supported, understood. When we think back to our childhoods (as our children will to theirs), these small acts of noticing can form the emotional foundation of "home" or "family": the place where we were "read," understood, held in balance. And in adult life—in marriage and business—isn't it easy to see whose emotional landscapes were not well read? The symptoms are the same—pouting, tantrums, icy withdrawal—but they get more convoluted as we get older. As parents we can be thankful for our six-year-old's dramatically furrowed brow, his slouchy posture, his mumbled responses, his big sighs. And when he doesn't even laugh at his sister's silly dancing you know—thank heavens that subtlety and subterfuge are still beyond him—that something is really bothering him. "Sweetheart, what's up?"

Symptoms that are missed or ignored tend to worsen, or disappear and reappear in a stronger form, until the internal conflict is addressed. There are a couple of reasons why noticing a child's soul fever can be difficult. Parents who are very busy and preoccupied, overloaded themselves, can miss the initial signs of a child's unease. This happens, just as it's possible to miss the first signs of a physical fever. And as parents, we don't want to develop our own hair-trigger response to a child's normal emotional ups and downs. A pout, a bad mood: These come and go. Like the sniffles, or a bump on the knee, their effects are temporary, easily shaken. But a soul fever lingers. Years ago it might have been called a growing pain, both inevitable and painful. And while it may not seem like much to us (compared with the stresses of adult life), there is some sense of loss associated with these growing pains. When you imagine the incredible rate at which children change and evolve, you can begin to see how their heart sometimes resists the adjustment. They must let go of comforts and assurances with one hand to have both hands free to reach ahead, to pull toward some new level of maturity.

Understandably, life's pace and pressures can sometimes distract a parent from the signs of their child's soul fever. Yet when a child's emotional distress is routinely ignored, they will usually, consciously or unconsciously, find other ways to solicit attention. Parental attention is the safest and most convenient, especially when one is displaying all of one's "nasty bits" (as one four-year-old described a tantrum). But if a child can't garner attention from their parents, then attention from someone else will do; and if they can't attract compassionate attention, any form of attention can seem like a worthwhile substitute.

On the flip side of parental busyness, what I've noticed often lately are children whose behavior is already so "pumped up," so frenetic and on edge, that it's hard to notice when they're emotionally agitated. For children whose "norm" has become an elevated emotional state, and whose daily lives are rushed and pressured, there's little equilibrium to measure against, no "set point" or normal temperature to judge by. When this is the case, children can very quickly get into trouble, manifesting extreme behavior just to say something quite simple: "I need a break."

Quieting Things Down

Physical Fever: There it is: a fever, an upset stomach, a nasty cough. Once we've noticed that our child isn't feeling well, what do we do? We stop our normal routines. Even as we're trying to figure out how we can possibly accommodate the change, we're making the announcement: "No school for you, love," or "Oh dear, let's tell Erin you can play another day, but right now you need to rest." Everyone else may gather at the table for dinner, but this child is off the regular eating routines and foods. They've been pulled out of the normal flow of daily life—the chores and activities, the comings and goings—and allowed to take a passive role, to be within the group while outside the action.

Soul Fever: So, you've noticed, and something is definitely up. No matter how fast they're spinning (figuratively, or, in the case of the little ones, sometimes literally), they're actually exhausted, quite undone. With emotional overload or soul fever, just as a physical fever, once noticed, it is time to stop normal routines. Children may resist this, but at times they seem to be almost pulling you to a stop with clingy behavior and an uncharacteristic avoidance of anything new.

As when a child is ill, there is now a shift in the normal flow of family activities, an accommodation that needs to be made. Certainly the child needs to take a break from after-school activities; they might even need to stay home from school. A parent decides the length and breadth of the change for a little one. For a middle school child, you might consult with the child, still making the final decision. And for a teenager, you collaborate on the best way to make sure they really take a step back, and out, from the pressures they are feeling.

Most children, no matter what their age, can reset their emotional clock given two or three quiet days. One restful, simplified weekend is usually enough to make the difference, to break a soul fever. It affords enough space and grace to loosen an emotional knot.

When there's a real problem that underlies the soul fever, I'm not suggesting that a quiet weekend will directly address the issue. But it will help your child maintain the resiliency they need to address it. Especially with older kids, who may be dealing with difficulties at school, with friends or romances, a quiet weekend is not a cure-all. But I still contend that it can be one of the best medicines. Our impulse as a parent may be to jump in and "make everything better," which is impossible, and more clearly so as our children mature. But their success in facing and resolving issues depends on their ability to work through their emotions, to regulate their physical and emotional energy. That's when a little retreat, a break in the normal routine, can really help.

Early on in my eldest daughter's second-grade year, she told us about a girl in her class, Myrna, who was often "silly and nasty." We weren't quite sure what that combination meant, but we could tell that she was wary of Myrna. Midyear, however, the silly/nasty threat seemed to be close at hand, and our daughter was clearly being affected. She did not want to talk about it. Yet she was dragging her way through breakfast and getting dressed, even though she usually couldn't wait to get to school. "You okay, love?" Her soft yes was unconvincing. She took a day off school, and between my schedule and her mother's, spent some time with each of us, at home and running errands.

The next day, I decided to bring some of the security of home to school. I walked her in that morning and lingered while she showed me her desk and recent work. I made sure to meet her after school that afternoon, and for the rest of the week. We would take our time, hanging a bit among her classmates before we walked home. We never addressed the issue head-on, and perhaps it resolved itself in a mysterious kidlike way. But over the week I could feel her step lighten, her shoulders settle, her mood become easy and playful again.

Parents of teenagers may pick up the signs of a soul fever in their child, but they won't necessarily know what's bothering them. I've found that (yes, this is a generalization, but one based on experience) with a girl, you may only need to say this once, whereas you might need to drop it casually a few times to a boy: "Something's up; I've noticed. I'm here if you want to talk about it." Even if your teenage son or daughter won't open up about what's upsetting them, you can still be available to them. And you can still suggest a pullback from normal routines. "You don't have to tell me what's up, but I can tell something's going on, something's bothering you. In this family, we pull back, take some quiet time. Let's figure out how we can do that for you."

A colleague of mine, Margaret, used to tell me about her fifteen-year-old daughter, who was busy at school and a competitive swimmer. Margaret said her daughter wouldn't slow down and resisted opening up even when a dark cloud seemed to be following her. When I suggested a pullback, Margaret rolled her eyes, but not too long after, she instituted a quiet weekend, missed training and all. The first weekend was enforced—"You mean I'm *grounded*?!"—but Margaret has since reported that her daughter now collaborates with her on making some downtime when she feels overwhelmed.

Margaret has also noticed that once that decision has been made, once they've cleared the calendar for a couple of days, her daughter is more apt to open up about what's bothering her, what brought her to this point. I think when your feelings are complicated (this could be a new definition of adolescence), it helps to know that if you *do* choose to open up, you'll have the time to talk it out. You won't have to try to explain the whole confusing mess on the way to swim practice or between dinner and your brother's bedtime.

That first time, Margaret's daughter felt she was being "grounded." It turns out she was absolutely right. I love this very American expression, "being grounded," because in this context, it fits. When an adolescent is overwhelmed, in a soul fever, the electrical current around them is so strong that they actually do need "grounding." They need to be brought back to earth, brought back to their more relaxed, resilient selves.

Bringing Them Close

Physical Fever: Normal routines are off, pajamas are on, and the sick child needs care. At this point, we bring them close . . . physically, and in terms of our attention. We watch them closely. There are complications to illness and fever, repercussions we want to avoid. We might cozy up with them, or make them comfortable in bed. In our house we have a box of special books and little toys that we get out when one of the girls isn't feeling well. Curtains might be drawn, a special "nest" of pillows made. Everything quiets down.

At this point we might also ask ourselves how or why this happened. Is there something going around at school? Is there anything we need to find out about, or seek help with? Do they need a doctor? Do we need a neighbor or friend to get a few things at the store?

Soul Fever: An emotionally feverish child is in need of care, too. Pajama time may be optional, but downtime is not. Your child will probably not be holed up in bed, but they can still have a period of ease, time that will feel different from everyday life. Simple pleasures they rarely have time for—getting out the paints, family stories, a building project—can occupy their attention while loosening their emotional knot. One-on-one time with a parent can be a welcome change.

Physically and emotionally, they need to be brought close. Sometimes a child who is "off their game" does not need pampering so much as a quiet assurance of our presence and availability. When we change the routine and quiet things down, we are placing an unspoken emphasis on relationship, connection.

Where do they feel safest, most at peace? For many kids the answer is home, but not for all. A friend of mine takes her eight-year-old son, Jason, fishing. "We do that in good times, so I figure getting out on the lake might help when he's having a hard time, too." Nature is a warm sensory bath that can counterbalance the cold overwhelm of too much activity, information, or "stuff." Time in nature calms and focuses; for most children, it takes only a few minutes for them to begin to explore. Watch as they seek out places that feel particularly right to them, as they gather symbolic objects—leaves, sticks, bits of moss—that they discover. You can't manipulate nature, it must be delved into; it's a vibrant but neutral canvas onto which a child can pour their creativity.

Studies have shown that patients who have even just a view of trees in a hospital setting recover more quickly than those who do not. It's no wonder; nature is profoundly healing, physically and emotionally. Neurologically, time in nature can bring a child out of the amygdala-based fight-or-flight response and into the higher functions of thought that are based in the limbic system (creative) and the frontal lobes (cognition).

There are complications to soul fevers as well as physical fevers, ramifications that we want to avoid. Little kids, under seven, will work themselves right into a storm of some sort unless or until their unease is acknowledged. Too young to regulate their emotions, they will act out until everyone, including the cat or dog, has felt the effects. As children get older they learn how to repress painful feelings . . . but not entirely, or for long. Especially in adolescence, unprocessed feelings can surface in all manner of seemingly unrelated ways: an extreme haircut, severed friendships, behavior issues at school.

By simplifying you offer your child support, and a container for the issues and changes they are working through. You also offer them a model, one that may be a lifesaver as they get older. This is the lesson they will take with them: A small period of downtime is a form of care, a way of being cared for. It's true, you may be the one doing the caring now, and insisting on limitations that they may resist, but you are also beginning a pattern that they can continue for themselves and will serve them throughout their lives.

So why is your child overwhelmed? You may be asking yourself that question, just as you would if they came home with a fever. What brought them to this point? Have they been doing too much? Has there been too much to'ing and fro'ing, especially for kids whose parents no longer live together? Is there a need for more consistency or balance in their schedules, their daily lives? Is school particularly stressful? With the current mania for testing in American schools (or, "No Child Left Intact" as I call it), is your child feeling the effects?

Is it time to reach out to others for guidance or help? In more serious cases of emotional issues, of course, professional help should be considered. What we are addressing here are common cases of overwhelm and upset, for which a day or two of downtime can be helpful. Still, you might want to consider if your child would benefit from a little time with someone whose influence is steadying and reaffirming. As children reach adolescence, they will naturally develop relationships outside the family with people who are in a position to be helpful. If your daughter loves and respects her dance teacher, a heads-up call might be worth making: "Ellen seems to be going through a bit of a rough patch" . . . would the teacher mind staying close, keeping an eye out?

"When your child seems to deserve affection least, that's when they need it most." I don't know which wise soul said it first, but I applaud them. And the saying has great relevance to the question at hand: How can we make ourselves available to a child who's in the midst of an emotional fever? It's one thing to cuddle up with a child who has the flu. They're certainly not at their best, and can be quite grumpy. They would rather hand you their used tissues and throw up in your lap than use the containers you've positioned all around them. But it's quite another thing to maintain a loving presence with a child who is exploring their inner shadow as they push every one of your buttons as though you were the elevator panel in a skyscraper.

Their soul fever can easily prompt your own unless you take care of yourself, as you care for them. I counsel this to any parent whose child is having a difficult time, especially if those difficulties are being felt throughout the home. Take at least a few minutes a day (longer or more often is better, but everyone can spare three minutes) to picture your child's absolute golden self, their "good side." This will give you the balance you need to look beyond the worst of a soul fever. It will help you with the questions that could surface, such as "Is this really my child, or was he raised by wolves?" If we can manage to hold a picture of our child's higher being in our hearts, then we won't need to be the Dalai Lama to get through their tough times. But don't fake it, or gloss over the exercise. Bring out the photo book. Just take a few minutes to look through, to see her leaning over the birthday cake with three candles on it, her ringlets shining in the light. Remember when they spent the entire week at the lake, playing in and out of water up to their dimpled knees? Remind yourself that the three-year-old still exists in the thirteen-year-old . . . the one who just told you that you could never, ever, possibly understand what it's like to be her.

If you can't put together enough lovely images to be your ballast in the storm, call their grandparents, godparents, or favorite aunt. Choose the ones who love your child to bits and tell them: "Look, this is your job as [fill in the familial relation]. Remind me of everything that is wonderful about Henry. And please . . . keep going until I say stop." This will be so helpful to you, right when you need it most. Some parents who've tried this have become addicted to the endorphin rush that accompanies those sweet memories. How much you avail yourself of it is your choice, but please don't forget to do it when you need to most. Take care of yourself while caring for your out-of-sorts child.

Running Its Course

Physical Fever: We don't often know how long a virus is going to last, but we do know that there's not much we can do to short-circuit it. We can't force the pace of an illness, or control the duration. Once we've done what we can to make a child comfortable, we generally have to let them make their way through the biological process that's already begun. We've acknowledged the illness, stopped our normal routines, and brought them close. We've simplified their environment, their activities, and their intake. We usually then find a balance between closeness and the space they need to rest undisturbed.

Soul Fever: A soul fever, like a virus, has its own life span, its own duration. We simplify not to try to control, bypass, or stop our child's emotional upheaval. Our efforts aren't a bribe, an alternative to a hard-edged "shape up and get over it." In acknowledging their discomfort and drawing close we are offering them support . . . through this, and by extension, through whatever they may need to face.

We figure out that an emotional tempest can't be shortened usually with our toddler's first tantrums. I knew this intellectually—honest, I did!—but I'll never forget the day I really learned it. Our oldest daughter was three, and having an absolute showstopper of a tantrum lying in the middle of our living room floor. There was the requisite scream-crying, the pounding of the fists, but then, as I stood above her, aghast, she also reared up and gave her head a good thwack on the floor. I was frozen (when my wife tells this story, she inserts this bit here with a kind smile: "Kim, the child development expert, was frozen . . ."), when my wife walked in, picked up a pillow from the couch, calmly placed it under our daughter's head, and wordlessly sat down and began knitting. Our little one quickly wore herself out crying and fell asleep right where she lay. Phew.

Nobody gets to skip the soul fevers and growing pains of life. In order to learn who they are, and what feels right to them, a child must grapple with these emotional upsets. It's all part of self-regulation. One mom told me her daughter Amy was having difficulty fitting in at a new middle school. She said that when Amy talked, she was speaking in different voices and inflections, taking on the speech patterns of the kids she was hanging out with. "I could tell when things eased for her; she wasn't 'trying on' different people, she was coming back to herself, speaking with her own voice."

Once we recognize the signs, and simplify accordingly, we can support a child as they make their way through an emotional process that—like a fever—has usually already begun. Your support doesn't "fix" anything, it just provides a loving container for them to process the things that are bothering them. With warmth you can help keep their emotions, their sense of options, and their behavior pliable. The roots of hopelessness and helplessness need hardened soil; you maintain fertile emotional ground around your child with the compassion of your noticing and caring.

If we respond to our children's soul fevers by simplifying, chances are we won't get lost in the hyperparenting jungle. The emphasis is not on us, not on parental heroics or histrionics, not on micromanaging our children's lives and every emotion. The emphasis is on creating a calming, supportive atmosphere so that they can get through what they need to get through. Simplifying is not about using guerrilla tactics to clear a path through life for our child. So often these tactics—the immediate urge to pick up the phone and harangue a teacher, or another child's parent—is a response to the worst parental nightmare: Our child is in pain, and there's nothing we can do. Simplifying is something we can do. By simplifying we take clear, consistent steps to provide our child what they need—time, ease, and compassion—to process what is bothering them.

A Slow, Strong Return

Physical Fever: Don't you love the little signs of recovery a child gives when they've turned the corner on an illness? One mother reports that her son is such a chatterbox that the worst part for her when he's sick is the quiet. "I can't count the number of times I've prayed for a moment or two of quiet when he's well. Yet it's the silence that kills me when he's sick. I hate to see him lying there on the couch, not saying a word. I breathe a sigh of relief with the first 'Hey Mom, guess what?' Then I know he's feeling better."

Slowly we reintroduce easy, solid foods as well as activity into our child's schedule. They might go back to school for a half day; they may get to play outside, or reconnect with a friend. You're careful to ease them back into regular life, especially if they've been sick for more than a couple of days. You may notice a change in them; they've grown up just a bit. Most of all, there will be a closeness between you. You've traveled this land of illness together and made it back to everyday life. You return with greater strength, and usually with at least one or two tales to add to the family storybook. While unpleasant for them, and at least inconvenient for you, this illness has brought you closer. You've made it through.

Soul Fever: We sure do know it when the emotional storm has passed, the fever broken. Our child, in his or her ease and brightness, is back. Even more noticeably than after a physical bug, children emerge from a soul fever stronger, with greater resiliency. Their feelings of overwhelm have receded and they're ready to dive back into the flow of life again. If we pay attention to our instincts, we monitor their reentry, especially if they're recovering from the effects of "too much." Can we ease them back into their previous schedule, or is a more permanent simplification in order? Are they doing too much?

You'll notice a change in your child with each passing emotional storm. They will take something from the experience; hopefully a sense of their own strength; certainly a sense that "things get better." Even if their unease remains nameless, unacknowledged by them, they'll know that you cared enough to support them through it. You didn't walk each step with them, but you eased their way. These experiences, never convenient or fun, bring us closer. "Take the day off work?! You've got to be kidding!" Quite often I hear that response to the suggestions I've described to you. It usually happens just after I've been told about a kid who's acting out in some way, clearly overwhelmed by something—or too many things—going on in his or her life. When I suggest that a little time off, spent together, could be helpful, the idea is sometimes met with amazement. "A day off? Why?! This is an absolutely crazy time for me!" Most parents are relieved and enthusiastic about the notion of trying a little period of connection and caretaking with their out-of-sorts child. But some find the idea vague and amorphous; they would much rather I handed them a phone number, or told them of this or that expensive purchase or expert who will "set things right." The more adamantly a parent tries to convince me that a break would be impossible, the more certain I become that both parent and child need to take a step out of their everyday lives, toward each other.

Our child's fevers—physical or emotional—can be downright inconvenient. Yet their well-being is going to cost us, and them, a lot more in the future if we ignore it now. What will we "save" in terms of heartache? What are the financial savings of occasionally scheduling a day or two's camping trip, or quiet weekend together—convenient or not—compared with the cost of long-term professional counseling? My fellow Australian and dear friend Steve Biddulph (author of *Raising Boys*) doesn't equivocate. He says, "If either parent spends more than ten hours a day at work, including travel, then their child will suffer. Fifteen hours a day almost guarantees damage. Emotional problems, addictions, suicidality, depression, poor school performance all are increased by parental absence through the workplace demands made on us. Children are especially vulnerable to the absence of the same-sex parent as themselves. Boys to dads, and girls to mums, although the opposite-sex parent is obviously also important. To have emotionally healthy children in today's America means making strong choices in the face of the consumerist economy."

By carving time out of our busy schedules we place an emphasis on connection. When we simplify our child's daily life and their environment, we support them, making room for contemplation, restoration. We also provide a counter to hopelessness and helplessness. A child can always refuse the support, though, and continue to grapple with issues, sometimes in increasingly self-destructive ways.

What do you do then? You continue to offer support, and alternatives, and with your love you counter despair. Just as most kids come through the average mix of childhood illnesses and scrapes, most kids manage their emotional upheavals and move on from them, stronger and more self-reliant as a result. Even when the going gets really tough—imagine an act of vandalism, or an eating disorder—the consistency of your love and support is the best you can offer. I've sat with parents who find themselves in extreme situations with their kids: in hospital waiting rooms, police stations, truly at a loss. I think then about love's constancy; about how we carry this parental love resolutely, wherever it leads us.

In other words, we're in it—loving and caring—for the duration. From her first high fever as a baby, when motionless, you held her upright all night, so she could breathe. On through the physical and emotional fevers of childhood and adolescence. The steps are fairly simple. The instincts kick in as you notice, stop the ordinary routines, and draw them close. You don't "make them better" when they're sick, yet your care and support allows them the ease to fight off whatever nasty virus they're grappling with. When they're overwhelmed by the pressures and pace of daily life, or when their "fever" is emotional, you can offer the same pattern of care to support them. Above all, you notice. And simplify. You draw them near, while affording them the time and space to work through their own issues.

In our sped-up world, this is as close to a panacea as we can offer our little ones: a step back, a bit of time and leisure to rejuvenate. Simplification, in a small dose. A detangler of emotional knots, it's an effective tool to remember and use in the swirl and bustle of daily life.

There are no great stunts, really. With care, and a bit of luck, there needn't be. The cape around your shoulders—the heroism of parenting—is well earned and deserved. But the cape is not for flying, or special effects. It is a symbol of heroic consistency. Heroic. Consistent. Simple. Lifelong. Love.

Imagine how secure your child will feel knowing that . . .

- when something is really "up," when they don't feel right, you will notice and respond.
- when they are overwhelmed—physically or emotionally—normal routines will be suspended.
- when their well-being is threatened, they will be brought close, be watched, and be cared for.
- when they are not well, they will be afforded the time and ease to recover their equilibrium.
- your love will accommodate, and look beyond, their less-than-best selves.
- they are deeply known and instinctively cared for.

THREE

Environment

If a child has been able in his play to give up his whole living being to the world around him, he will be able, in the serious tasks of later life, to devote himself with confidence to the service of the world.

—RUDOLF STEINER

The threshold to a child's room can seem like a border checkpoint; to cross it is to pass into a foreign land. In relation to the rest of the house, a child's bedroom can be otherworldly, with its own terrain, microclimate, and definitely its own laws of physics. More items than there is physical space for somehow find purchase on top of piles, overflowing baskets, or in drawers jammed open. Under the bed there is some sort of superconductor magnet, sucking down all manner of things (who's brave enough to check?) to rest among the layer of dust bunnies.

Walls are often invisible, plastered with posters, pictures, pen marks, plaques, and "wall units" (a form of vertical storage for things that no longer fit on the floor). Topographically, the stuff functions as an archeological image of the child's commercial life so far: the deeper you dig, the earlier the toys. The room's pastel color scheme and basic furniture—bed and now bureau where the changing table once was—are no longer visible, buried under a thick overgrowth of multicolored, ever-growing, and expanding stuff.

Of course, not every kid's room looks like this. And certainly not every day. This image is surely an exaggeration. But based on my sampling of children's bedrooms, I'm certain that many parents would recognize some aspect of their own children's rooms in this picture. It is an image by no means limited to wealthy or upper-middle-class families, either; the quality of the "stuff" may differ, but the quantity can be similar across class lines.

In my lectures and workshops, I've found that the issue of stuff—the sheer quantity of toys, books, and clothes that accumulate around a child—strikes a nearly universal chord. After giving a lecture with a broad overview of "simplification," much as we covered in Chapter One, I usually suggest breaking into smaller groups to discuss issues more fully. When I ask parents to choose which of the four levels of simplification—environment, rhythm, schedules, and filtering out the adult world—they would like to focus on, the room tilts toward "environment" as most parents head in that direction.

Why do most parents want to begin by considering their child's home environment? Why do they gather, hypothetically, at the threshold of their children's rooms? There are two reasons. Certainly when one's considering a big change, it's easiest to begin with the tangible, the clearly doable. Simplification is a process, a lifestyle change that has several layers and takes time. It requires, as it builds, commitment. I have to agree that the environment we make for our children at home is an excellent place to begin simplifying. As a starting point it has traction. Simplifying your child's room is eminently doable, and most people find that it provides results and the boost they need to continue.

Most parents also connect, personally and emotionally, with the issue. They are deep in conversation, already sharing their own moments of recognition and realization, as they gather. Despite what differences they might have—in terms of background, culture, income, or politics—they find plenty of common ground when they consider how their children's rooms (and their homes and lives) have become deluged with "stuff." They've already acknowledged, at some point or another, or perhaps several times a day, that this surfeit of stuff is oppressive. Yet perhaps never before had they thought of it as potentially harmful to their children. This profusion of products and playthings is not just a *symptom* of excess, it can also be a *cause* of fragmentation and overload. They hadn't considered how too much stuff leads to a sense of entitlement. Or how too much stuff relates to too many choices, which can relate to a childhood raced through at far "too fast" a pace.

As I listen, I'm taken with the sense of surprise so many of us feel around this issue. It's as though parents realize they're on a runaway train, but they can't believe they never noticed it speeding up. Even in the span of one or two generations, there has been a sea change, a flood of items marketed to parents for their children. Or, more often than not, marketed directly to the kids. I sometimes jot down some of the comments I hear at workshops. I remember one mother saying, "My parents are quite respectful of my husband and me as parents; they don't ever say much about what they did differently or what we should do differently. But I've noticed that whenever they come to visit, they are *amazed* by the number of toys Jared has. We don't even think he has that many, compared with his friends, but my parents are truly taken aback, literally flabbergasted."

As David Elkind points out, it's only been in the past fifty years that inexpensive, mass-produced (overwhelmingly plastic) toys have flooded onto the market "in mass quantities and seemingly endless variety."[1] In his history of play, cultural historian Howard Chudacoff sets 1955 as a watershed year.[2] The Mickey Mouse Club provided a powerful new venue for toymakers, and for the first time Mattel began advertising a toy—the Thunder Burp gun—outside of the Christmas season. Almost overnight, Chudacoff asserts, children's play became less focused on activities, and more on the *things* involved, the toys themselves. In researching her book *Born to Buy,* sociologist Juliet Schor found that the average American child receives seventy toys a year.[3] No longer reserved for special occasions, toys have become staples of family life, appropriate as purchases any day of the year.

Ubiquitous, too. A dad in one of my environment workshops was bemoaning how toys are no longer just in toy stores; they're everywhere he goes. "It's like walking through a minefield, any time I'm trying to get errands done with the kids. The gas station, the grocery store . . . There are always toys, always right by the counter where you're standing, ready to pay. The other day we ran into the post office, and even there . . . There were little stuffed animals for sale. Who would want a little postal animal, for heaven's sake? My daughter. As soon as she saw them." Toys are everywhere, and nearly everything a child might need or use is now marketed as a toy: flashing shoelaces; transforming soap; character-driven school supplies, vitamins, and bandages; books with musical microchips; even scratch-and-sniff clothing.

In the workshop discussions, I've noticed an interesting progression, one that rarely fails to unfold. Early on, there are finger-pointing comments about which one in the couple is the most avid consumer, the biggest "pushover." A mom might share how her husband "bribes" the kids with toys for good behavior as the husband (who really didn't want to come to this lecture anyway!) crosses and uncrosses his legs, shifting about on the metal auditorium chair. The comments are more pointed, of course, when the targeted spouse is not there. But invariably, as parents trade stories, they come to acknowledge that the weight of consumer pressure is huge, and felt by all, moms and dads alike.

Companies have found that they can enlist our children in their marketing efforts. By targeting kids directly, they can use "pester power," meaning a child's ability to nag their parents into purchasing things they might not otherwise buy, or even know about. Just how powerful is "pester power"? While couples may differ over whether Mom or Dad is more susceptible, researchers have found that children directly impact more than $286 billion of family purchases annually.[4] Marketers have more than taken note, increasing their spending on advertising to children from $100 million in 1983 to more than $16 billion a year now. And it's working. The average ten-year-old has memorized three hundred to four hundred brands, and research has shown that by the age of two, kids can recognize a specific brand on the store shelves and let you know—with words or the ever-effective point-and-scream—that they want it.[5]

Clearly nobody is completely immune to the marketing forces arrayed against us. Yet the less exposure a child has to media, especially television, the less vulnerable they will be to advertising's intentional and unintentional messages. In her wonderful book *The Shelter of Each Other,* Mary Pipher discusses some of the unspoken lessons that advertisements teach us, and particularly our children:

- to be unhappy with what we have
- "I am the center of the universe and I want what I want now"
- products can solve complex human problems, and meet our needs
- buying products is important

These messages, over time, create both a sense of entitlement, and a false reliance on purchases rather than people to satisfy and sustain us emotionally.[6]

I once offered a lecture called "Entitlement Monsters and the Parents Who Enable Them." I thought parents might be reluctant to attend, given the title's provocation, but the room was packed. We've all met a child, or many, who believe that the world spins to please them. They have everything imaginable, yet they feel beleaguered, cheated. Life's many gifts and pleasures have made them somewhat passive, world-weary at a young age. Yet that passivity has an aggressive "chaser": If they feel they're being denied, they can exhibit outrage, and razor-sharp negotiation skills.

How does this happen? Too many choices.

QUITE SIMPLY:
Too much stuff leads to too many choices.

What's so bad about choice? As adults, as Americans, as consumers, and as a society that values individuality, we love the notion of choice. And we love to give our children choices—like gifts—about everything they see, want, or do; about every aspect of their lives. We think that these choices help them on the road to becoming who they are. We think choices clarify a child's personality, their emerging sense of themselves.

I strongly believe the opposite is true. All of these choices are distractions from the natural—and exponential—growth of early childhood. Let me frame it as an understatement: *Young children are very busy.* Their evolution in the first ten years of life—neural, social, and physical—makes what we do as adults look like standing still.

Children need time to become themselves—through play and social interaction. If you overwhelm a child with stuff—with choices and pseudochoices—before they are ready, they will only know one emotional gesture: *"More!"*

Carl Jung said that children do not distinguish between ritual and reality. In the world of childhood, toys are ritual objects with powerful meaning and resonance. To a child, a mountain of toys is more than something to trip over. It's a topographical map of their emerging worldview. The mountain, casting a large symbolic shadow, means "I can choose this toy, or that, or this one way down here, or that: They are all mine! But there are so many that none of them have value. I must want something else!" This worldview shapes their emotional landscape as well; children given so very many choices learn to undervalue them all, and hold out—always—for whatever elusive thing isn't offered. *"More!"* Their feelings of power, from having so much authority and so many choices, mask a larger sense of vulnerability.

We are the adults in our children's lives. We are the grown-ups. And as the parents who love them, we can help our children by limiting their choices. We can expand and protect their childhoods by not overloading them with the pseudochoices and the false power of so much *stuff.* And as companies spend billions trying to influence our children, we can say no. We can say no to entitlement and overwhelm, by saying yes to simplifying.

Those parents at my lectures who convene in the environment workshop are invited to create a mental image of their children's rooms. Stand with them, in those hypothetical doorways, or go right to the source, and identify the most obvious form of clutter. The answer, usually, is toys.

Toys

Imagine all of your children's toys in a mountain at the center of their room. You've rounded up all of the outpost piles wherever they gather and grow throughout the house. The large bin of bathtub toys, the pile near your phone (which sometimes allows you to talk a moment longer), the ones stuffed into bins and drawers, the revolving bunch that always end up on the kitchen table . . . add all of these to the heap.

QUITE SIMPLY:

The number of toys your child sees, and has access to, should be dramatically reduced.

The pile needs to be halved, and halved again, and perhaps again. The first removed half will probably be discarded, the second removed half will probably be both discards and some toys to be stored, and the third halving will give you your keepers. However the percentages work out for you, you should be left with only a small fraction of the toys you had before. I realize this advice transforms me into a sort of Scrooge in your eyes, a figure—I can hardly imagine what they'd look like—who's the opposite of every benevolent gift-bearing character in every popular movie and advertisement. Bear with me.

We'll look at this accumulation of toys more closely, and I'll make suggestions about which to keep, which to store in a "toy library," and which to throw away. We'll discuss the notion of fixed toys and those that engage a child. But for now I would ask you to simply ponder the sheer quantity of toys your child has, and consider what might happen when that number is reduced.

We are told, often and in so many ways, that this toy and that toy will somehow develop our child's imagination. If one such toy is beneficial, surely ten more will increase their imagination tenfold. How wonderful to envision the potential of even *more* toys—especially this very elaborate one and those dozen or so small ones—to delight, and stimulate our children? We see the toys as assets, and why stop there? Increasingly we see them as *necessary* to the growth of our children's imaginations. Needless to say, our involvement is also critical as the procurers of these vital commodities. Our motivations are generous; they fit with our deep desire to provide everything we can for our children's well-being.

Yet these basically good impulses can be manipulated. Advertisers would have us believe that our kids have no inner life at all, except that which toys—particularly their own—can provide. Their pitches suggest that our children's imaginations are blank slates waiting for the right, or newest, or most perfect combination, of toys to imprint its magic.

The attribution of creativity has shifted away from children, who come by it quite naturally, to the efforts of executives in toy company boardrooms, who claim the power to "develop" and "stimulate" creativity. An overemphasis on toys co-opts and commercializes play, making it no longer a child's natural world but rather one that's dependent on adults, and the things they provide, to exist.

Our generous impulses can also go awry. After all, if toys are seen as universally beneficial, then we have an unlimited pass to buy, buy, buy, and buy one or two more. What started as a generous desire to please and provide can assume its own life. It can become addictive, feeding our own needs rather than our children's. Overworked and undernurtured, we parents sometimes use toys, or stuff, as a stand-in for relationship. Our kids' joy fills an empty space within ourselves. We may be feeling disconnected, tied up in our many responsibilities, distracted by all that we have to do. A fast way to "connect" with our kids—and surely "fast" is better than "not at all"?—is to give them something new.

We buy toys with a degree of compulsiveness that children pick up on. What does it say to them? As the mountain of toys in their room grows, it also speaks. It speaks as loudly as advertisements, and its messages are the same, I believe, as the ones Mary Pipher identifies. What comes through to our children, loud and clear, is "Happiness can be bought!" and "You are the center of the universe!"

Isn't it a joy to watch a child with a new plaything? It really is a pleasure. As parents, we delight in their ability to focus on something so exclusively, to give themselves over to it in the "flow" of play. We can't get enough of it. However, that natural ability can be derailed by having too many things to choose from, too much "stuff." Nothing in the middle of a heap can be truly valued. The attention that a child could and would devote to a toy is shortened, and eclipsed by having too many. Instead of expanding their attention, we keep it shallow and unexercised by our compulsive desire to provide more and more and more.

Ironically, this glut of goods may deprive a child of a genuine creativity builder: the gift of their own boredom. I'll cover this more extensively in Chapter Five, on schedules, but essentially, boredom is the great instigator and motivator of creativity. The frustration of having "nothing to do" is usually the start of something wonderful. We rob children of opportunities to test their own creative mettle when we step into every breach and answer every sigh with another toy or offer of entertainment.

So, here is the paradigm shift that I am suggesting for toys: Less is more. No special toys, or quantity of toys, is necessary to develop a child's imagination. Children use and grow their imaginations quite naturally. They only need time to do so. Plenty of open-ended time, and mental ease.

QUITE SIMPLY:

As you decrease the quantity of your child's toys and clutter, you increase their attention and their capacity for deep play.

A young couple, Sue and Mike, attended a workshop of mine in New Hampshire. As we broke into small groups, they announced that they had transformed their children's rooms after they had listened to one of my CDs on simplification. The rest of the parents in this group were contemplating such a move, so they were very interested to hear how Sue and Mike had accomplished it in their home.

Sue and Mike had two kids, a five-year-old daughter, Elise, and Mikey, a three-year-old son. They started their story by describing the way their kids would fight, rather than play, with the toys that they had.

"We had a lot," Sue said. "I'm not even sure how it happened, but between us, our parents, and all of their uncles and aunts, we had tons of toys." Confronted with this pile, Elise and Mikey would behave consistently, but very differently from each other. "Elise loved to organize them. She loved to sort the toys, and she was forever making little arrangements, and lining them up in different configurations," said Sue. "And screaming," Mike added.

"Yes, she was often screaming, because Mikey loved nothing more than to break the toys, and mess up her arrangements!" As they talked we could all see that they were not describing an occasional upset, or what a "bad day" *might* look like at their house. "It was constant," they both said, and Sue admitted to reading every book on siblings and sibling rivalry that she could get her hands on. But when a friend lent them my CD, both parents really connected with the concept of simplification, and they established their first beachhead at the toy pile. "It took us two or three days, but we had, in effect, an 'anti-Christmas,' " Mike reported, reducing the number of toys to maybe a tenth of what they had before.

Everyone in the group wanted to know the same thing: "What did your kids do?!" Both parents agreed that at first, their kids hadn't noticed. It wasn't until the final reduction, when they put most of the toys that they had not thrown out into "toy library" storage, that the kids saw the difference. "At first, they just stood there," Sue said. "Mike and I kind of held our breath. We explained that some of their toys were in storage and might come out again. But really, we hardly finished saying that when they started playing. They each found something they hadn't seen for a long time and started playing."

Sue and Mike had been concerned that their kids just did not, and could not, get along. Certainly there's going to be friction among siblings, but I think Elise and Mikey were often reacting not so much to each other, but to a feeling of overwhelm. Elise's response to all of those toys was to try to control them, to herd and classify them, while Mikey's response was to pound them. Elise was constantly barring her little brother's way to protect her sense of order, but this would only send him into further paroxysms of destruction. She continually sorted, overcontrolling in her behavior, while Mikey created chaos, clearly out of control in his behavior.

Sue and Mike went on to describe the things they had noticed since they simplified. Their kids' fighting had dissipated (not disappeared, but eased up considerably), and they were now much more focused on their play. As Sue and Mike described how Elise and Mikey played now, I could see that in many ways they had become "unstuck"—they weren't fighting constantly, or fixed in their separate, obsessive roles ("Elise the Organizer" and "Mikey the Destroyer"). They were free to focus on their play, and they seemed to be progressing through the play stages: parallel ("I play this while you play that"), cooperative or crossover ("If we use your bricks and mine we can build a bigger house"), sociodramatic ("I'll be the witch and you can be the little boy in the woods"), and game play ("Let's say that if someone touches the line, they're out").

Mike mentioned one other thing about their recent efforts. "It was fun," he said. There were some raised eyebrows in response, but when he seemed to want to take it back, Sue clarified. She said the work wasn't exactly fun, but that she and Mike had felt a real sense of shared purpose simplifying the kids' toys and room. They had worked together, and both had shared in the sense of accomplishment, as well as the excitement, as they noticed their kids settling down, and into, their play. There were nods of understanding in the group as Sue admitted that she and Mike hadn't felt like they were both "pulling together, rowing in the same direction" as parents for a while.

Evidently Sue and Mike were *also* progressing through the stages of parental play! After a long period of parallel efforts, they were experiencing a welcome stage of crossover, or cooperative parenting.

The Power of Less

In years of helping people simplify their lives and homes, I've come up with some basic guidelines for how to reduce the amount of stuff we are surrounded by. Our focus here is on the child's environment, so we'll give special emphasis to their room. However, unilateral changes will *not* be possible given children's well-developed sense of fairness (that is, their ability to see through hypocrisy). If the entire house is cluttered, with every surface covered, every crannie crammed, then your streamlined, simplified child's room will not last. Some form of homeostasis among the rooms will develop—either their room will reclutter, or its simplicity will prove your inspiration for decluttering elsewhere. However it happens, the more consistent you can be in simplifying throughout the house, the more wholeheartedly your commitment will be understood and embraced.

What's the magic number of toys a child should have? There are no absolutes, of course. One night after a lecture a mom asked, "If fewer toys are better, is it best to have none at all?" No, I'm not advocating complete toy deprivation. A half dozen or even a dozen toys may be too few for children beyond eighteen months of age. Beloved toys are sacred; they stay. And there has to be a good mix of toys. We'll address the keepers and the mix after we create some space by reducing the pile.

QUITE SIMPLY:

A smaller, more manageable quantity of toys invites deeper play and engagement. An avalanche of toys invites emotional disconnect and a sense of overwhelm.

If you have a large number of toys, you'll need to whittle that quantity down considerably. This is best done without your child. . . . That is, if you want to get the task accomplished. By yourself you can declutter dramatically, guided by your own sense of what toys have "staying power" for your child. When you're finished, they may greet the results with a question about one or two things that they miss. However, if you try to declutter with your child, whether they are three years old or twelve, they will likely argue to save everything in the pile. They'll profess undying love for all of the things they never play with, the toys that have been broken or long forgotten. Again, this is a job best done without them.

It would be wonderful if you could donate your undamaged, usable toys to charity. But the unavoidable (and liberating) first step is to throw many of them out. In any given pile there are usually a good number of toys that are broken, unrecognizable, or separated from whatever used to make them whole or give them meaning. Toss them in to the "out they go" trash bag.

One principle is vitally important, and it will be your most trusted guide to simplifying your child's toys. Ask yourself, "Is this a toy my child can pour their imagination into, or is it too 'fixed'?" By "fixed" I mean is it already too finished, and detailed, too much of one—and only one—thing? Does it "do everything," or can a child change it, manipulate it, dream into it? Is this a toy that "does" so much (this button pushes the ejector rods, this button triggers the lights, this button launches the missiles), that my child's main involvement will be sitting there pushing buttons? Is this toy so complex that it can only break?

Let me illustrate the concept with a few stories. It seems there was a study done (proving the theory that in academia, the stranger the study, the greater the funding) that looked at the amount of "violence" that poor Barbie has suffered over the years. The question behind the study is one I think most parents can attest to: Why are there so many "Barbie parts" per square inch of your average sandbox or toy pile? Why has poor Barbie so often lost her head, or a limb, in service to her owner? Why is she being treated so unkindly? Is this an unconscious, feminist, politically correct statement on the part of our young daughters? Who knows, that might be part of it. After all, Barbie looks like nobody any of us knows.

But more to the point, I believe, is that Barbie and Ken are pretty finished pieces of work, to say the least. They can be dressed differently, and changed superficially, but their expressions, their bodies, their "images" are fairly fixed. Compared with a simple doll, one that can be cuddled, and transformed through play, Barbie does not invite much emotional investment from a child. Toys that are very fixed or conceptually complex usually—not always, but usually—get either left or pulled apart. As you excavate the toy pile, I think you'll find that there is often a lot of collateral damage done to these fixed toys. The less emotional investment they invite, the more damage they sustain.

The toys that endure, in reality and in our memory, are often the simplest ones. The less they do, the more they can become, in play. When you think back to the toys you treasured, the ones you might still have as an adult, they are often quite elemental. Granted, fully digitalized robotic dinosaurs didn't exist when you were a kid (or, speaking for myself, when I was a kid), but even within the range of your childhood (from stuffed bears to plastic ovens), the toys you remember are probably from the simpler side of the spectrum.

In the 1970s, architect Simon Nicholson wrote about his "Theory of Loose Parts," which is sometimes cited now in the design of play spaces and structures for children. What he noted was that the degree of creativity and inventiveness possible in any environment relates to the kind of variables in it. In other words, in play children use what they can move, and what they can transform with their imagination. In nature, the rock pulled up from the streambed becomes a mountain, the pile of sticks becomes a house. The creativity is not in the things themselves, it is the force with which children move, imagine, and design with them. This flexibility is the difference between fixed toys and open-ended toys.

Isn't it interesting that the thrust of most toy companies now is not toward flexibility, but toward more complex and technological toys? In noting how toys and gadgets are merging, *The New York Times* reported that such companies as Fisher-Price, WowWee, Hasbro, Razor USA, and others, in response to faltering toy sales in recent years, have responded with more and more high-tech toys.[7] One reason for this is "age compression." Many companies that market to children have decided not to promote their products simply to the age group for which they are intended or appropriate. Arguing that kids are maturing faster these days (KAGOY, a marketing industry term, means Kids Are Getting Older Younger), they reach down to younger and younger kids, hoping to expand their markets, hoping to pull a child along faster, commercially if not developmentally.[8] Children (especially girls) as young as six are now being targeted for tween products. "We are definitely seeing a trend in young girls as young as 8 or 10 years old receiving their first cellphones," said Jeff Nuzzi, director of global marketing for THQ Wireless. "We like to call it the mobile rite of passage."[9]

The trend toward more high-tech toys speaks to the presumed need for more and more stimulation to hold a child's attention. This notion has been sold to us so aggressively not by any one advertisement, but by the cumulative whole. It is the endgame of the commercialization of play. It asserts that play requires products, and that parents must constantly increase the quantity and complexity of toys to capture their children's attention. In a world as sped-up and hypercharged as our own, surely the last thing our children need is more stimulation.

Yet the siren song of the "industry of play" is catchy, and alluring: "This incredibly complicated, high-tech toy has it all. It is the one that will hold your child's attention. *This* is the one." Sadly, I see how many parents have unconsciously, yet wholeheartedly, accepted this idea, continually buying the toy of the moment. It can become an addiction, both for the givers and receivers.

QUITE SIMPLY:

If you give a child less and less complexity, they become more interested, and this cultivates true powers of attention.

This is a paradigm shift, and as such, it seems counterintuitive. We've been told to think, and move, in another direction for so long.

And toys are just one analogy, one part of a different way of thinking about children and their needs. By simplifying the number and complexity of our children's toys, we give them liberty to build their own imaginary worlds. When children are not being told what to want, and what to imagine, they can learn to follow their own interests, to trust their own emerging voices. They can discover what genuinely speaks to them.

As you simplify, you allow children to pour their attention, and themselves, into what they are doing. When they're not overwhelmed with so many toys, kids can more fully engage with the ones that they have. And when the toy is simpler, children can bring more of themselves to that engagement. There is freedom with less: freedom to attend, engage, and absorb. Toys that don't do things can become anything, in play. When we don't try to fill children's minds and toy chests with prefabricated examples of "imagination," they have more freedom to forge their own, to bring their own ideas into play.

Our parental roles are simplified, too, when the world of play is realigned with kids rather than consumerism. When we refute the notion that our child's development is a race we have to win, and that their imagination is for sale, we step off a consumer treadmill. Our kids gain time and freedom to more deeply explore their worlds, and we are liberated from a false sense of responsibility and control. Rather than providing the newest in an unending list of "must-have" toys, our generous impulses can be harnessed to provide in simpler, more powerful ways. We can provide for our children by safeguarding their time and opportunities for open-ended imaginative play.

Getting Started: The Discard Pile

So, the primary push in simplifying toys is to reduce the quantity and complexity of your child's playthings. Here is a checklist to keep in mind as you dig your way through the pile, deciding which to discard. Remember, you are the final arbiter; this list is simply a guideline. Whether you embrace the ideas behind it or not, the list may at least give you food for thought. Even if you follow your own criteria, your goal will hopefully be a much smaller pile in the end. Those toys that are not discarded may be divided into keepers that will find a place in the room, and others that will be put into storage, and may later be "recycled" into the room as others are "recycled out."

10-Point Checklist of Toys Without "Staying Power"

1. BROKEN TOYS

   Large or small, old or new, unless it is among the handful of dearest toys, if it's broken, toss it. Include in this category the ones that "you'll fix as soon as you call or write the manufacturer and get replacement parts." If it is truly dear, and you can fix it or get it fixed, consider keeping it, but remove it until it's repaired.

2. DEVELOPMENTALLY INAPPROPRIATE TOYS

   You don't want toys that your child will "grow into" in a few years. As you go through the toy pile you'll notice that the simpler, more basic toys have a longer developmental life. A solidly built dump truck can be played with for years and years; the same applies to a beloved doll. Most toys, though, especially those tied to something specific—a character, television show, age range—have built-in "expiration dates." Prune toys as regularly as you streamline clothes. As with clothes, give the toys your child has outgrown to parents of a younger child. This helps you simplify, and helps others break the cycle of consumerism. If you're sentimental about some of those dear old toys, you can keep them for yourself, in storage, but don't "store" them indefinitely in your child's mix of keepers.

3. CONCEPTUALLY "FIXED" TOYS

   So many toys in the average toy pile are detailed, molded plastic characters from movies, comic books, or television shows. Ninety-seven percent of American children six or under have products based on TV shows or movies.[10] They may evoke memories of the original entertainment that inspired them. They may also point down a road of commercial possibilities, with more and newer products, "sequels of stuff." Taken together, though, a Teenage Mutant Ninja Turtle next to Darth Vader next to Hannah Montana next to Dora the Explorer, all beg the question: Whose imagination is being celebrated: Hollywood's or the child's?

4. TOYS THAT "DO TOO MUCH" AND BREAK TOO EASILY

   Chances are, the exploding lunar rocket that shoots flames and collects rock samples no longer does either. These specialized functions are prone to mechanical failure. And like other very fixed toys, the rocket doesn't tend to morph into anything else in play. Its own rigid concept takes the place of, rather than inviting, the child's imagination.

5. VERY HIGH-STIMULATION TOYS

The toys that strive to re-create a video arcade experience—complete with flashing lights, mechanical voices, speed, and sound effects—set the "stimulation bar" very high for your child. They are designed to entertain, and, like adult-sanctioned jolts of espresso, to "excite." My issue with these toys is that they add to a frenetic, cumulative whole. So many things children experience today come with a rush of adrenaline. From increasingly in-your-face advertising and programming, movies designed for sensory overload, children's increased access to adult news and media . . . many aspects of a child's daily life have been "dialed up" several notches.

Frequent bursts of adrenaline will also increase the cortisol levels in your child's system, which are slower to build but also much slower to decrease. These hormones don't differentiate between real and simulated stress. And the physiological effects of consistently elevated hormone levels are the same regardless of what triggers their release: so-called "entertainment," or real danger.

When children are seen less as impressionable beings to protect, and more as a gold mine of a market to exploit, the competition for their attention is fierce. Advertisers feel the need to scream to be heard. Add to this the prevailing assumption that greater and greater levels of stimulation are necessary to hold a child's attention. In a world as hyperkinetic as ours, why would we need to "entertain" or "stimulate"? Why willingly hijack a child's equilibrium? Individually, are these toys damaging? Is a roller coaster ride? No, but I believe we are seeing the effects of children whose nervous systems have been calibrated to "high"—the new "normal"—as a result of so much collective, daily sensory stimulation.

6. ANNOYING OR OFFENSIVE TOYS

As you can see, some toys will fit a number of these categories. Even if these aren't high-stimulation toys (and they often are), they're toys that offend the senses in some way. They are often "favorite uncle toys," purchased by someone who doesn't have children, or who knows that they'll only be visiting for a short time. They make an awful noise, or project an offensive attitude, or they may be quite simply ugly. Toys that are truly offensive to the parents, but not the child, still qualify as chuckable. Early childhood is a period of exploration and sensory development. Toys that feel good and are made of natural materials invite exploration. With the prevalence of cheap, plastic toys on the market, it is easy to gather dozens and dozens of them without much effort. However, when divesting your home of toy and clutter overload, you *can* be selective. Consider the sensory and aesthetic beauty of those you keep.

7. TOYS THAT CLAIM TO GIVE YOUR CHILD A DEVELOPMENTAL EDGE

This or that remarkable new toy will not make your child more creative, socially adept, or smarter, despite all the claims its manufacturer makes. Once we reclaim our child's creativity, and the wonders of their developmental growth as intrinsic—internal, and theirs alone!—we, and they, will be freer. As parents we won't feel so pressured to "exercise" and "supplement" what they are naturally driven to develop. And children will have "play" back, as their rightful domain, rather than simply having tickets to our culture's commercialized version of play. If you feel pressured as a parent to buy a toy because you fear that without it your child will "fall behind" or not "measure up" to other kids his or her age, chances are it is not a toy you want to buy. I'm not suggesting that such a toy might be harmful; I'm suggesting that thinking about toys in this way can be. Not only is it an expensive, slippery slope that can lead to overload, it also derails "play." Play is not a race. It is not an advancement opportunity.

8. TOYS YOU ARE PRESSURED TO BUY

Are you a victim of "pester power"? Most parents are, at one point or another. A study noted that the average number of requests a child made for something was eight, but 11 percent of the kids surveyed admitted to asking for something they wanted *more than fifty times.*[11] If you see this "something" in your child's toy pile, you've already given into the pressure. Isn't it helpful, though, to see these much-desired toys now buried and forgotten? It can remind us that we are all—children and parents alike—victimized by such aggressive marketing. You can put a stop to it in your home by limiting your children's exposure to advertising, and by not taking the bait.

Some toy companies offer children incentives to keep them involved with their brand. Like "pyramid schemes" for kids, these toys come with access to a website that offers kids games with points, and rewards that they can accrue. Children are encouraged to "invite your friends!" to the site and are thus drafted into the company's viral marketing plan.

Included in this category are "fad" toys. These are the ones that play on your child's fear of not having "what everyone else has." It can be difficult to say no, but the difficulty, believe me, is temporary. Fads are self-regulating; they fade out quickly. And in no time a new toy will be the one to have. Parents who give in to fads have to keep up with each new one; those who hop off that train don't. As a child grows into adolescence, not only will peer pressure increase, so will the prices of the latest "must-have" gadget. And while individual instances or occasional indulgences in this competition (for that is what it is) may be harmless, cumulatively such a path can erode a child's sense of morality, their view of what's important in life. The longer you play along with the "keeping up" and "one-up" game, the more difficult it can be to stop.

Soon after my eldest daughter turned eight, one of her friends got a very expensive, much-admired doll as a present. In the months that followed, several other girls also got these dolls. These pricey dolls would easily fit into the "fad" category, but I include them here since they changed the dynamics of play between girls who had been friends for years. For a while all was well. Play didn't focus exclusively on the dolls, and there was sharing within the group. However, soon the once-harmonious social mix of six girls was seriously split between the "haves" and "have-nots" with anger, hurt feelings, jealousies, and conflicting loyalties circulating like a swarm of bees among them.

A couple of us parents of the "have-not" girls spoke to one another. Together we confirmed that whether we could or could not afford these expensive dolls, we would not give in to the pressure. In a week or two we noticed that the hurt feelings had cleared. The "have-not" girls had moved on, involved and engaged in other things. The "have" girls were feeling somewhat isolated in their exclusive play with the dolls. They began to seek out the others, interested once again in the larger group, what was happening, and what they were missing.

9. TOYS THAT INSPIRE CORROSIVE PLAY

Many parents assume that this refers only to "guns" or weapons. Actually, any kind of toy can sometimes inspire play that isn't joyous, or even pleasant. This is a "you know it when you see it" category. To address guns first, though, it's clear that boys will often make sticks or any manner of things into play weapons. That doesn't concern me so long as the weapons are imaginary, and the play does not physically harm anyone. However, fully detailed plastic assault rifles are a step beyond. Even if they don't actually shoot, in their specificity and detailed singularity they seem to condone and even glorify violence. You may find studies to support either side of this issue, but I personally have no doubt that violent video games, movies, and television shows also negatively affect a child's play, and their interactions with others.

10. TOY MULTIPLES

Do you remember the story of the sorcerer's apprentice? The sorcerer's young apprentice, left to tidy up the workshop, soon tires of fetching water and mopping the floor. Using magic he is not fully in charge of, he conjures up many brooms to do the work for him. Soon, however, he is surrounded by these madly sweeping brooms, pails, and water. The rising tide of water threatens to drown him. The same thing can happen with toys. They can multiply, seemingly by magic. Let's say your child has a favorite stuffed elephant who sits in a place of pride on the bed when it is not being hauled about. You and your spouse and any family member who sees this human/elephant love story can be inspired to re-create it by purchasing stuffed elephant siblings, other jungle animal cousins, or stuffed "friends" of every kind. Soon the bed is covered with them. There are too many to carry around, or properly "care for" with the occasional cooling dust bath or invitation to tea. Names have been dispensed with, and the original elephant looks a bit threadbare suddenly, surrounded by so many new, robust but unhugged companions.

You are going to have more than a few blocks and balls, multiple crayons, doll clothes, and games. In fact, there will be plenty of "multiples" in your child's mix of toys. However, if one speedy race car is a delight, that does not mean that three of them will be delight cubed. If your child has many versions, or copies, of the same toy, consider reducing the number to a more manageable and lovable little group. This is especially important if the original toy (not the "clones") is one your child has imbued with special affection and loyalty. Our best intentions to increase the circle of love surrounding our child can have the opposite effect. By overwhelming a true connection with too many superfluous ones, we can send a message that relationships are disposable.

The Antidote

Have I thoroughly depressed you with this list? If it doesn't downright dampen their mood, it gives most parents pause. We're so accustomed to thinking of toys in purely positive terms: "Fun!" "Educational!" "Guaranteed to please!" It's no wonder that our children's bins and rooms are overrun with them. Who wants to consider what "evil lurks inside the toy chest"?! Who wants to look at the unadvertised, unintended, and not-so-positive effects that some of these toys have on our children? Or to consider how having so many toys can affect their attention and their sense of entitlement?

I applaud you for persevering. And after the doom-and-gloom session we've just had, I understand you need an antidote. You need a glimpse of what a simplified play environment can be, and what it can offer your child. Coming right up.

So as not to leave you sitting among piles of toys, some to be discarded, stored, or kept, I'll make a few suggestions for organizing. From there we'll take a look—hopefully an optimistic and inspiring one—at what you've been working toward in simplifying your child's toys and play environment.

Organizing What Remains

Congratulations are in order once you've slogged through the pile and pulled out most of the excess toys. At first it's fun, digging around for that plastic exploding disaster from Grandma, or the one with the high-decibel whine, and tossing them gleefully into the discard pile. (By the way, to avoid hurt feelings, you can label a storage box with the name of the gift giver for easy retrieval. "Grandma" or "Uncle Bill" toys can then reappear when they come to visit.) It's a real pleasure to declutter, to see clear surfaces again. It's calming, for you and your children, to be surrounded with clean lines and a simpler palette rather than a riot of shapes and colors.

Once you've identified all of the discards, you'll be left with a group of toys that are fine, undamaged, but not members of the keepers group. These toys can be put into storage, forming a toy library. In the future they can be brought back into the child's room, and back into play, but only on a "lending library" basis. In other words, for every toy that reenters the room, one from the room must be put into storage. This isn't a rule imposed for the sake of pickiness; it's a finger in the dike of our culture's flood of "stuff" just waiting to reenter your home. I've found that until parents have really embraced simplification, they must be careful not to reopen the "stuff" floodgates. However, I've also seen that once they've simplified enough to appreciate the changes it inspires, no vigilance is necessary. The process, and choices involved, become second nature.

Ideally, you want a small number of beloved toys at hand and visible at any given time. Beyond those, you can have others that are accessible (in baskets or bins), but not visible. Either they are under the bed, and can be pulled out to be played with, or they are covered by a lid or by fabric. You can use whatever organizing system you wish, but you want to dramatically limit the visual clutter. My preference has been to have some large baskets, covered or draped with colored fabric.

By keeping the toys low—at a child's level—and movable (that is, in baskets or carts that can be pulled out), you are inviting a child's participation in cleanup. If the bin or toy chest is unmovable, a child will usually clean up . . . one . . . item . . . at . . . a . . . time. First they'll bring this one over to dump in the bin, then they'll go back for this very interesting one, which really needs to be looked at more carefully, because really, when it is connected with this one over here. . . . The child is fully involved again, but not in cleaning up. If the basket can be slid to the child, then he or she can use both hands to tidy up, staying right there, engaged, until the task is done.

By displaying and playing from one basket at a time, a child is better able to focus while playing, and to clean up. Upending huge bins of toys sometimes seems like a bonanza, a luxury of possibilities. In daily life terms, however, doing so just creates, and re-creates, chaos. Areas of clutter around the house tend to be hot spots for difficulties with transitions and discipline. The forces of time and space naturally collide where there is too little time and too much stuff. Kids tend to spin out in response to too many things, making cleanup and transitions even more problematic.

How many toys can your child (depending on their age) put away, by themselves, in five minutes? Let that be your guide. Reinforce the notion by storing most toys out of view and by saying, when necessary: "That's enough toys out now."

I'll make more suggestions for organizing as we continue. However, after such a prolonged focus on what *not* to keep, one longs to consider the keepers. After all of the work of discarding, let's consider play, and what it can be when simplified. Hopefully, where once there stood a mountain of playthings, you now have a relative "molehill" of beloved toys.

Simplified Play

You are the best judge of what delights and engages your child. You know which toys fit them developmentally, which ones they cherish. I think you'll be amazed by how many toys really will be forgotten—not even missed—if they disappear. On the other hand, you know which of your child's toys have currency over the long haul. While one might be up on the shelf at the moment, you know it's just on hiatus. It's a keeper; it won't be out of circulation for long. You know the ones that are carried around, the ones that have made a place in your child's heart, their stories and conversations, perhaps even their dreams.

Even more than with the discards, I am going to address the keepers in general terms. Rather than list toys that may or may not fit your child, I'd like to discuss some ideas about play, to paint some images that are not tied to any particular toy, or to any Hollywood script. I'd like to begin with this assumption (which I'm hoping you'll grant me, now that you've slogged through an overgrown toy pile): Kids don't need many toys to play, or any particular one. What they need most of all is unstructured time.

Hopefully, you'll see that in simplifying your child's toys and play, you are also simplifying your parental "duties." You don't need to stimulate or enrich play. You don't have to control it. Sometimes we parents help most by getting out of the way, while being available. We can provide time, opportunities, and resources. Play is an of-the-moment affair, as any parent knows who's fielded an urgent request for "feathers!" or "a really floppy hat" or "something we can use for a grocery cart." The resource providing can be tricky. But by allowing rather than controlling, we give children a sense of freedom and autonomy. Their play is open-ended, the choices and decisions are theirs to make, and the discovery process includes self-discovery.

QUITE SIMPLY:
Children's play flourishes when we "let it" rather than "make it" happen.

So I'll offer no list of "must-have" toys. Instead, consider play at its simplest: what it can do and be for kids, what needs it fills, and what develops naturally from it. There is nothing novel in what I'll suggest, but these simple elements of play are worth reconsidering. They may remind you of some activities and pastimes that don't rely on hordes of toys. They may also suggest new directions for our parental generosity, our natural desire to provide for our children.

Moving away from things and toward experiences, we can be indulgent with time and opportunities for exploration. We can be lavish, unsparing with the space and time kids need to move and be physically active; bounteous with opportunities for them to connect with nature and others. Our generosity can stretch and expand in response to their need for make-believe, art, purpose, music, and joyful, busy involvement.

A mix of toys should definitely be part of a child's world of play. It just shouldn't be the overwhelming center. Within the following descriptions you will see places for some of the toys you've already identified as beloved, your child's keepers. You may even be inspired to add to the mix you have, to round it out with some simple toys that could inspire new directions in their play.

Trial and error. The long process toward a baby's first steps is driven by her desire to see and experience more of the world. From turning her head to the side, to pushing up on her elbows while lying on her belly, and eventually to rolling over, each phase requires repetitive trial and error, and great effort. It's a personal struggle, but it is also a re-creation, in miniature, of our evolution as humans into vertical bipeds. Re-creating all of human development takes time, even if most infants manage it within a year and a half or so. It requires many hours of "floor time," of stretching, scootching, and crawling about.

There has been a dramatic rise in "sensory integration" therapy in the past ten years, which strives to build neural connections and pathways that were not established naturally through these early childhood activities. In our hurry to have our children walk, or in our anxiousness to serve them, we may cause them to skip stages essential for neural development. Instead, when we let the process happen—without trying to hurry or help it along—we are allowing the development of our child's brains and bodies. We are also helping them sow the seeds of their own curiosity, attention, perseverance, and will. All of these faculties will continue to grow and develop through play.

Touch. Children use and develop all of their senses through play. Touch is the most prevalent of these for small children, and so they put *everything* into their mouths, that most sensitive of touch organs. A child's sense of touch metamorphoses into their awareness of the world, and their awareness of their own body, and boundaries: of self and "other." A child who does not fully develop their sense of touch through explorative play can become hypersensitive to their own personal space and hypersensitive (or not fully aware) of another's. Consider your child's play environment through various lenses of "touch." Natural materials, ones that invite touch, will inspire your little one's explorations, their sensory safaris.

Outside, they'll want to dig, feeling the give of dirt warmed by the sun, or the cool viscousness of mud. But what will they be touching in their room, in their indoor play? What textures and weights, what angles and smooth lines? Not every toy will provide this, but it is wonderful when a toy engages more than just a young child's fingers. When a little one buttons a doll's sweater, sits it up, and cradles it in their arms, he or she is using small and gross motor movements, yes. More to the point, though, they are putting more of themselves—almost their whole bodies—into the connection, the interaction. Rattles, nesting cubes, cloth dolls for babies, silks and scarves, heavy woolen blankets and cloaks, the pliancy of beeswax and clay as they warm to touch, a basket of smooth pebbles that change color when wet, solid wooden blocks and shapes, gnarled roots and sticks, beanbags.

Food preparation offers a parade of sensory delights for children: kneading damp, stretchy bread dough, its aroma as it bakes, stirring all manner and consistencies of liquids, forming shapes with cookie cutters, seeing butter melt and spread into the warm craters of toast. Even toddlers can have their own "real" kitchen tools, such as a workboard or mat, apron, wooden spoons, vegetable brushes, rolling pin, pots and pans, whisks and spatulas, with cloths for polishing apples and tidying up. Garden tools also should be real: a wheelbarrow or garden cart, garden gloves, with a small, but real shovel, rake, and trowels.

I think it is important that, whenever possible, what a child touches be real. A plastic hammer has no solidity, no weight or heft in the hands of a five-year-old. Even small versions of real tools are preferable to such blatantly false imitations. Granted, a child must be taught how to use real tools, and monitored for a time. But with such play comes the bonus of genuine involvement and mastery. A small worktable or bench, preferably right alongside the larger one used by Mom or Dad, can involve a child to lesser and greater degrees over many years.

Imagine the tactile pleasure of a tree stump, and an old-fashioned turning hand drill. For some kids, the pulling and pounding may lead to genuine skills. More likely it will just be time spent happily doing and fixing. Blocks of wood with nails hammered in, basic wooden boats—building things, building a sense of themselves.

The airport I often fly in and out of has one of those bright plastic playhouses plopped in the middle of a barren room. I've never seen a child near it. Each time I pass by I imagine how happily populated the room might be if, instead of the fake house, there were boxes of wooden blocks, and wooden stands and easels, stumps, planks, cloths, and large clothespins or clips. Imagine the construction that would take place! And not only by kids . . . I picture travel-weary adults joining in as well.

Pretending; imaginary play. It starts with imitation, and takes flight from there. The six-month-old baby learns to wave, or to imitate a simple clapping rhythm they hear you make. Soon, as they enter their second year and beyond, they will be role-playing and pretending, using imitation and imagination to create elaborate stories and worlds of their own making. Much has been made in recent years of how this make-believe play helps children develop critical cognitive skills known as executive function. Executive function includes the ability to self-regulate, to amend one's behavior, emotions, and impulses appropriately to the environment and situation.[12]

Make-believe is open-ended play at its most flexible and creative. Anything at all can be used in the service of an idea or fantasy. And it is just this kind of flexible thinking—the pot that becomes a hat one minute, a steering wheel the next—that will serve a child their entire life. Children draw meaning from the world through this play; a lack of it leaves creativity and identity weak. The choices made in fantasy play build a foundation of individuality and guard against a child becoming a passive receptor for concepts and ideas that have been prepackaged for them.

Once again, the more elaborate the "prop" for pretend play, the less a child flexes their own "imaginary muscles." A fully detailed princess bed, complete with turrets, drapes, and a drawbridge, can provide a huge initial liftoff for castle fantasies. But with so little left in court to imagine, and so few fantastical choices to make, a child may just hang up her princess robes. She may wander out of the bedroom kingdom in search of a little more space and new people to become. Dress-up clothes, hats, and accessories are wonderful play tools that I think deserve a place in every child's mix of keepers. Here again simple choices, rather than elaborate or character-specific outfits, will provide the most varied and sustained possibilities for pretend play. Items can be recycled in and out of your little collection with an occasional trip to a charity resale store, such as Goodwill.

Experience. Children need experience, not entertainment, in play. The more kids can do, see, feel, and experience for themselves in play, the more connected they will feel to the world, and the less overwhelmed. We live in an information age, where kindergarten-age children know all about the tropical rainforest. Yet have they thoroughly mucked about in their own yards and neighborhoods? Have they grown their own plants, taken mud baths, climbed trees, dug for worms, or seen a robin's nest close up?

Imagine a day spent playing with the four elements. Campfires may be rare treats, and the warmth of a wool sweater may have to stand in for the heat of fire on most days. But there is elemental bliss associated with the combinations of dirt and water; muddy, marshy mucking; sand poured and molded and pushed; windy days; breaking up ice with sticks; sliding or trudging through snow; standing on the shoreline border of earth and water. Excellent toys for all of this "primal" exploration are buckets, nets, shovels and kites, scoops, bubbles, baskets, and containers for pouring and collecting.

Purpose and industry. My friend Anna told me the story of her son Jacob's "Christmas breakfasts." When Jacob was five he became fascinated with mixing up concoctions in the kitchen. Anna would let him use some vinegar, a few rarely used spices from the cupboard, whatever she could spare. Jacob loved his "work," pondering each addition with great concentration and focus. His name for each of these often malodorous brews: "Christmas breakfast." Anna would sometimes find an unexpected (and unsupervised) "Christmas breakfast" in the oven, or in a cupboard. She's convinced Jacob has a future—probably not as a chef, but as a chemist.

Children love to be busy, and useful. They delight in seeing that there is a place for them in the hum of doing, making, and fixing that surrounds them. I throw my torn jeans or holey socks into a basket and purposefully sit down one evening to mend them. Needles are threaded, doll clothes added to the heap, and together my daughters and I get to work.

Honor your child's efforts with real tools for their work, their own apron hung where they can get to it whenever the need or desire strikes. A pocket organizer hung on the back of a door might include space for a child's small broom and dustpan, a dust cloth, and other "tidying up," pet feeding, cooking, or laundry tools.

So often a child's play models adult "work": being a storekeeper, a truck driver, a teacher. Especially as children reach school age, they need opportunities to be industrious, to build a sense of autonomy and mastery. A wonderful counterbalance to "entertaining" children is to involve them in a task, in the "work" of family life. Home is the environment a child will know best, and they need to affect their environment through their own efforts. As small beings they can feel like inferior, passive observers of all that happens around them. A sense of industry—of busyness and purpose—counteracts feelings of overwhelm. And isn't it easy to feel small and inconsequential in a world so awash in information, so threatened with issues such as global warming? Children who grow up as little doers, making Christmas breakfast and participating in the chores of daily life, will already have an inner gesture, a posture toward competency, activity, and autonomy.

Nature. Nature is the perfect antidote to the sometimes poisonous pressures of modern life. In his book *Last Child in the Woods,* Richard Louv makes an eloquent and compelling case for the importance of nature in children's lives. "Modern life narrows our focus until it is primarily visual, appropriate to about the dimension of a computer monitor or television screen. By contrast nature accentuates all of the senses."[13] Louv offers scientific evidence for what most of us know intuitively: that time in nature is restorative, that it helps us recover from the stresses of daily life and improves our capacity to pay attention. In its complexity and sensuality, nature invites exploration, direct contact, and experience. But it also inspires a sense of awe, a glimpse of what is still "un-Googleable" . . . life's mystery and magnitude.

For those who live outside a city, the yard is often the first "frontier" of nature. Whether in parks, yards, empty lots, nature preserves, scraggly wild patches, or well-preserved wilderness areas, nature is an ideal environment for play. And a childhood full of opportunities and time for exploring nature is a rich childhood indeed. We don't have to aim for spectacular natural settings. How satisfying it is for a child to know a place—however modest—and to know it deeply. To explore it repeatedly, to know it in all of its seasonal faces, to identify one's own favorite little spots and crevices in it. It's also wonderful to have a variety of natural places and spots to explore. Children feel more grounded to where they live when they can learn to identify some of the common plants, birds, and animals they see in their yards and neighborhoods.

Children have a deep need for their own special places, humble or grand. The almighty cardboard box speaks to this need, as does a fort made from a table and blankets, or a more free-form version made from rope, cloths, and clothespins. A "summer bed" with a camp lantern on the porch on summer nights, a storage loft swept clean and transformed into a new play landscape. The outdoors offers wonderful possibilities for special places. A tree house, or even a climbing tree with a branch wide enough for a perch. My friend's daughter, Amy, used to read and play in a mossy spot next to an old lilac bush on the side of their yard. It was her special spot, a place to be alone. A place to play or read, or just to sit. One day Amy was amazed to find a perfect little snakeskin at her special spot. She took it as a gift and a wink; it was confirmation that other creatures, at least, had noticed her there.

Social interaction. On a recent visit to a child-care facility I saw a group of children sitting on the floor in a semicircle around a television. The man on the screen was leaping about, singing a song that was designed to get the kids up, kicking and clapping along with him. The poor guy was giving it his all—you had to give him an A for animation and effort. But the children were just sitting, motionless, watching. There is no vitality to a screen. Children need interaction with others, with human beings, to build social skills and their own individuality. There is no substitute, no "virtual" alternative to the vital, identity-forging power of relationships. Social skills can't be stimulated by technology. In a world that increasingly relies on various forms of technology, none of which involve human touch, we find ourselves even further removed from one another.

Here's another snapshot. A client of mine told me the story of her son Phillip's recent sixteenth birthday. "We gave him the option of a party. 'Great,' he said, 'I'll just have some of the guys over.' About six of his classmates showed up around nine in the evening, each of them carrying a laptop, speakers or some other equipment. They all went down into the basement, and when I went down later, they were spread out around the room, each thoroughly involved in some sort of virtual play. It was interesting; they seemed to like being together in the room, but all eyes and comments were directed straight ahead, at the various machines."

We'll talk more about screens and technology in Chapter Six. Screens and gadgets are here to stay, and will be part of most children's lives as they reach Phillip's age. However, this also continues to be true, as it has been since the advent of our species: The primary predictor of success and happiness in life is our ability to get along with others. Screens won't help. Family, where membership is automatic, and hopefully lifelong, is the first laboratory of identity and social interactions. Parents who talk, play, cuddle, and engage their babies, often and with pleasure, build a foundation of feelings that will prepare those small beings for widening circles of socialization, as toddlers and beyond. In relation to others a child learns how to act, and learns who they are. Much of a child's socialization—years of practicing, pretending, role-playing, learning, and refining codes of conduct—takes place through play.

Like magnetic fields, babies attract people to them. Facial gestures, eye contact, nuzzling, clapping, and rhyming games begin the lifelong interplay with others. From about the age of two, a toddler can form a bond with a special doll. It is a defining relationship, a magical window of identity, wherein so much is processed, felt, and learned. Again, the simpler the doll, the more a child can project onto it and draw from it. Cloth dolls with simple features, often handmade, tend to be more expensive than plastic dolls. However, considering what they can do and be for a child's developing sense of self, they may be worth the investment. Tea sets, wooden animals, trucks and blocks, the loose democracy of the sandbox, the swing set, foursquare and hopscotch, jacks, pick-up sticks, puppets and puzzles, games of hide-and-seek and catch, cards and board games, checkers and chess. What joy to discover, again and again in life, how unpredictable and expansive pleasure becomes when shared with others.

It is an interesting window to a child's development to see how close they want to be to the family while playing. Infants thrive on closeness; they're most soothed and happy in some form of warm embrace. Toddlers want to play—even if they're playing alone—where they can see and be near others. You've noticed their preference for right under your feet. Sometimes rooms in the house need to be shifted for the early childhood years, so that a play space is made near the kitchen, or heart of the house. From preschool through the first couple of years of primary school, children still want to be close. Kids six to nine will crave more privacy in their play, but they will still "return to base camp" to check in and see what is happening, flying in and out like a flock of noisy seagulls. From the age of nine or ten, kids will really want their own space, preferably with a desk or table at which they can do projects, hobbies, and crafts. As a child reaches the preteen years, their play reflects the fact that their sense of identity is "under construction," a process that requires more alone time. While teenagers still want you to be available emotionally, they have a developmental job (separating from you) that makes physical proximity more difficult. They will still need it, but increasingly on their own terms.

Movement. Children need to move. They need to run, skip, jump, climb, hop, and twirl; they need to wrestle, to roll about, to throw and catch balls, to feel their bodies move in space. Science has conclusively proven that rough-and-tumble play helps shape the brain, pruning excess cells, branchings, and connections in the prefrontal cortex.[14] Yet scientists are still conflicted about the main developmental purpose of play. Is it imperative for neural growth and shaping? Does active play help a child "practice" the movements they'll need for survival as adults? Does it help develop social and behavioral flexibility?

While the scientists ponder, children will continue their impromptu games of tag. Through movement they'll build balance and coordination—undeniably; they'll also develop vitality and a lifelong predisposition for activity. The Kaiser Foundation estimates that American children age six and under who use screen media spend an average of almost two hours in front of screens every day.[15] Movement counters the passivity of our devotion to technology. A childhood rich in physical play, in time and space to move, builds more than physical strength. It expands your child's lifelong access to fun, health, and connection with others. That's reason enough to move. These and other toys inspire active play: bikes and balls, skates, swings and scooters, climbing ropes and jump ropes; play structures or gates to climb over, tunnels to climb through, balance beams, Hula Hoops and basketball hoops, blocks, trucks, and construction toys, sleds, snowshoes, marble runs, hopscotch, and foursquare.

Art and music. The image that comes to mind when I think about children and art is not a refrigerator covered with drawings. It is an earlier image: a one-year-old's pudgy legs half hidden in a mudhole, the hose nearby still dribbling water. Registering on his face is delight . . . delight at the mud's cool sludginess in his toes, but also a delightful growing awareness of what he can *do* with that black glop. Children need to create. They need to make art, to feel and see and move their worlds in new directions.

From clay pinch pots to cutouts, the wet pushing and slapping of a ball of wool being felted, to the exuberant wash of color on a page, art invites the senses and movement; it opens up imaginary worlds, relaxes and channels attention in concert with fascination, and makes for playful purpose and industry. With or without tools, art is primal, nourishing play.

Maryanne came to see me about her six-year-old girl, Esme, who was having trouble falling asleep at night. When I looked at various aspects of their daily lives, it became clear that what Esme needed was more art. A lack of exercise is often the issue when kids can't sleep, but a lack of creative expression can also make the transition into sleep difficult. As the daughter of a mathematician and an engineer, Esme's home life was very organized and streamlined. She was a sweet girl, somewhat timid, and quite precise in her movements and speech. She needed to experience the flow of creativity, to relax her very focused and directed attention. The creative process involves a letting-go of conscious thoughts and ideas, and such opportunities for artistic release during the day help a child surrender into sleep.

There should always be a place in a simplified children's room for a big pad or roll of paper; sturdy crayons (thick for toddlers) and pencils; paints; some kind of modeling medium, such as beeswax, clay, or Play-Doh; fabric; scissors; glue; and some dedicated space for art. As children reach school age, they can begin some simple crafts. Whittling and knitting, for example, develop graphomotor skills just as children are beginning to write. Beadwork and sewing, woodwork and candlemaking, papier-mâché and ceramics. Especially when schools are dedicating less time to art, parents can make sure that art, play, and crafts are richly valued at home.

Music, like art, is an essential form of playful expression. From a mother's heartbeat in the womb to the rhythmic cadences of nursery rhymes and lullabies, music surrounds even the youngest among us. Music can help children move and learn to coordinate their movements, channel energy, express their emotions, and connect with others. In the next chapter, which is all about rhythm in daily life, we'll look at the sense of security and predictability that rhythm affords a child. As for creative rhythm making—music—these and other instruments of your own making can be fun: wooden rattles and egg shakers, drums, bells of all sorts, pennywhistles, harmonicas, and simple recorders, lap harps, thunder shakers, and rain sticks.

Books

The same principles you used to simplify toys can be applied to other forms of clutter in your child's room. Books are often the second major form of excess, given that books are viewed in the same light as toys. As parents, we want to promote reading (play), so we figure that the more books (toys) our child has access to, the more they will read (play).

Who could argue? The premise seems logical, and it is based, again, on generous parental intentions. Storytelling, the precursor and larger context for books, will be addressed in Chapter Four. We'll look at how stories nurture children, and how repetition is such an important part of the process. Stories can offer young children great security and assurance: stories that are heard again and again, lived with, anticipated, and known deeply. For now, I would just like to make a few practical suggestions around books, in keeping with this chapter's primary goal: simplifying the child's environment.

Hopefully, you have just taken major steps to reduce the number of toys that surround your child in their room. You've created space and visual ease. You've also created mental space and calm, making it possible for your child to engage with the toys they have rather than being overwhelmed by too many. You can do the same thing with books.

For children before the ages of eight or nine, you might have one or two current books accessible at any given time. A dozen or fewer beloved books may find a permanent place in the room, perhaps on a bookshelf. These are books that your child will return to again and again, and you may choose to rotate books in and out of this favorites group as your child grows. At seven or eight you can add reference books about subjects your child is interested in, such as insects, horses, or airplanes.

QUITE SIMPLY:

We honor the value of something (like reading) in our child's life by fostering a deep—not disposable—relationship to it.

Books offer such delight and satisfaction to children, conjuring magical worlds and bringing the wonder of our own right into their hands. How could it be possible to have "too many" of such good things?

It is a bit easier to imagine the "too much of a good thing" principle with books when our children have entered the "series" section of the library or bookstore. A child who is racing through "Number 23 of the Magic Tree House Series!" in a rush to pull ahead of their friend is not reading so much as consuming. When a desire for the next thing is at the heart of an experience, we're involved in an addiction, not a connection.

Sadly, though, anything can be commercialized and trivialized through overexposure and excess. By establishing a consistent level of "enough" (simplicity) rather than too much (overload), we leave room for our children—room for their imaginations and inspirations, room for them to build relationships with the things that they play with or read.

We've all noticed children's love of repetition. As we settle in to read to our three- or four-year-old child: "Again? We've read *Curious George* for the past three nights! Are you sure you want to hear it again?" Even as our kids grow into independent readers we often express surprise when we see them reading a book that we know they've read before, or when they ask to hear the same family story that they've heard so many times, they can recite it from memory.

Repetition is a vital part of relationship building for children. By repeating experiences and scenarios in play, as well as in storytelling and reading, kids are able to incorporate what they learn. Repetition deepens the experience and relationship for a child; it helps them claim it as their own. Children up to the age of seven or eight can be told and read one story repeatedly for a number of days. The consistency and security of such repetition is very soothing for young children.

As with play, kids do not need any one magical book, the newest bestseller, or an endless stream of new books, to foster a love of reading. They need time, and mental ease. They need the time to read deeply, and sometimes repeatedly. They also need stories that leave some room for their imagination. You can evaluate the books you choose for your child with similar criteria to those I mentioned in evaluating toys.

Is it developmentally appropriate? There is a great deal of "age compression" in books as well as toys. I've noticed it in several forms. Sometimes children's books are written more for the adult reading than the child listening. They are full of little jokes and asides that mean nothing to the child. Some have very adult themes, especially as children reach "middle reader" level books. Because books are classified by reading level rather than content, parents of independent readers need to monitor whether their child should read a certain book just because they can.

Mary, a client of mine, told me this story about her daughter, Ashley, who was a very precocious reader. When she was eleven, Ashley came home with a novel she had checked out from the school library. Mary had heard of the novel, and knew that it was a very popular coming-of-age story more appropriate for teen readers. She read through it that night and confirmed her impressions. Mary spoke with Ashley the next day before school. She told her that the book had been getting a lot of attention, and she understood that Ashley wanted to read it. Then she gave her a choice. They could either read it together, now, and be able to talk about it as they read, or Ashley could wait another year to read it herself. With a great harrumph, Ashley chose to wait.

Is the book based on a product or television character? As we saw with toys, product marketers have children firmly in view. The pressure to buy is intense and pervasive. There are books based on television characters, movies, even on products such as M&M candies or breakfast cereals. I think we can draw "lines in the sand" around our children. We can say no in our own homes to the commercialization of childhood. When you picture reading with your children, or them reading alone, imagine the circle of light around them as an "ad-free zone."

Does it tell an unfolding story or is it "all over the place"? Like a toy that does too much, some books are very fragmented, graphically intense, and lacking cohesion. Is the book designed to engage the child's imagination, or to "stimulate"? This distinction is important because kids take a book's images into their sleep. A book read at bedtime nourishes a child's dreams. The images and the archetypes of the story follow a child into their sleep and into the unconscious "practicing" for life that they do while dreaming.

I am not suggesting that everything a child reads needs to be conceptually "neutralized"—all bunnies and flowers, peace and love. Can a seven- or eight-year-old child read a fairy tale in which the little tailor mouse's tale is cut off, or a dragon attacks? Yes, I believe that a story with room for a child to "imagine into it" affords them some distance, some power and grace to manipulate the images and story in their own mind. I am more concerned by books that are like flashing billboards. Some books are designed to provoke a reaction rather than engage the imagination.

Another way to judge a book is by the play it inspires. Books that are read to a child, or that they read, are often taken right up, incorporated into their play. Is the play engaging? Does the interaction go well? Or is the play corrosive, causing more issues and problems than fun?

Clothes

With the exception of teenagers, the younger the child, the more times a day he or she will dress and undress. Can you imagine a time-elapsed film of a day's wardrobe changes for an infant, or an active three-year-old? Don't forget the shoes-and-jacket shuffle at the back door (times ten), the pajama interludes, the "what's that food?" T-shirt game, or (cue the *Space Odyssey* music) the long, very long, extremely long "let's play in the snow" suit-ups. Clothes are some of the most transitional items of childhood. Almost as soon as they fit properly, children grow out of them. And the transitions of "in and out of clothes" punctuate each day.

When you simplify a child's clothes, you simplify daily life. Each one of the transitions around clothes is made more difficult by clutter and excess. As you did with toys and books, you can reduce the number of clothes available to your child to a manageable, accessible, and streamlined mix. The clothes in your child's wardrobe or bureau should fit now. Clothes they've grown out of can be given away or stored, and clothes that are still too big should be left in storage. All but the current season's clothes can be labeled and stored in boxes or bags. I save those little silica packets used in packaging (you see them sometimes in shoe boxes, or with vitamins), and throw those in with clothes to prevent moisture.

When the only clothes available are the ones that fit your child, and the current weather, the closet is no longer a jungle to be hacked through. Even a three-year-old will begin to recognize the pattern of drawers, and be able to get a shirt or a sweater themselves.

At any given time your child may have some clothes from friends or relatives whose children have outgrown them. There may also be gifts, and one or two items for special occasions. Beyond these, your child can have a mix of fairly basic items. Your little one's clothes don't have to make a "statement" beyond the obvious ones: "I'm dressed and ready for school" or "I'm comfortable and ready to play." Your child has better things to do than to be a walking advertisement for mall stores or brands. Simplify your choices in shopping: If you find a pair of jeans that fits your child, and your budget, consider buying a few. Having fewer choices simplifies getting dressed. Young kids can still adopt all sorts of flash and style, playing with different looks, roles, and fashion statements in their dress-up play.

QUITE SIMPLY:

By simplifying clothes you ease transitions. You offer freedom from choice and overload, while still allowing for the slow and sure development of personal expression.

Variety and style are usually much more important to parents than to preadolescent kids. "Choice" is so often a false distinction, when a child is more interested in what they are going to do, once dressed, than in the clothes themselves. As adults who value individuality we are so convinced that children need variety and style to assert their individuality. But the identity building that children do through play is much more fundamental than any external look they may adopt. By limiting choices in the early years you give children the time and freedom to develop an inner voice. Simplicity provides the ease and well-being to develop a strong sense of self. And believe me, there will be no lack of personal expression—through fashion and otherwise—when that strong sense of self reaches adolescence.

Scent, Lighting

Before we turn off the light and close the door to your child's room, here are a few more suggestions for simplifying.

The amygdala, the ancient part of our brain, is the area associated with olfaction, or smell. Most of us have read or heard concerns about the ill effects of toxic chemicals in some cleaning and home care products. Many products, from "air fresheners" to candles to various soaps and cleansers, come with their own mix of chemical scents. So in a world that booms and buzzes, especially for children, you also have a cacophony of smells. Too many smells. All of these competing, chemical perfumes get the amygdala firing, and cortisol and adrenaline pumping.

Simplify the smells and perfumes in your home, particularly in your child's room. One of the things that quiet the amygdala and promote a sense of safety and well-being for a young child is their own, albeit very subtle and fine natural scent, and the smell of their mother or father. When we surround ourselves with chemical smells and perfumes, we miss out on an opportunity to calm and connect with our children. Be careful of perfumes and these chemical scents, particularly in an age when so much adrenaline is pumping through our little guys' systems.

I travel a fair bit, giving talks and workshops, and when I am away, my wife snuggles into bed with our girls to read before bed. One of them will grab "Daddy's pillow" and add it to the mix so that my scent can also be with them as they listen and relax into sleep. Little ones find this sensory connection very soothing.

QUITE SIMPLY:

Too much stimulation causes sensory overload. Adjust the tone and volume not only of sounds, but also smells and light in your home.

An easy way to minimize the sounds in the home environment is by softening some of the reflective surfaces. Many people have wooden floors and ceilings, and a lot of wood and glass in their homes, which offer clean lines and a natural aesthetic. However, children sometimes have difficulties with auditory processing. Some kids have trouble having the auditory senses that they take on board actually make sense to them both on the brain-based level and also a visual-spatial level. In other words, environments where noise bounces around a lot can confuse children. When your children are young, it may serve to have rugs on the floor, and to drape some cloth on the ceiling in their room. It does not need to stay that way forever, but particularly up until the age of about eight, you can take steps to soften and simplify the acoustics in your home.

Consider the different levels and varieties of light in your home. Beyond the natural light from windows, we may have fluorescent lights, and the flickering glow of computer and television screens. School-age kids can spend a good part of their day in the often harsh lighting of the classroom. Again, this is a simple suggestion, but I have found it wonderfully powerful to have at least one point in a child's day that includes the light of a candle. It may be just before bedtime, an interlude between day and night. If you are nervous about candles in the house, you might want to incorporate it into bathtime, when you have a whole tub full of water nearby. Children love the light of a candle and the magical circle of its glow.

Winters in the Northeast are long and dark. My eldest daughter, who gets up earliest for school, loves coming down in the morning as there is a candle lit just for her to eat her breakfast by. Somehow the darkness of the outside adds to the peace of a candlelit morning. Like an inhalation, the light draws us together as we start the day.

Children who have trouble sleeping at night sometimes have lighting systems more elaborate than airport runways. I suggest slowly weaning them off their various lights: the light in the bathroom, the hallway, the three night-lights, and the bedside light kept on "while they fall asleep." Let natural light be the last that is curtained at night and the first that is welcomed in the morning. Most small children can sleep right through loud noises, but they are very sensitive to light. Especially for children who have no nighttime concerns, wean them gradually off every light, even night-lights, so that the quality of their sleep will be deeper and more nourishing.

As you close the curtains, and turn off the last light, sit for a moment in the darkness of your child's simplified room. Imagine it as an environment. Their childhood paths, like dotted lines, will extend from here . . . out into the yard, to friends' homes, to school and the wider world, but those lines will always pivot back. The dotted lines return, around the apple tree and through the open windows of a summer evening or through the black closeness of a cold winter night, to the circle of light around their beds. To stories about the day, or the angle of an open book shared in the moments before sleep.

By simplifying, you've taken steps to curb the excess that threatens childhood's natural rhythms and growth. By starting at home—embracing experience over things, and "enough" rather than always more—you've made room. You've cleared out space, literally and emotionally. You've made a container for relationship and the slow unfolding of childhood. You've allowed room for your child's own imagination and their explorations through play.

It's a small environment, an even smaller circle of light we draw around those we love. But for a while, when they are young and growing, we adults can offer the protection of more time and ease, less speed and clutter. We can be the stewards of our child's home environment, setting limits and saying no to too many choices, too much stuff. As we'll see in the next chapter, we can also increase the security of the environment we make for them with rhythm and predictability.

Imagine your child's room . . .

- uncluttered, and restful to the senses.
- with soft light and colors, and a sense of order and space.
- with room to move and play, to draw and build.
- without toys that are broken, forgotten, or heaped in piles.
- with a few of his or her most beloved toys in sight and the rest in one or two baskets on the floor, covered with cloth.
- with a place for a handful of books, while others are stored, ready to be cycled in once these are thoroughly read and enjoyed.
- as a peaceful and secure place for sleep, with the natural scents of home and minimal or no night lighting.

Imagine . . .

- watching your children create new worlds and new ways to play with their toys, instead of their requiring new toys to play with.
- opening your child's bureau or closet and seeing space around a few clothes that fit her and the current season.
- your children's own real tools and their happy sense of purpose as they work and play at cooking, cleaning, and gardening.
- your child being able to live deeply and repeatedly in the "now" of a story or his or her play, rather than always eyeing what's next.

FOUR

Rhythm

Life today for most families is characterized more by randomness and improvisation than rhythm. Tuesday wash day? Cookies and milk after school? Sunday roast beef dinner? With both parents usually working outside the home, these kinds of weekly markers may sound more quaint than realistic. Family life today often consists of whatever is left over, in terms of our time and energy, when the "work" of the day is done. Whenever I ask a mother or father to describe for me a "typical day" in their home, nine times out of ten they begin by saying there is no "typical."

There aren't many people whose lives are still characterized by the rhythms of the earth, by the sunlight in a given day, the growing or fallow seasons, the cycle of a crop's harvest. Yet our lives are still influenced by rhythms: academic, work, sleep, holidays, and circadian, to name just a few. Work and commuting schedules may rule the clock, but they are regularly irregular. They can change and evolve, overlap and fall short in ways that we have trouble keeping up with, and keeping straight. We impose the rhythms of our children's lives. And as those patterns become less natural, regular, or decipherable—"Don't forget, we're heading into third quarter selling season, so I'll be late all this week"—they are well beyond a child's sensory world.

A baby's first lullaby is its mother's heartbeat in the womb, a powerful rhythm that we try to re-create with gentle sounds and rocking in their first weeks, months, and even years. You can always recognize a new mother or father, can't you, even when they're away from their baby? They're the ones in the grocery store line, or at the bus stop, gently (and unconsciously) swaying back and forth. Whether babes in arms or toddlers on their fathers' knees, little ones crave that motion . . . the rocking motion. The tempo is echoed in their breath, the beating of their hearts. Rocking is also the surest path to sleep, a rhythmic road of harmony and calm.

Just as night is replaced by day, children learn that there are movements and changes that, with their regularity, can be counted on. Games of peekaboo reinforce the notion that things disappear and reappear. A child's sense of security is built on these predictabilities. The rocking motion continues on the swing, and the rhythm is then picked up in language with repetition and rhyme.

Day becomes night becomes day; when we're hungry we are fed; the people we love leave and return. These rhythms correspond to a child's way of knowing their world. With security they can venture out—with the promise of a return, they can explore—and this cycling will be their pattern of learning throughout their lives. Children depend on the rhythmic structure of the day—on its predictability, its regularity, its pulse. They benefit from dependability and regularity throughout childhood, but especially in the first three years, when the greatest learning takes place unconsciously. Not only can children find security in the patterns of daily life, they can begin to find themselves. In the day's most regular rhythms, its high notes—the meals and bathtimes, the playtimes and bedtimes—young children begin to see their place in the comings and goings, in the great song of family.

In talks or workshops, when I begin to address the importance of rhythm in daily life, there is always a corresponding noise from the audience: parental fidgeting. I'm certain that for some, especially the couples who managed to come together, it took all the planning of a high-level military operation just to get them in the same room at the same time. And here I am, going on about rhythm. Rhythm? Some blended families have teenagers and toddlers whose schedules have little musical commonality. Some parents' work schedules gap where they don't overlap, or change just as soon as the family has adjusted to their patterns. Rhythm? Imagine how that sounds to the mom whose "typical day" goes something like this: starting at six with breakfast, kids dressed and lunches packed, kids to school, hectic workday followed by important client dinner, a mad rush home to tuck the kids in, dishes, line up backpacks for the next day, and its then—at 10 P.M.—that she notices the slip "reminding" her that tomorrow is her day for "Second Grade Special Snack"! Rhythm?

Meals, sleep, work, school, play, sports, errands, day care, classes, appointments, and friends: Those are a lot of pieces to fit into any framework. To do so with a sense of rhythm and regularity is asking a lot. It's asking more than some of us can manage. In fact, the mere subject of rhythm can bring tears to some parents' eyes.

Here is my good news/bad news response to these very understandable frustrations: Increasing the rhythm of your home life *is* one of the most powerful ways of simplifying your children's lives. If you see that as bad news, here's the good news: It will also simplify—not complicate—yours. And it can be done. It *can* be done.

QUITE SIMPLY:

Increasing the rhythm of your home life is one of the most powerful ways of simplifying your children's lives

What is so overwhelming about the notion of rhythm is that we assume we need to organize all of the moving parts of our lives into a full-scale symphony. Parenting is hard enough. While parenting involves a lot of "conducting," the whole concept of rhythm—or anything approaching music—can seem impossible. And for some families it will remain elusive. Not to worry. Even if your schedules and lifestyle defy all taming, I'll show you how to give your children greater predictability and transparency. These techniques will provide a sense of security, and they often establish a toehold for a more rhythmic home life, much to everyone's surprise. And benefit.

It has been my privilege to work with many families, and to speak with a great many more over the years. Along the way, I've developed and gathered lots of ideas and techniques that work, ideas that have been "tested" in busy homes. You can choose from these to establish more consistency in your own home. The primary rhythm of this chapter itself will be stories, from which you can gather ideas for your own family. Some will take, others may not, and some may serve as springboards for new ideas. You'll know the keepers, though, with great certainty. Your children will embrace, and rely on them, as though life made no real sense before doing "favorite things" at dinner (for example). Your reaction might be more subtle. At first you may realize that all of the worries you had about committing to this or that now regular part of the day/week/month have vanished. What's more—surprise!—you find yourself looking forward to this new little ritual as much, or more, than your kids do.

We'll address the major chords of a child's daily life: meals and bedtime, and expand out from there, with many ideas for establishing "notes" your child can count on in the pattern of their days. By surrounding a young child with a sense of rhythm and ritual, you can help them order their physical, emotional, and intellectual view of the world. As little ones come to understand, with regularity, that "this is what we do," they feel solid earth under their feet, a platform for growth. Such a stable foundation can facilitate their mapmaking: the connectedness that they are charting in their brains, in relation to other people, and in their emerging worldview.

Meaning hides in repetition: We do this every day or every week because it matters. We are connected by this thing we do together. We matter to one another. In the tapestry of childhood, what stands out is not the splashy, blow-out trip to Disneyland but the common threads that run throughout and repeat: the family dinners, nature walks, reading together at bedtime (with a hot water bottle at our feet on winter evenings), Saturday morning pancakes.

A rhythmic home life has a pattern and a flow. Its cadences are recognizable, and knowable, even to the youngest members of the family. Because the primary patterns—daily, weekly—are so well established, life's other sequences—seasonal, annual—fit smoothly over well-worn grooves. The tempo of a rhythmic daily life, as described by a child, would sound something like this: "This is what we do on school day mornings . . ." "Before we leave the house we . . ." "When I get home from school, I . . ." "When my mom or dad starts dinner, I . . ." "Before bed on winter evenings, we love to . . ." "The thing I love about Saturday mornings is . . ." "When one of us is sick, we always . . ." "The special thing we do when someone's birthday is coming up is . . ."

We are connected by the things we do together. There is a regularity, a consistency to what we do as a family.

QUITE SIMPLY:

Rhythm and ritual are what we aim for;
predictability may be what we can achieve.

"That's nice," you might be thinking, "nice maybe for a family living on the prairie a hundred years ago. But my family is way too busy to have any kind of rhythm to our days." My response to your imagined comment is this: The busier your life, the more your children need and will benefit from the establishment of a sense of rhythm. I would also say that you can start with *any* point in your day—from dinners together right down to teeth-brushing time—and make it more rhythmical. I'll show you how, and I'll bet that you will then continue on, establishing more beachheads of rhythm and regularity throughout the day. Finally, let me reassure you that even if rhythm remains elusive, you can still provide your kids more security by increasing predictability in their daily lives.

Predictability

So, what is this cousin of rhythm: predictability? What I mean by greater predictability and transparency is illustrated very handily by the story of Justin, a six-year-old boy with whom I worked. Justin's parents contacted me because he was refusing to get out of bed in the morning. Justin was mounting what I came to think of as "the pajama defense." His thinking—or unconscious logic—went something like this: "If I stay in my pajamas, then nothing much can happen to me, and certainly nothing bad."

There is a simple beauty to the argument, isn't there? I considered it myself, ever so briefly, but I'll save you some time: Your children would *love* the idea of your mounting a pajama defense, but your spouse will *never ever* go for it!

As I came to know Justin, I realized that he led a very unpredictable life. Both of his parents were salespeople, with extremely hectic and flexible schedules, and a lot of traveling. Each worked for a different pharmaceutical company. Some mornings Justin took the bus to school, sometimes one of his parents dropped him off, some mornings one of his parents would get him up early to drop him at a friend's house to be taken to school by the friend's parents.

School pickup was also erratic. Some afternoons Justin was picked up for a playdate that had been arranged while he was in school. Sometimes he would be picked up by one parent and learn that the other parent had left unexpectedly for a trip and would be gone for a few days. Occasionally after his mom or dad picked him up at school, they would have to continue going on their sales calls, and Justin would do his homework or read in doctors' waiting rooms until dinnertime. While dinner was always a part of the daily equation, the what, where, and when of it was ever changeable.

The better I came to know Justin and his parents, the more certain I was that the concept of rhythm did not, and would not, work in this family. Justin's mom and dad were paid, partially, for their willingness to be adaptable, to travel and to keep hours that were more convenient for the doctors they served than for them. I came to see also that (and perhaps this was why they were good at what they did) by nature, both parents were very flexible, go-with-the-flow people. Their son Justin was clearly the most "fixed" entity in their lives. They were working toward a plan; Justin's dad was aiming for a position in corporate sales that would require less travel. In the meanwhile, I could also see that they were doing everything they could to keep Justin "covered": safe and protected.

But there's a gap between "safe" and "secure," and Justin had devised a way to fill in that gap for himself: He was staying in pajamas until further notice.

Justin's parents and I worked on ways to increase predictability and transparency in his daily life. Predictability is understandable. By transparency I mean that we, as adults, have an understanding of how our day may proceed. No matter how hectic it promises to be, we can picture how it might play out. Children need some level of that clarity. They may not be in control of their day, but they need some access to the "picture," the understanding of how it might proceed.

So every night, one of Justin's parents would sit with him and "preview" the next day. This was hangout time, not a hurried "coming up next" rundown of the following day's highlights. It doesn't have to be at bedtime, or in bed, but it does need to be a guaranteed relaxed, not-rushed period of decompressing. Justin might talk about what happened that day, or his current theory about UFOs, or whatever was on his mind. His mom or his dad would talk about the next day, and what might happen.

Children live their lives pictorially, especially when they're really young (under seven). They need "visuals." Your intention here is to create a picture that they can then "live into" the next day. This doesn't mean you have to have everything figured out, but you do need to give them some markers, some elements that they can count on. Justin's mom or dad would often mention what the weather was supposed to be like, and point to where his clothes ("with your new sneakers, because you have gym tomorrow") were laid out. They would tell him how he was getting to school. They might even say "Either mom or I will pick you up after school. We don't know who yet, but there you'll be, waiting at the apple tree, and you'll look up to see either my red car or mom's blue truck pull in."

It is very helpful for children to take this picture, this sense of clarity, into sleep. Whatever happens in those mysterious, healing processes of sleep, you can be sure that if your child has a concern, you'll hear about it the next morning. "Dad?" "Yes?" "I was thinking, Mom's truck isn't really blue."

What this previewing of the day does is say "there is no hidden agenda here." You are giving your child markers, and so including them in the process of your days together. It's true, as the adult and parent you govern the movement between those markers, but you are not entirely imposing your world on theirs. You are establishing yourself as "captain of the ship" in a way that would be comforting to any small being afloat on a large ocean. So, instead of never really knowing what might happen, the child is able to see that there is someone in charge. This person (the "captain" or "co-captains") not only have a handle on things, but they've just shown you the "log book," and you understand how you fit into the picture.

So, while your child may not know the pattern of your days by their consistency and repetition (rhythm), you can provide markers and previews of their day, thereby letting them know what to expect (predictability).

QUITE SIMPLY:

With "predictability," a child knows what to expect.

A single mom I knew used to do this previewing with her little daughter in the sandbox. Her sandbox was actually inside—a sand table more than anything—and she used to sit there with her four-year-old and talk about what the next day would be like. As she spoke, she would move a little car around in the sandbox, stopping at the wooden "school" or "grocery store."

You set the mood, and create an expectation for the day not only with what you say, but how you say it: a comfortable place, restful eye contact, an unhurried, relaxed approach. You don't want to go over every single detail of what might happen every moment of the next day. You know the expression "too much information"? That applies here, as such an approach would surely increase your child's anxiety rather than security. Let the process, as well as the message, be comforting.

In general, for greater predictability, you want to try to reduce the ways that your children are caught by surprise. I often see toddlers being scooped up from behind by their mom or dad. Granted, if you are in a busy parking lot or a dangerous situation, you need to use any means you can to protect your child. But otherwise, I think of this approach as a mini-shock, a surprise that, when done habitually, says "my world rules" instead of "we're doing this together." Imagine instead that wonderful way that kids sort of bend their knees and jump up, face-to-face with their mom or dad as they're gently lifted. Up we go! That kind of "working together" is comforting for the child, and gives us parents the illusion that we might still be able to pick them up when they're ten or eleven.

Your three-year-old is engrossed in play, but you know you'll need to leave in a half hour to pick up your husband at the train station. Perhaps you could discuss the train schedule with Katie, and the relative probability of an on-time arrival? (No, she's three!) Wait until the last minute, grab her, and go? (No, she's three; a little warning helps.) "Love, soon Mama is going to say that its time to clean up. Not now, but in a few minutes I'll say that, and then we need to start with the blocks and clean up. We'll clean up, then we'll go get Daddy at the train station." These sorts of "advance notices" can help increase security and ease.

If your children are older, approaching or in adolescence, family meetings can do what previewing does for younger kids. Sometimes tied to Sunday supper, the meetings take place with everyone hanging out for fifteen or twenty minutes beyond the cleanup of the meal. The previous week is reviewed: What worked? What didn't work? What were those things we meant to tell one another, before we forgot? The following week is then discussed, with everyone's plans, and the necessary logistics, rolled out on the table. It may all be quite complicated, but as the pieces come together, what lingers, with the smell of dish soap and the last bite of dessert, is this: We're in this together.

QUITE SIMPLY:

Rhythms establish a foundation of cooperation and connection.

One of the simplest, purest forms of stability or predictability in daily life is politeness. It is a level of communication and interaction that can be counted on, that builds trust. When you ask me for something, you say "please"; when I respond to your request, you say "thank you," and I say "you're welcome." What could be more predictable? In the flow of the day's words, noises, shouts, and various utterances, this polite exchange stands out for children like a nursery rhyme, secure and familiar. It is also a code. In its regularity, politeness affirms and reaffirms our connection; the way we treat each other.

Some people may feel that politeness, especially for young children, is a form of blind obedience, or enforced conformity. I take a different view. Politeness is one of the simplest ways to establish a base beat of predictability in the home. Points of politeness throughout the day are like the lights of a suspension bridge, securing and connecting.

We are so concerned with safety as parents. (I'm sure you've seen kids going out to ride their bikes or skate, dressed in so much padding it is a miracle they can move.) Politeness practiced in the home is a very basic, simple way to give children deep feelings of safety. Even if your schedules are untamable, your thoughts and days as cluttered as can be, a form of predictability is established with politeness. In a rushed, often rude world, a line is drawn around your family when you speak to one another with respect. Count on it; your children will. They hear and feel it, like their own heartbeats. They often seem to forget, but not really. The rhythm is internalized: Notice how quickly they look up if *you* forget a please or thank-you.

Establishing Rhythms

We've talked about how children feel when their daily lives are rhythmic or at least predictable. Rhythm calms and secures children, grounding them in the earth of family so they can branch out and grow. The implication of rhythms is that there is an "author" behind how we do things as a family. Parental authority is strengthened by rhythms; an "authority" is established that is gentle and understandable. "This is what we do" also says, "There is order here, and safety."

For parents, the advantages of rhythm are equally pronounced. Rhythm carves the necessary channels for discipline, making it more intrinsic than imposed. Where well-established rhythms exist, there is much less parental verbiage, less effort, and fewer problems around transitions.

Parents also suffer the effects of a chaotic, arrhythmic home life. When life is a series of improvisations and emergencies, each day different from the next, children don't know if they're coming or going. As parents at least you know. You know that you are coming *and* going at the same time, crazy busy, and no matter how adept you may be at "multitasking," you feel stressed by it all. Beaten down, mentally and physically. Yes, rhythm makes children feel more secure. Absolutely. But a sense of rhythm makes adults calmer, too, and less plagued by parental craziness. With consistent structures in place, you'll feel less like a Border collie, constantly nipping at your children's heels.

"All well and good," you may be thinking. "But how does one impose order on chaos? If my life were more regular, rhythm would be easy. But it's not regular, it's crazy."

The good news is that you can start small, gradually establishing little islands of consistency in your daily life. If your family life is a piece of music, what does it sound like now? Which points of the day can you begin to connect with others, so bits and phrases of a melody emerge? We'll consider an average day, looking at opportunities for rhythm and regularity along the way, but any repeated note of the day can be made more rhythmic.

What are your children's "flashpoints" or difficult periods? For a lot of kids, transitions are the trickiest: getting out the door in the morning, coming to dinner. The flow of the day will be improved when more rhythm is brought to those points. However, start small. Choose basic activities that need to be made more consistent, and work up from there, slowly changing the composition of your days. Once you've established some routines and rhythms you can more easily tame the day's stickiest wickets.

QUITE SIMPLY:

Any repeated "note" or activity of the day can be made more rhythmic.

When you build rhythms when your children are quite young—between two and six—they'll be soaked up naturally and eagerly. Little ones are already very process oriented, with strong body clocks. A small investment of effort on your part will yield lifelong habits and rituals. However, the process will need to be front-loaded, with parental closeness and interaction for a couple of weeks before your child will be performing the task and following through on autopilot. Make sure your commitment is complete—especially for these first attempts—and you'll lay the groundwork for success with this and future routines.

Let's use teeth brushing as an example. To make it consistent, you have to ground it either to another dependable activity or a specific time. If bedtime is anywhere between 7 and 10 P.M., you can't use that as an anchor. Walk them through the steps, stay close. Secure each step: Where's your toothbrush? See, right next to mine. How much toothpaste? That's right, about the size of your thumbnail. We need to brush for two minutes. Ready? Let's turn over the egg timer. There you are, good.

In his book *Secrets of Discipline,* Ronald Morrish beautifully identified the steps that parents need to take with their child: Start small, stay close, insist, and follow through.

To make any activity more rhythmic, it's helpful to connect the process with a bit of melody, especially for kids five or under. The steps along the way can be sung—no arias needed, just a singsongy delivery. Washing hands before dinner? That's it! "A little soap, a little water, rub and scrub until the bubbles come!" Hand washing is then tied (in time) to the meal, it is tied (in feeling) to the physical sensations involved, and it is tied (aurally) to a little melody, heard and also sung. All of these small connections help to ritualize the activity; they help your child "file" it in their view of an orderly world.

If you are establishing rhythms for the first time with an older child, the process may take a little longer (a month), but the method is the same. (Though for kids seven or older you should probably stick with a nonmusical, spoken delivery!) Your involvement (start small, stay close, insist, and follow through) is even more important, since compliance is less assured as a child gains in age and independence. You want to be sure they reach the point where the process is automatic and unquestioned. That's when it will feel like success.

With a child seven or older, who has rarely done the same thing in the same way at the same time any two days in a row, again, you'll want to start small. Begin with a humble task that will either be pleasant or help them in some way, such as hanging up their favorite baseball cap and backpack in the same place every day when they come in from school. When your child has mastered these, and felt some benefit from them ("At least I don't have to search for my hat anymore, Mom. . . ."), then you can point to these advances as inspiration for bigger changes and more consistency.

With older children, you'll need to discuss the change beforehand and consult with them about the best way to adopt it. Especially for kids approaching adolescence, make "what's in it for them" clear, even if the primary benefit will be less nagging from you. You don't need to plead a case; you can keep it short. But you should let them know that besides the obvious benefits (getting to the bus on time, feeling more on top of their schoolwork), this change will also mean that they are taking more control of their own lives. And you will notice.

QUITE SIMPLY:
Rhythm builds islands of consistency and security throughout the day.

Anything can be made more dependable with repetition and care. The necessity of waking up in the morning can be made into a small but pleasant ritual. When you sit on a young child's bed and sing or hum softly for a minute or two—or just sit—they wake to a loving presence. If you have an early riser, you can prepare a tray for them, with quiet things to do until the others wake.

Dressing in the morning can be made so much easier with a little preparation the night before. We make "scarecrows" of our daughters' outfits for the day by completely "dressing" a hanger, topped with a hat in the winter. This saves time, but also helps propel kids into their day by limiting the opportunities for choice and conflict. For kids with sensory integration problems, it helps to have clothes laid out that have already been vetted for scratchy labels or bumpy bits.

Breakfast tends to be less formal than dinner, but it doesn't have to be completely on-the-go. You can anchor breakfast with some rituals of connection and security. It's an ideal time to preview the day, verbally walking your child through what they can expect. Do you sometimes wish your kids opened up more about their days, and what's on their minds? Sit down across from them in the morning, as their blood sugar is replenished over breakfast, and as they reflect on whatever they processed in their sleep the night before. You never know what you'll hear!

For kids who are studying an instrument, after breakfast can be a good time to practice. If they don't enjoy practicing, the chore is then finished first thing. Meanwhile, though, especially for kids who tend to be grumpy in the morning, playing music will usually balance their mood. It brings them right into the brain's center of creativity, or limbic system.

The islands of consistency and security that rhythm builds throughout the day are like breaths. Such intervals allow a child's brain to maintain balance, and to flow through its willing, thinking, and feeling centers. If constantly on the run, and always reacting to changing circumstances, a child will default, or return mentally to a form of amygdala hijack. They operate from the part of the brain that is quick to react, but less able to consider things thoroughly or flexibly.

Once in a workshop a dad shared with us his clever way of building an "ejector" rhythm into the mornings. He and his wife were having trouble getting their kids out the door. Wake-up, dressing, and breakfasts all went fine, but then there would be considerable foot-dragging. One kid would go missing, shoes would be "lost", excuses made. The final push took forever. It makes sense. When the house is warm and cozy, why not linger? So they incorporated a new rhythm into the mornings. Once each child was dressed he or she had a small chore to do before leaving. Whether this was carrying out the compost, feeding the cat, or making the bed, somehow the call of "Come on! Out we go!" was more welcome, coming on the heels (or in the middle!) of a chore.

When the emphasis in school is toward testing, the day's pauses are often cut or shortened. Recess, art, music, movement: Again, these are the intervals that allow a child's brain to maintain balance, to process information. In teaching to the tests, schools try to "insert" more, bypassing themes and longer curricula processes, increasing regimentation and fragmentation. An average day may include "units" on Egypt, insects, long division, Spanish, and sentence diagramming. The more fragmented their school day, the more children will benefit from consistency at home.

The time between school and the evening meal is an important transition period. Some kids are involved in after-school programs, for others there may be a succession of lessons or activities before dinner, and still others are involved in sports. Many parents feel that their kids benefit from some sort of cathartic release, a way to "go crazy" and expend energy after school, so they add a scheduled activity or two to the end of each day. Some kids really do need to move—to run around, climb a tree, ride their bikes—especially after sitting in a classroom most of the day. But after-school time is also a great opportunity for free, unscheduled time. Having time for open, self-directed play is a nice balance to the rules and schedules kids follow at school. What a delight it is for a school-age child to set their own agenda; what a blessing, even, to be bored.

Not all activities, done regularly, constitute a sense of rhythm. After all, a strict regimen is rhythmic, but only in the driest, most lifeless meaning of the word. A rhythm's value comes from the intentions behind it. As you consider increasing the rhythms in your family life, ask yourself: Would this make life easier, more balanced? Will this help with what we need to do? More importantly, will this contribute to the way we want to live?

In their consistency, rhythms establish trust. They offer children a sense of order . . . the joy of anticipation and the security of things to be counted on, every day. Busyness, change, and improvisation will still have keys to your house, but they won't entirely rule the day. Not when rhythms are honored. Consistency will gain a foothold. And as you consider adding new rhythms to your family life, remember: In addition to consistency, the best daily life rhythms offer connection.

QUITE SIMPLY:
The rhythms of family life provide consistency; the best ones also offer connection.

I'm not suggesting you schedule "group hug" breaks throughout the day. (More power to you, though, if you can manage it.) What I am suggesting is that connection builds through small, unplanned moments. Cleaning up after supper is just something you do as a family; no big deal. Not exactly a well-oiled machine, but somehow—with a lot of reaching over and around, different styles and speeds of engagement, the occasional crashes and heroic saves—the job gets done. It is when your six-year-old son, playing to a full audience, first made up his signature robot dance. When the baby actually sits quietly, transfixed by the motion all around her.

Relational Credits

Music is as much about the spaces between notes as it is about the notes themselves. As a (frustrated, would-be) guitar player, I know the importance of the pause. As you're coming down off one note and preparing for the next, or when you hold a suspended seventh, the space is absolutely critical to the piece. In parenting, too, it is often in the intervals—the spaces between activities—that relationships are built.

Here is the simplest example, an exchange that, especially for boys, is likely familiar to you. You pick your son up from school, and he's barely in the car when you ask: "How was school?" "Okay." "Just okay?" "It was okay, regular." "What happened; what did you do?" "Nothing." We parents find this stinginess in conversation maddening. But wait. Later that night, as he's lying on the living room rug, his head propped on the dog's back, he may be more inclined to turn to you and share more: "Hey Mom, you know my new science teacher, Mr. Elway? Today he said that I could do my project on black holes, which is so awesome, because that's *exactly* what I wanted to do it on!"

Moments of pause, when nothing much is going on. Or the passage, the interval between one activity and the next. Ironically, it's often not the activities themselves but the moments leading up to them, or away from them, that provide windows into how our kids are doing. Unfortunately, some kids have very few pauses in their daily lives, going from one activity to the next without a chance to process their thoughts or feelings. Or a child's parents might be so busy and overscheduled that they present a moving target, unavailable for these unplanned moments of connection.

A sense of rhythm in the home can increase these moments of pause. There's something about being there consistently for kids that allows them to "pick their spots" and open up to you when nothing much is happening. You're familiar, consistent, and predictable.

There are two points here, and they're intertwined. One point is that by being a parent who commits to regularity—to books every night, dinners together, the winter walk, the "favorites things," the regular notes of the day and week—you become, by extension, a parent kids can be with, doing nothing. I sometimes think of it as "the old shoe phenomenon." As such a mom or dad, you prove yourself regular, trustworthy. By those habitual commitments you are saying, "Yes, I may be 'an old shoe,' but I am *your* parental old shoe."

QUITE SIMPLY:

Relationships are often built in the intervals, the spaces between activities, when nothing much is going on.

The other point is that these moments of doing nothing—together—are critical. I remember in one of my workshops a mother mentioned that she couldn't imagine being alone for any period of time with her father. Even as an adult she wondered what she would do if she needed to take a long car trip with her dad, or if they somehow found themselves in a rowboat together for a couple of hours. There was nothing scary or threatening about her father, she was quick to add. But despite all those years of growing up in the same house, he was a stranger to her, and she didn't know what they would have to talk about without other people or distractions around them.

Simplification establishes an unspoken emphasis on relationship. By eschewing some of the distractions that could easily consume our time and attention—limitless media, activities, and *stuff*—we leave our emotional door open for our loved ones. We acknowledge the claim they've already staked on our attention. Simplicity establishes a connection with our children that is "bankable." By that I mean that we have "relational credits." In difficult times we can count on, and draw from, this connection.

A deep comfort in one another's company is what we look for in family; it's what we want our children to feel. A sense of ease that doesn't depend on a shared interest, activity, or conversation. This reassuring connection is often effortless when they're young. We are, after all, the family architect; we build its structures, we set its emotional climate. As our kids grow toward independence, however, there are more opportunities for hits and misses in our emotional timing and connection with one another. A father may find he hasn't too much to offer in the depth of his daughter's "horse phase," when all her thoughts, conversations, and dreams are equine. Likewise, the son that Mom used to play Wiffle ball with is now playing a bass guitar in the garage. If she opens the door to look in, he and the four other guys (one with multiple piercings) will turn and say, in unison, "'Sup?"

How your child (and you as their parent) fares during their adolescent years is determined by the years that proceed the first rush of hormones. It's at least partially predicated on those moments of pause that you've shared as they grew up, those relational credits that you've built up. Such moments of security and ease form a well-worn groove of connection. What you hope is that the relational habit life you've established together continues right through adolescence. The bond is habitual, unconscious. It is just the way you are together, always have been.

Does hanging out together when they're young make their adolescence a breeze? Hardly. Not even close. Adolescence is a developmentally turbulent time, and it can be intense, for teens and for their parents. But relational credits, the emphasis you've put on being there for them, and with them, can make things easier for you both, during their adolescence and other difficult times. Here are two examples from my recent experience.

A father and his daughter came to see me. The daughter was having some problems academically, but as we were talking, a completely different issue surfaced. The girl, Lily, was in seventh grade. It seems that in her small school community there had recently been two parties with no adults present, at which sexually explicit "games" had been played. Lily mentioned that it was she who had spoken to her father about these parties, and she had told him how uncomfortable she and several other kids had felt. Lily's father contacted some other parents, and the parties had been stopped. Many conversations between participating kids and their parents had taken place, and the whole thing had been handled without Lily being outed as the one who had first gone to a parent.

As Lily told me about this I said how impressed I was that she had shown the courage to talk to her father like that. "Well," Lily said, "my dad and I, we're pretty tight. I mean, I knew that he would listen. I knew that he would hear me out at least; he always does that. And I just kinda thought that if he could figure out a way to work things out, he would help." In fact, Lily's father had been listening quietly while she described the whole incident to me. Listening—waiting, pausing—seemed to be something he had made a habit of. So would it always play out like this between Lily and her father? I don't know. But I was certain that no matter what, *she* was certain her father would listen to her. Considering what can come a young girl's way at this time in her life, that certainty is a very powerful thing.

One other point about Lily and her father. A woodworker, Lily's dad had his workshop in the basement. He wasn't always there when Lily and her brother got home from school, but whenever he was, the door to the basement was open. Both kids knew that they could come down and talk to him as he carved or sanded. He would sometimes stop, turn off his machines, and just sit opposite them at the old shop picnic table. But more often the talk was just part of the flow of the afternoon, as much a part of it as the work. I mention this because we sometimes feel we have to create a "sacred space" (dim the lights, cue the Gregorian chants) for communicating with our kids.

Not so. Anyplace will do; the sawdust is optional. The point is to create space in one's time and attention. Your intention, and your commitment to it, will make that space sacred for you and your children.

QUITE SIMPLY:
Committing to rhythm builds trust and relational credits: a connection that is "bankable."

Sometimes it helps just to remind children that such a safe space exists for them. One afternoon a few weeks ago my older daughter was coming home after school. As she walked down the driveway toward the house she began to cry. By the time my wife reached her and held her the tears and words were spilling out. "Unbearable!" I heard as I walked over to sit near them. It had been an awful day at school. There was so much noisy "yammering" in class that they had not had a second recess, and she had not heard the story, or had a chance to finish her painting.

Isn't it tempting to jump in with a solution? Absolutely tempting to quiet their quivering little chins, and dry their eyes, with a failsafe, can't-miss solution. But to do so consistently says "I'm in control of your life" and "I know how you feel." We aren't. And we don't, really. And while it may seem a comforting thought to "know how they feel," it also denies them their own feelings.

Soon both sisters were playing, reclaiming the day somewhat in their own way. But when the subject of school came up at dinner, our eldest was clearly still upset. "Darling, whatever happens at school or anywhere, you also, always, have a place here, at home. We are here, your mom and I, and your sister." The tears came again, but she jumped up to hug me, relieved. I wasn't "fixing" her day, I was just reminding her that she had a safe place, a haven. I mentioned to her that I was going to fly the next day to Chicago, "one of the biggest airports in the country." I told her that as I was walking through this busy airport, bustling with noise and people hurrying here and there, I would probably think of her and her mother and sister at home. "Really?" she asked. "Yes," I said. "That picture is with me wherever I go."

My friend Laura's daughter, Alison, is fifteen. She's a bright, wonderful girl, very much loved by those of us who know her. When I ran into Laura recently we talked about the teenage years. For all of her charm out in the world, Laura said, Alison could be quite rude and hostile at home, especially toward her. Rolled eyes, monosyllabic responses, straight down the "Adolescent Behavior" checklist. Alison's nastiest comments seemed to be reserved for her mother. "You know what's strange, though?" Laura asked, lowering her voice to a whisper. "At dinner she can look at me as though I've sprouted a second head, and still, almost every night, she plops down on the couch in front of the fire with me, her head in my lap!"

That's not so strange, really. Alison's full-time (developmental) job right now is to push Laura away, but on her "time off" she does what *also* comes natural to her. She can think of her mom as an alien one minute and, thanks to their broad and deep connection, snuggle with her the next. Adolescents can forget their current mission in life long enough to live in the well worn groove of their connection to you. And as parents we need those moments of connection to get through the rest. Their hormones can't repress the heart muscles entirely; those are trained and exercised by years of quiet, simple connection.

Relationships are forged in pauses . . . the ordinary, incidental moments that have extraordinary cumulative power. Every night, as a family gathers for dinner, they do "favorite things." One by one, they mention something special from the day . . . something they did or saw, something that stood out. For the children it can be the dragonfly wing they found on the fence post, the mastery of tied shoes, the neighbors' new kitten. For the parents, it can be an opportunity to make an acknowledgment: "Today I noticed how well you two made a plan and cleaned up the play space . . . and with no arguments. That was so helpful." This simple affirmation—not overblown or sentimental—can be very powerful. When done regularly, it has all of the power of ritual, bookending the flow of time, focusing our attention and love. The day becomes colored by this evening moment, as you find yourself looking, wondering: What will be today's "favorite thing"? What beauty can I notice in my child's actions today?

Rhythms are like a place set for you at the table. An unquestioned invitation to participate, connect, and belong.

Family Dinner

In my years as a Waldorf teacher I noticed a curious phenomenon. A regular part of the kindergartner's day is the preparation of a snack. This process might include chopping vegetables for soup, peeling apples, or kneading dough for loaves of bread. Invariably parents would be dumbfounded to learn that at school their son or daughter ate whatever the snack was—vegetable soup or a warm porridge—with gusto.

"Impossible! Taylor only eats two things: bow-tie pasta with butter, or waffles." Vegetable soup? How could this be? Throughout the year, parents would figure ways to visit the classroom at snack time, looking for the trick, the sleight of hand that would explain this miracle. They would look at the kindergarten teachers searchingly: "There *is* something magical about her . . . but what can it be?"

The magic, it turns out, is in the process. Children who've had a role in preparing a meal assume ownership of it. More simply: When children make the food, they're less likely to throw it, or refuse it. In the wonderful world of the Waldorf kindergarten, "snack" is not just something to eat, it is an event. There is reverence associated with the whole process: the preparation, eating, and the cleaning up afterward. Everyone is involved.

Social scientists have scrutinized the importance of "the family dinner" since the 1980s, when it was clear that this once-sacred ritual was on the endangered list. Numerous years and studies were devoted to chicken-and-egg questions: Was it the quality of the time together that determined the effects? Were kids who did better in school more likely to come from families who ate dinner together, or was it the eating together as a family that influenced the kids' better grades?

The answer, again, is in the process, not the particulars. Tonight's dinner may not be a gourmet triumph, the conversation might ramble, and uninvited guests may join the family gathering: bickering, or underlying tensions from the day. Process, it turns out, allows for bad nights, bad moods, even (heaven forbid) bad food. Process (or rhythm) braids those particulars, with the golden moments, too, into a strong, unifying bond. This is what we do together, and mean to one another, good day, good meal, or bad.

QUITE SIMPLY:

The magic of rhythms is in the process, not the particulars.

Studies have shown that the more often families eat together, the more likely it is that kids will do well in school, eat fruits and vegetables, and build their vocabularies, and the less likely they will smoke, drink, do drugs, suffer from depression, struggle with asthma, or develop eating disorders. The National Center on Addiction and Substance Abuse (CASA) at Columbia University did a ten-year study that found, among other things, that family dinner gets better with practice. The less often a family eats together, the more likely the television will be on during dinner, the less healthy the food, and, as rated by the participants, the more meager the talk and less satisfying, overall, the experience is likely to be.[1]

Blending the wisdom of the kindergarten, social scientists, and our own instincts, we can at least say this: The family dinner is more than a meal. Coming together, committing to a shared time and experience, exchanging conversation, food, and attention . . . all of these add up to more than full bellies. The nourishment is exponential. Family stories, cultural markers, and information about how we live are passed around with the peas. The process is more than the meal: It is what comes before and after. It is the reverence paid. The process is also more important than the particulars. Not only is it more forgiving, but also, like any rhythm, it gets better with practice.

In Chapter Three we limited clutter and excess in your child's environment by simplifying toys, books, and clothes. Consider applying the same principles to food. My purpose is not just to declutter your pantry but to declutter the choices, judgments, and power issues around food, especially for young children. First, though, in keeping with our current emphasis on rhythm, we'll look at simple ways you can emphasize the process around dinner. Or, to put it another way, we'll look behind the kindergarten's magic curtain to reveal how you, too, can serve vegetable soup that your child will eat.

The rhythm of dinner begins with its preparation, not the first bite. However you can manage it, involve your children. Even young children can poke the eyes out of a potato, wash lettuce, or just put forks by each plate. It takes more effort on your part in the beginning, but it lays a path for regular, more efficient help in the future. It also gives kids a stake in the meal, a "pride of authorship" that will influence their eating and their behavior. "How do you like it?" they'll ask everyone, several times.

Involving kids in the food preparation will also help ease the transition to the table. If you're pulling a child away from play, it is easier to pull them into an activity than it is to pull them into a chair. "Come on, Emma, I need you to give these peas a bath!" A child involved in something, in the flow of a task, is in a rhythm of their own. By involving them in the preparation, you build a ramp up to the meal.

This easier transition is important, because you don't want strong emotions—the lockdown of fight-or-flight—stirred up with your food. What can kids do with powerful emotions, when they so often feel powerless? Well, there are three areas where kids can exert control and win: eating, pooping, and sleeping. More to the point: not eating, pooping, or sleeping. When hauled out of play, kids can be ready for a fight. You sit them down to a plate of food and they've found a fight they know they can win. You can't make them eat, it's true, but with a little ramp building you can even the odds.

It's nice to have some sort of symbolic start to the meal. My family observes a moment or so of silence. (We started with ten seconds). Some families share a prayer or a blessing; some observe the lighting of a candle. Again, the particulars are up to you. A family I know keeps a basket of Christmas cards they've received near the kitchen table. One night a week a card is chosen from the bunch and the sender is remembered, for just a moment, before the eating begins. All of these are essentially a collective breath, and a thank-you, whether religious or secular. Thanks to the cook(s), the farmers who grew the food, to those we love, or to the good fortune that brings the family together, safe and hungry!

The dinner table is one of a child's most consistent laboratories for learning social skills (and impulse control); it's democracy in action. It's true, it may be a rare meal when you don't cringe once or twice, imagining how your "dinner theater" might play to a wider audience. Your family may not be ready for that audience with the queen yet. But most of the rules are principles of basic fairness and graciousness. Plates of food are passed, silverware is used or bravely attempted, nobody leaves the table until everyone is finished; we ask and tell one another about our days.

Involving everyone in the cleanup is an ideal way to ramp down from the meal to the evening rhythms and activities. This continues the democracy of the meal: If you eat it, you might help prepare it, but you surely help clean up from it. The connection built through the meal continues, but on the move, as everyone assumes their own tasks, working together.

Simplifying Tastes

For most families today, the pillars of too-much certainly apply to food. We generally consume too much of it; we're overwhelmed by too many choices and too much information (advertising and marketing); and "too fast" applies both to what (fast food) and how (on the go) we eat. A sense of overwhelm, especially for children, can be the basis of poor eating habits and lifelong control issues around food.

Like the issues around toys and clutter that we explored in Chapter Three, food is another area of our daily lives that has become bloated (excuse the pun) with excess and pseudochoices. While I don't claim to be an expert on nutrition, no dietary expertise is needed to lose some of the weight (again, sorry . . .) we feel around our family's food choices. Just as I did with toys and clutter, I'll offer some general guidelines on simplifying food.

Instead of a hypothetical "mountain of foods" in the center of your kitchen, imagine the huge expanse of your grocery store. Many now are the size of airport hangars, with the least processed foods (those that existed fifty years ago) located around the periphery. Intense marketing pressures are brought to bear on our food purchases. And like toys, foods are being marketed as entertainment, as treats that children deserve to enjoy. Who are we, as parents, to say no to their pleasure? Then there's peer pressure. Food marketers, like toy marketers, capitalize on the notion of social acceptance, or "membership," around food choices. "Tell your friends!" The pressure then circulates back to you, as marketers urge children to apply pester power to their parents. Lost your appetite?

My first suggestion for simplifying food, as with toys, is to limit choices and complexity. Simplify the number of food options available to your kids, and simplify the tastes and ingredients of those options by backing away from highly processed and sweetened foods.

To simplify foods we can follow many of the same principles we used sorting through the toy pile. These basic guidelines can accompany you down the aisles of your supermarket: Is this food designed to nourish, or to entertain? To stimulate? More simply, is this food designed, or was it grown? Did it exist fifty years ago? Is it unnecessarily complex, with ingredients you can't identify or pronounce? There are seventeen thousand "new food products" introduced to shoppers in this country every year.[2] Simpler foods, like simpler toys, tend to be the ones that last. And when you simplify your child's food choices as you did with their toys, you release them from the pressures of too much; you allow for the development of lifelong healthy eating habits.

Remember the high-stimulation toys we identified in the toy pile? They were the ones with the screaming sound effects, flashing lights, and revolving dials, designed to put your child's nervous system into cortisol-induced overdrive. Here is a food parallel, quoted directly from the Frito-Lay website: "Turn up the volume of your snacking with the amped-up spices, high-decibel cheese, and the awesome crunch of Doritos brand tortilla chips. The bold flavors like Doritos Nacho Cheese and Cool Ranch are the loudest tasting snacks on earth."

The problem with such foods, leaving aside their health effects, is that they hijack your child's taste buds. They set the stimulation bar so high, children lose the ability to recognize and differentiate subtler flavors. The tastes (thanks to additives) have gotten bigger and bigger, more complex. How can a carrot compete with Hot Wings and Blue Cheese Doritos? Next to such extreme flavors most foods can't attract your child's attention, much less their interest.

QUITE SIMPLY:

Food is meant to nourish, not entertain or excite.

I think of Doritos, and so many other snack foods, as "big-hit" flavors. (Clearly I'm not alone; they're even promoted as such!) Such big-hit flavors (usually additives and stimulants) set up an addictive cycle. As we grow accustomed to in-your-face flavors, we crave more, we need more to deliver the bigger and bolder "hits," or physiological reactions we've come to expect. Children's little systems can be hijacked, recalibrated by the hyperactivity-inducing effects of food additives, sugar, and caffeine. Such foods are the enemies of rhythm. You can't flow through speed-crash-and-burn.

The first step, then, in simplifying your children's food is to wean them off these highly processed snack foods that have little or no nutritional value. You can make a dramatic cold-turkey stop, or you can ease off them. Based on what I've seen and heard from numerous families, it takes about a month to clean your child's palate of such big-hit flavors. This surprised me—I thought it would take longer—but a month seems to be the average. When backing off extreme tastes, offer bold textures but healthier choices. A banana won't be a good substitute for Doritos, but crunchy baked vegetable chips will work in a pinch and get their food choices moving in a better direction

To wean your family off sugary sodas, create your own "soda fountain" at home with seltzer water and juices. The bubbles will help your kids transition off sodas. You can even begin with really sweet concoctions . . . then back off the sugar. The sodas you are weaning them off are going in the opposite direction: 7UP has more than tripled its amount of sugar in the past twenty years; the average can of commercial soda contains the equivalent of ten teaspoons of sugar.[3] Back off the sugary sodas and the caffeine. As the sugar is reduced, what flavors begin to appeal to them? You can make it clear that these are not strictly "alternatives" to more highly processed snacks; these are now what's available at home. The detox process goes only in one direction: toward increasingly real (as opposed to processed) foods, with increasingly simpler and more natural ingredients.

The younger your children, the easier it will be to simplify food. But you can change course when your children are older; it can be done. Don't let a difficult few weeks stop you from establishing a new direction. The grumbling will be short-term; the benefits (and you'll notice them quickly) will last. You have to embody this kind of change, fully commit to it. Do not present it as "an experiment" or an "interesting learning experience."

If your children are teenagers, let them know that these changes are here to stay. There will be eye rolling, and yes, grumbling will echo through the halls. And no doubt you'll be approached with a very persuasive argument. It will go something like this: "But that's ridiculous, *everyone* drinks tons of this stuff! Janet drinks triple what I do! And the candy? Are you *kidding* me? Bob's parents have *boxes* of it, and they *give* it to us! You can even get it at school!" Listen to all of it; don't interrupt. Let them assure you that the very things you've eliminated at home are actually present (accepted, offered, and enjoyed) every single other place on earth. You can then say, calmly and with reassurance, that given that these things are so widely available, the fact that they will no longer be available at home should not present much of a sacrifice.

You can't control what your teenage son or daughter eats (or does) every minute of the day. But you can be firm and clear about what happens at home. And don't forget: Over time, with rhythms and predictability, "what happens at home" naturally evolves. It becomes accepted, anticipated, and depended on.

When children—especially young children—have too many choices before they develop good judgment, they can easily be derailed: by marketing, their own desires, and by their developing wills. It's entirely normal for a kid to be drawn to a sweet confection that's bright pink and shoots flavor sparks when stirred into their cereal. (I made that up, but it will no doubt be on the market within the year.) It's also normal for a young child to want to exert control when and where they can. But as their parents, do we want these understandable tendencies and a legion of advertisers to co-opt our kids' health? Or their lifelong relationships to food?

Surely you know kids who've negotiated or stonewalled their way into a very narrow alley of food preferences. I call them strictly "red and white food" kids. Bread, pasta, sweets, and the occasional red sauce. By vacillating between carbohydrates and sugars they move back and forth between comfort and vigilance: a common reaction to stress. Stress also makes kids reject newness, so they remain stuck in the alley as it gets narrower. Here's more bad news: Such power issues around food will almost certainly spill out to other areas. But there is good news.

Through more than twenty years of helping parents simplify I've come to a curious realization. I didn't understand it for the first couple of years, but parents continued to mention that as they simplified, their kids became less and less picky about food. The pattern was consistent. Whether parents just simplified food, or simplified more extensively, by increasing the sense of rhythm and regularity in their children's lives, control issues around food substantially lessened or disappeared. Why? Because as kids begin to feel less overwhelmed, as their lives become more predictable and less out of control, they feel less of a need to exert control over food. Simplification has broad effects.

QUITE SIMPLY:

As parents simplify, their kids' food issues diminish or resolve quite naturally.

Food should be a source of nourishment for children, not entitlement, entertainment, or empowerment. If you concede your authority around food to young children, they can adopt habits that may affect them throughout life. You actually limit their options by giving them too many choices, too young. We know that a person's food preferences are formed over the first few years of life. We also know that this process is primarily social: Kids try and learn to enjoy foods—whether spicy, bland, nutritious, or processed—that they see others enjoying.[4] By simplifying food at home you give young children time to try a wide variety of healthy foods and to develop a well-rounded set of preferences.

Another benefit of breaking out of the "red and white food alley" is this: When we expand our food horizons we expand in other ways, too. I've yet to meet a child who is broadening their food preferences who isn't also making intellectual or emotional leaps. Food is fundamental, and our relationship to it is a watermark of our relationship to life.

One other point before we answer the age-old question "What's for dinner?" I've passed this tip along for years now, so I have firm confirmation that it works. If you want your child to try a new food (or food group), you need to have them try it at least eight times. We tend to give up too soon, setting up a detour around all forms and varieties of lettuce, say, or beans, after just one frowny-face reaction. What I've noticed is that you start with a very small quantity (let's use broccoli as an example) and offer it with butter and salt. You'll want to offer it again—at least seven more times, however you want to prepare it—while decreasing and then eliminating the salt. The flavor comes through as the salt decreases. The process is gradual enough to almost—almost—guarantee acceptance: eight tries, and they have a food for life.

Simplifying Dinner

I've suggested that you move toward fewer options and simpler flavors by sorting out "big-hit" processed foods. My next suggestion is designed to simplify the family dinner. It will make "What's for dinner?" easier to answer—perhaps even an obsolete question in your house. What's for dinner? That's easy: What day of the week is it?

Family dinners get much simpler when they're predictable: Monday pasta night, Tuesday rice night, Wednesday soup, and so on. By suggesting this system, do I have Mom or Dad (or whoever cooks) in mind? Well, yes, regular meals make preparation easier. But I recommend the practice mainly because it is so deeply grounding and affirming for kids.

Hopefully, by now you accept the idea that rhythm secures life for children; it forms a foundation for their growth. In the wash of life, the comings and goings, sleep and wakefulness, work and play, car pools and more car pools, the evening meal is a red dot with a large arrow pointing to it: You Are Here. It is a pivotal opportunity to establish rhythms that will ripple out and be felt—in other parts of the day, in our kids' behavior, and in our connection as a family.

We are here. This is now. The first argument for regular meals on regular nights is that it helps family dinners actually happen. Instead of marshaling tremendous energy, inspiration, ingredients, and creativity every evening, certain decisions are already made. There can be variation within each night's staple; pasta night could include a range of possibilities. But you are not staging a new Broadway production, from concept to performance, every night.

You never make one meal anyway, right? When Bobby doesn't like crunchy, Sara is allergic to green foods, and Maryanne has gone vegan. One mom told me that she felt like she was spinning plates to get dinner on the table, furiously running to keep six concoctions in the air. Once dinner was on the table, she was so exhausted that she could snap at the slightest comment that didn't sit well.

For the cooks, the consistency of regular meals can forestall that moment when, leaning into the open but empty refrigerator, we throw up our hands and call the whole thing off. The regularity (and simplicity) extends back from the meal to the preparation, to the grocery store, and to the shopping list.

So, I've lost you, or you're beginning to suspect some strange cult-like associations on my part. After all, isn't variety the American way? Haven't I seen how cookbooks are swallowing all the other sections in the bookstore? How could I possibly suggest tying you down to such a routine, to such boring regularity?

Variation is possible with this system, as I mentioned. This Wednesday night's soup might be quite different from next week's, depending on what's available. But there's a larger point here, one that relates to all daily life rhythms. The description of them may seem routine, but the experience of them is usually not. There are so many currents in day-to-day life, so many modifications, permutations, and variations on the wave, that rhythms tend to act as buoys, not anchors.

Also, rhythms make stepping out of them a real treat. "I know it's soup night, but we're going out for dinner!" A sense of rhythm sets a steady beat, but allows for wonderful high notes. Children react to such unexpected pleasures with genuine appreciation. Occasional high notes are welcome against a steady rhythm. Very different from this are the tones of continual escalation. That song, by another name, is entitlement.

Many years ago I heard from a mom who had adopted this suggestion, and simplified it further. One weekend she made a couple of big trays of lasagna and a big pot of soup, freezing several dinners at once. She figured that 20 percent extra resourcing (her word for shopping and prep work) had yielded an 80 percent higher dinner yield. By profession, this woman was (I am not kidding) an efficiency expert. At first I found this level of organization a bit scary, but she's absolutely right. It can be wonderful, after a particularly busy day, to be able to have dinner already prepared. We went out and bought an old secondhand freezer so that we could do the same. When there is more time around a meal, there is a greater sense of ease all around.

Chances are there will be a less-than-popular night in the lineup. That's okay. Wednesday night is soup night, and your kids will eat it. If they don't, chances are also good that they won't suffer irreparable damage. Soup day will come and go. They may start worrying about it on Monday, they may skip their soup dinner once or twice with a great show of disdain, but before long the objections will be forgotten; slurping will punctuate the conversation. Consistency also teaches us that some things do not change, though we may wish they would. Not everything bends to our personal preferences.

If this seems extreme, it's because we're no longer used to thinking of dinner as a group event. All that is missing is the flashing neon "Diner" sign over our homes as each person in the family eats what, when, and where they want. The kids eat (something, usually either red or white) in front of the TV, Mom makes a salad, and Dad grabs food on the way home to eat later, reading the paper. There are no rules, no need to change in any way for anyone else. No sense that there may be something to gain from coming together.

QUITE SIMPLY:

Consistency reinforces values that are larger than personal preferences.

My friend and colleague Jack Petrash (author of *Navigating the Terrain of Childhood*) has raised three children: two grown and one in high school. He told me that evening meals were sacrosanct at his home. This was fine for many years, but as his boys got older, they tried to get out of it. They had places to go, things to do; dinner with the family had competition. Jack and his wife, Carol, held firm. They also decided that they would spend thirty or forty dollars extra every week on food so that the boys' friends could come over often and have meals. They figured that even with high food bills, compared to, say, the costs of family therapy, they were coming out ahead. So much would be discussed over the course of those meals. As parents, Jack and Carol had a view into what their teenagers were thinking, doing, and what their friends were like.

It's appropriate for teenagers to begin to chafe at long-standing family rhythms. It is their job, developmentally, to complain. That doesn't mean that in response we should pack up our traditions and call it a day. Consistency and connection at home pay some of their highest dividends during adolescence. CASA found that a majority of teenagers who ate three or fewer meals a week with their families wished they did so more often.[5]

You may have doubts about whether "core meals" on regular nights would be a good idea for your family. Again and again I've seen how grounding it can be for children, so I hope you'll give it a try. You needn't make any announcement; no grand speeches will be necessary. You'll be into the third week before your children notice the pattern. Well before that, though, I think you'll see that dinners have become a bit simpler and more consistent.

Sleep and Pressure Valves

The dishes are done, and any leftovers have been put away. Do you find yourself now mentally assessing the odds of an on-time bedtime? Do you rate the energy level of each child against the chances that his or her lights will go out, and eventually yours, at a reasonable time? It's impossible for a child to go from full tilt to full stop at bedtime. In fact, I think of a child's process toward sleep as beginning when they wake up in the morning. What kind of day will this be? How rhythmic? Will it include activity, and opportunities to pause, to process what has happened?

When you think about it, falling asleep involves a sort of leap of faith, a "letting go" that requires trust. I sometimes say to my daughters, when turning out the light, "It's okay now . . . Fall right back into your angel's arms." Sleep issues often stem from problems with anxiety and trust; what kids need to "let go" into sleep is a greater feeling of connectedness.

Let me share with you the idea of "pressure valves," rhythms that you can build into your child's day. Pressure valves offer security and (like the best of rhythms) connection. A pressure valve lets a child release emotional steam. When they can let it go during the day, they can more easily "let go" into sleep.

Henry had had problems ever since he started school. Boys and school don't always coexist peacefully. It's an alliance that often has to be helped along, nurtured. Henry's problems at school were being made worse by the fact that he was having trouble going to sleep at night.

Henry's mother, Sue, was a single mother. I think of Sue often to this day, because I learned something wonderful from her. You may find it useful as well.

Sue and I talked about increasing the predictability and rhythm of their days together. When I mentioned how she could preview the following day for Henry, she said, "That's just what I've begun to do! I call it 'making a grit sandwich.' " This I had to see. At the end of the day, when Henry was getting ready for bed, she would lie on his bed and begin with a question. "Henry, love, what was a good thing, a courageous thing about the day?" "Well," Henry would say, giving it some thought, "at recess, in foursquare, Theo said that Jerry was cheating . . . but it was just that he hadn't seen the hit, really, so I said, 'Jerry wasn't cheating!' " "Really? You stuck up for your friend? Good for you. What was the hardest thing today?" "Well, probably when we had to do those counting things again, you know? I told you about how in math now we have to make piles with those beads and then put them together?" "Yes, you mentioned that Tuesday." "Yeah, well I still hate that stuff, but I got it more today." "You understood it better?" "Yeah." Sue's responses would be minimal. She would not offer psychoanalysis, no ready fixes or judgments on the day, so much as the quiet validation of bearing witness. Listening and noticing

Henry, meanwhile, was unpacking his day for her. Imagine a suitcase full of thoughts and emotions from the day. With her questions, Sue opens the suitcase and allows Henry to take each thing out to show her. She would then ask him about the next day. "What do you think will be the hardest thing about tomorrow?" "Oh, volleyball! We're doing volleyball in PE and I suck at it!" "What will be the best thing?" "Recess! Cuz, like, that will be so cool, we've already picked teams for kickball and I am on Joseph and Lucas's team, which is awesome. . . ."

Out it all pours . . . Henry's fears and disappointments, his hopes and dreams. Dreams are not always huge things, after all. They can be quite small. But they illuminate our thoughts, our perspective on life. Sue has not only beautifully unpacked the day with Henry, she's previewed the next day. And because Henry is having some difficulties at school, she has left him with what she calls "a grit sandwich." In other words, he has expressed some of the things he is having trouble with, but those things are cushioned, or contained (picture some very soft bread) by other aspects of his school day that are pleasant and exciting for him. Sometimes, especially with quiet little ones, you may not get a ready rush of responses to your questions. That's all right, too. They have, meanwhile, thought about their day, in the comforting light of your attention.

QUITE SIMPLY:
Two or three "pressure valves" built into the day will help a child fall asleep at bedtime.

How can you help your child release the pressure of their day? I think there should be at least two, hopefully three or four such "pressure valves" built into the day's routines.

Especially for kids who have trouble getting to sleep at night, it helps to think about the day as a mirror into what might happen at bedtime. What kind of day will this be for them? "Another way to look at it," a father once said in a workshop, "is 'Am I going to be able to watch the game tonight?' " If your child hasn't had opportunities during the day to release pressure, he or she may have trouble at bedtime. And if you think of pressure in strictly adult terms, you miss the fact that today your child's brain will be processing information and building neural pathways, and her body will be growing at rates that will make what you do today look like a whole lot of standing still.

A baby's or toddler's naps are built-in pressure valves. A quiet rest time during the day is something to hold on to for as long as possible. Even an eight- or nine-year-old child can benefit from an hour of calm in the middle of the day, whether they spend it resting or in some quiet activity. Actually, we could probably all benefit, regardless of age, from such a practice. Once a child is school age, and not having a rest period there, you can still implement one during the summer months or on weekends. Keep the concept alive—even after your kids graduate from their midday naps—that rest time is something we do when we can. Won't sleep during the day interfere with your child's ability to drift off at night? Most kids older than six won't sleep during rest time, and if they do, it's because they really need more sleep than they're getting. But a half hour or an hour of quiet, restful solitary time during the day is restorative at any age, and a habit worth cultivating.

An after-school ritual can serve as both a pressure valve and a bridge between the worlds of school and home. The proverbial after-school snack can do the trick. Do you remember Marie, from Chapter

One? Marie's mother had arranged her work schedule so that she was home when Marie was done with school. I suggested she make a habit of having a little snack with Marie as a transition ritual. "But she doesn't talk to me!" she reported, after a week. Who says she has to? A moment of connection can be silent. As Marie comes to rely on her mother's presence during this time—sitting there, moving about the kitchen, looking through the mail—she'll use that connection to suit her needs.

As I mentioned, my family observes a moment of silence right before dinner. I think of this as a pressure valve. Quite honestly, we started with ten seconds of silence and gradually worked our way up to a minute. We'll probably work up to two minutes and that will be our limit. No, it isn't an hour of meditation every day, but any parent with small children will probably be impressed. I know I am, most every night. The kids are quite itchy, without fail, for the first bit, but then they relax into it.

You may be wondering: What's the point of having a moment of silence? If so, I challenge you to try it. Around our little table each night there is a sort of collective sigh as we relax into this one quiet moment. The point of holding this silence is to deepen one's attention. We aren't always aware of the tension we're carrying. If you have to be quiet for a moment, chances are your shoulders will drop a bit and you'll be aware of your breath, perhaps for the first time that day. For a child who talks or moves or fidgets quite continuously all day, this moment of quiet stillness will be *very* noticeable. A moment of silence not only releases the tension of constant doing, it presents a remarkable alternative: just being.

For some boys and industrious types, work can serve as a pressure valve. Such work might be doing a project: hauling rocks in a wheelbarrow, digging a hole, building with blocks, catching lizards, or climbing a tree. Ongoing projects that kids are anxious to get back to right after school can be wonderful pressure valves. Any activity a child can "lose himself in" allows for a release of tension, and the mental ease needed to process the day's events. Whatever the means, active deep play is an excellent pressure valve. As kids reach the preteen years, sometimes hobbies or collections—the beginnings of deep passions—and organized sports can serve the same purpose.

One small suggestion I have for a pressure valve I've mentioned before: the lighting of a candle at some regular point of the day. Part of your family tradition might be to light a candle before dinner and let one of your children snuff it out at the end. For small children, the light of a candle creates a magical world. It concentrates their attention and narrows their focus to a small, golden circle. Again, this is a very simple thing. But you may be surprised by how powerfully soothing it can be.

One mother really made me laugh when she reported that her little son seemed to equate candlelight with some sort of primal truth serum. "Aren't most kids quieted by candlelight?" she asked me. "Not Jared! When the candle's lit he opens his little heart (and mouth) to recount his deepest wishes for the earth and every creature ever known, as well as his thoughts, hopes and dreams for himself, his friends, pets, teachers and our mailman. It's very dear, but honestly, as I light the candle now, I think to myself, 'Hold on to your hat!' I never know what will come out!" Now, *that's* a pressure valve!

No gadgets or special effects necessary. We have what we need to help our children balance their lives, days, and energies. Each little pressure valve, each opportunity for release and calm, is very small, insignificant. But imagine tucking in a child—your child—when they have had some of these moments throughout their day. Imagine a greater sense of ease and calm in their little bodies, in their breathing, as you lean down to kiss them good night.

Sleep is the ultimate rhythm. Everything your child does and who they will be are affected by their sleep or lack of it. Low self-esteem? Too little sleep is one of the first things I look for. Without sleep we're reactive, unable to approach new things or changing circumstances with strength and resilience. Sleep is the required rhythm to a strong "I am" sense of self. Because a child's brain is still developing, and so much of that neural growth and pruning happens while they're sleeping, a deprivation of even one hour can have intellectual and behavioral consequences. According to studies done by Dr. Avi Sadeh of Tel Aviv University, the performance gap caused by just one hour's less sleep was equivalent to the normal gap between a sixth-grader and a fourth-grader. In other words, your sixth-grader who's going to school sleepy may be learning (and behaving) at a fourth-grade level.[6]

In my experience, most children between two and six need eleven hours of sleep. From ages six to eleven, some kids can do well with ten hours, but that number will go up again—to eleven or even twelve hours—during adolescence. Unfortunately, most kids don't get anywhere near these numbers. Half of all adolescents get less than seven hours of sleep on weeknights. According to studies conducted by the University of Kentucky, by the time they are seniors in high school, kids average only slightly more than six and a half hours of sleep a night.[7]

Bedtimes should be some of the family's most inviolable rhythms. I counsel a twenty-minute window—ten minutes grace on either side of an otherwise fixed time. Bedtimes that vary or are vastly different on weekday and weekend nights have the same physiological effects as jet lag. You might also remember that sleep your child has before midnight is worth more than that of a postmidnight hour. Your child's internal rhythms are set so that the deeper somatic sleep happens earlier in the night.

Bedtime Stories

Stories are wonderful pressure valves. The day's events and the questions stirred up by them can be given flight by the adventures of mythical creatures and fantastic lands. Children recognize themselves in the characters; they sense their own worth as they feel the heroine's fears, experience her bravery, compassion, and hope. They follow along with their heads and their hearts, recognizing the consequences of deeds, navigating the path of right and wrong. As they ask themselves "What would I do?" or "How will it end?" their own day releases its hold, washed by the power of imagination.

I've never met a child who didn't like a good story, well told. Such a child may exist; I've just never met them. Most children delight in stories, to imaginary worlds spread out before them as they snuggle close to the teller or reader. Nothing is required of them; they can relax into their bodies and their breathing as they conjure all of the details in their mind's eye. Stories have their own richness and rhythms, a musicality of language that children love. I'm sure you've heard images and phrases from stories come through in their play. Kids learn about the world through stories, and about a world of possibilities that stretch far beyond their bedroom walls. By lending their hearts and emotions to the characters, children carve out their own identities and dig inner wells of compassion and empathy.

Stories affect the way children learn to narrate their own lives, and influence the stories they will tell themselves. Einstein once said, "If you want your children to be intelligent, read them fairy tales. If you want them to be more intelligent, read them more fairy tales." It is all there, in fairy tales: truth, beauty, goodness, struggles and second chances, mistakes, conflicts, promises, and magic; archetypal lessons for a lifetime.

In Chapter Three we discussed how small children thrive on repetition, and it bears repeating. A child under four's most common response to any story—read or told—is usually "Again!" Even for older kids, ages four through eight, it can be very affirming and relaxing to reread or retell familiar stories several times. With repetition the story becomes deeply known—not just tasted—and assimilated into the child's learned experiences.

What are the family stories we tell over and over again? They're tales with beloved characters, tales of humor, of danger and fear, hardships and heroism. "Remember when Anna cut her cheek and had to get stitches? Remember when we finally got home from the hospital and had milkshakes for dinner?" The worry and relief are transformed in the retelling; with repetition the story becomes like a family creed: "Look at our strength! See what we can do!" We relive the memories, but we also reinforce what we believe about ourselves. What does your child value most about your family? You can tell by the stories they ask to hear, again and again.

Sharing stories and reading with your children is a rhythm that extends your power as a parent. Food and shelter you may have covered; college can seem like a remote possibility on a good day. But can you provide a childhood rich with stories? Remarkable! In doing so you offer security and connection—true of the best of rhythms. You also provide magic, with the circle of light from the bedside table as the stage. You throw open doors with stories, to other lands, to the magical, to the past and the future; you emphasize the importance of now while introducing the infinite.

A bedtime ritual of stories can be a very valuable path of connection and communication. This point is best illustrated, coincidentally, by a story; the story of Amber and Lola.

Amber was well into her first-grade year, age six. She was doing very well in school, eager to go each day, and happy with her world there. The day Amber's mother, Lola, came to see me, she explained that there were no issues at school. But at home Amber was very angry and short with her. Lola went on to say that her brother, who lived in California, was seriously ill. He had been sick for some time, but it was now clear that he was dying. She had been making a trip west every few weeks, staying for about five days at a time. A single mother, Lola had worked hard to build a strong network of family and friends with whom Amber felt at home. Still, Amber was terribly angry with her mother . . . not only for leaving, but for being sad.

"What are you telling Amber about what is happening?" I asked her. "I am being as honest as I can," she replied. "She loves her uncle, and knows that he is very sick. I think she deserves the truth. I didn't want to make up some story about it." In her words I heard the echo of what I wanted to tell her. "Yes, she deserves both," I said. "She deserves both the truth and stories. But she needs more stories now, to help her with the truth."

I suggested that Lola speak to Amber about this difficult time indirectly, through the stories she told her at bedtime. I suggested that she tell stories—or one story, in various forms and repetitions—about someone in a scary situation who finds a way out. He or she might be lost in a forest, truly lost, in a dark and perilous place. There were dangers involved, and challenges to be overcome, but there was also, eventually, light and change. There was a resolution, a better place that the protagonist (who, by any other name, would be Amber) would find her way to.

I ran into Lola much later, possibly even a year after that day at my office. She told me that her brother had passed. She also said, with a sort of embarrassed smile, that night after we met, she had felt irritated by my advice. "Please understand," she explained. "This was a very difficult period for me. I was overwhelmed, and it annoyed me that your 'prescription' was fairy tales. But it really worked. . . . The stories soothed her. She got through it." "Does she ever ask for that story now?" "Yes!" She seemed surprised by the question. "She does ask for it, and I tell it to her still. She doesn't want any changes to the story, but it feels different to me now, when I tell it." I knew why. "You believe it now yourself, don't you?"

Children need to nurture themselves, and stories can help. Very powerful, healing balms, stories give children the strength and the images they need to make sense of their world. In Amber's case, her mother was her "world," her safety, and to see her mother shaken was not only frightening, it was maddening to her. How could this be? It conflicted with the proper order of things. The stories gave Amber an outlet for her feelings, reassurance, and the hope that the world's "order" might one day reassert itself.

Most of the answers a young child is looking for can be found through story. This is a good example of the difference between our worlds as children and adults. As adults, we sometimes assume a direct correspondence between our worlds. So we figure that communication in a difficult situation should be direct, and thorough. After all, with all of the facts at hand, anything can be understood. Yet children are not fully emerged in the world of facts, nor do they process information the same way we do. They need simple truths, plainly spoken, especially in response to their own questions.

But children also need containers for the truth, for situations that may be difficult for them to understand. With stories they have an arena for their own feelings and questions, a place to process the truth through their imaginations. With the stories, Amber was able to develop a relationship with analogy, and through that analogy to cope with reality. Stories give young children wings, letting them fly free of the tyranny of facts.

Lola learned the power of story when she and Amber needed it, in the midst of a difficult situation. But it was one of those lessons that as a parent she'll remember and use again. We often have hunches about what our children need, what they may be grappling or having difficulty with. Sometimes a story can have no real parallel with your child's reality, but it can still be a gift, a bridge to a new perspective. It can present images that create a mood as palpable as a cool breeze coming through an open window. Stories can speak of beings and powers well beyond our control, of small kindnesses with enormous consequences, of courage and humor and the wonder of home. In their images, their malleability, and possibilities, stories offer emotional engagement and release for children. They offer sustenance.

As we end our look at rhythm, I hope you've found examples of regularity and connection that you can build into your family's daily life. I also hope that you've come to see rhythm as a remarkable gift—no savings plan necessary—that will provide lifelong dividends to your child.

Imagine . . .

- your family's days acquiring a sense of order, rhythm, and flow.
- difficult transitions being smoothed by reliable patterns.
- a growing sense of consistency in your home, and with it the joy of anticipation and the security of things that can be counted on daily.
- the opportunities for connection and moments of pause increasing as rhythms take hold.
- the security your child will feel having a mental picture of how their day will proceed.
- your child having a place in the tasks and rhythms of daily life, their roles growing as they do, from involvement toward independent mastery.
- family dinners becoming more regular, the food familiar and comforting, the connections evolving with repetition.
- having a family fortune of stories that you share.
- your family's sense of identity growing along with the number of activities you do together.

FIVE

Schedules

Take rest; a field that has rested gives a bountiful crop.

—OVID

Twelve-year-old Dylan is in an all-year soccer league and preparing for his test for a purple belt in tae kwon do. He plays the trumpet in both band and jazz orchestra, and has, on average, between one and two hours of homework a night. Dylan's mom, Carol, a financial consultant, described Dylan to me as "laid back" in comparison with his nine-year-old sister, DeeDee. "He hasn't found his real passion yet, but we are going to make sure he's exposed to all sorts of possibilities." Two years ago Carol noticed that among DeeDee's many after-school activities, she seemed most interested in gymnastics and horses, so Carol got her started in vaulting, a high-level combination of the two. "That was the end of our free time!" Carol says, "But DeeDee loves, it; she is absolutely driven." Most weekends Carol or her husband, Rob, take Dylan to a soccer tournament while DeeDee and her coach load up the horse trailer and set off for a vaulting competition in a neighboring state.

Carol and Rob are smart, busy people, devoted to their work and their family. They're equally involved in the effort it takes to raise kids, to help them get what they need to succeed in school and to pursue their interests. I met Carol after she wrote to me to take issue with a comment I had made about "overscheduled kids" in a radio interview.

Carol listens to a lot of radio, needless to say, given the time she spends driving the kids around.

The factor I failed to take into account, Carol insisted, was motivation. She felt that the term "overscheduled" was overused. Some parents may push their kids into activities, driven by a desire to see them achieve, or by a need to have them occupied while they—the parents—are at work. "That's not us. Rob and I want to give our kids opportunities that we never had as kids." She acknowledged that for children, activity without interest could be stressful. But when kids love what they're doing, when they're self-motivated, then their busyness is productive, exciting, and even energizing.

Carol and I exchanged several letters, and I had the pleasure of meeting her when she attended a lecture I gave near her hometown. We've remained friends, which pleases me. Carol could have been offended when I compared her children to crops, her efforts as a parent to farming, but she wasn't. More on that in a bit.

First I'd like to make it very clear to you—as I did to her—that I'm all for kids being active, and engaged in all sorts of interesting pursuits. I don't believe in childhoods spent in lotus positions: serene, quiet, and stress free. Children thrive on activity. My daughter's highest praise for an afternoon well spent is "Before we knew it, Daddy, we were playing *really* hard!" We all delight to see a child flushed and happy, a little out of breath with damp curls pressed against their face, fully involved in something they love.

It wasn't just my comments about "overscheduled kids" that Carol took issue with; she was responding to an issue that has been debated for some time now in the media. It was in the early 1980s when David Elkind's now-classic *The Hurried Child* first questioned whether kids were being pushed toward adulthood or "super-competency" because parents lacked the interest or time for child rearing. His more recent *The Power of Play* looks at what he feels has been lost in the rush toward early maturity. In *Children of Fast-Track Parents* (1989), author Andrée Aelion Brooks noted a growing trend among upper-middle-class parents seeking extracurricular enrichment for their grade-school-age children. Brooks saw a competitiveness in this increased focus on children's "accomplishments." In 2001, Alvin Rosenfeld and Naomi Wise's *The Over-Scheduled Child: Avoiding the Hyper-Parenting Trap* looked at "parenting as a competitive sport" and how it has led, among other things, to a loss of leisure time for parents and children.

So these trends and the debate around them have been with us for nearly thirty years. But just how much have things changed in that time, in essentially one generation? How do today's kids spend their days, compared with how their parents spent theirs as kids?

Some activities have remained fairly constant since the early 1980s: kids ages six to eleven still spend a good chunk of their time every week watching television, though they now pass increasing amounts in front of a computer screen, too. They are in school about eight hours a week more now than they were in 1981, and the amount of time spent in structured activities (for example, sports, art, classes, church, social activities) has doubled: from 11 percent in 1981 to 20–22 percent in 1997.[1] Time spent doing homework has also doubled. Fifty-two minutes per week did the trick in 1981, while kids ages six to eight spent 128 minutes in 1997, on average, completing after-school assignments. And that was before "No Child Left Behind"; a 2006 poll of parents conducted for America Online and the Associated Press found that elementary school students were averaging almost an hour and twenty minutes *a night*.[2]

Overall there is less free time for kids today; as much as twelve hours a week less.[3] According to University of Michigan researchers, in 1981 the average school-age child had 40 percent of the day for free time, after sleeping, eating, studying, and organized activities, but by 1997 the figure was down to 25 percent.[4]

Some parents, Carol included, feel that they've been unfairly blamed for these changes. And is it really so bad to be busy? Why aren't their busy kids seen as fulfilled rather than frantic? What is wrong with wanting your children to have as many opportunities as possible? I don't think blame is instructive or productive here. I don't think the central issue of "overscheduled kids" is motivation—either the parents' or the kids'. Most parents are driven by good intentions. Very few moms or dads (except, perhaps, on a bad day) would claim to keep their kids busy just to be left alone. Even given the very real, daily difficulties involved in juggling family, work, and personal responsibilities, most parents would take offense at the notion that they were rushing their kids, shortchanging them of a childhood. In wanting to provide for their children, here again parents act with generous motivations. But just as too many toys may stifle creativity, too many scheduled activities may limit a child's ability to direct themselves, to fill their own time, to find and follow their own path.

We've all known kids who need an organizer—between school, classes, sports, clubs, meetings—to keep track of where they need to be when. Or toddlers who have full schedules with varied child-care arrangements during the week, on the go and adjusting to different caregivers and social situations. Or kids whose days are so programmed that unscheduled time—even a spare fifteen minutes—seems strange, instantly "boring." Are such relentlessly busy kids happier when they enjoy what they're doing? Absolutely. But is there an emphasis on enjoyment, or accomplishment? Satisfaction, or competition? And motivation is difficult to untangle between parent and child. Is a child motivated by their own love of what they're doing, or is their motivation colored by a desire to please? In either case, I don't believe a child's love of an activity protects them from the stress of doing too much of it, too young. I think an interest, if genuine, is sustainable over time. What's more, a healthy interest requires time and the ballast of leisure and other interests for it to deepen and endure.

QUITE SIMPLY:

Too many scheduled activities may limit a child's ability to motivate and direct themselves.

Balance and *control:* These are the words that come to my mind when I think about overscheduled kids. Three words, actually: *balance, control,* and *fertilizer.* Children need free, unstructured time. They need time to do "nothing"; time to do handstands. Or to figure out a way to get the ice-cream truck to continue straight down the block without *always* turning at the corner. Or to make a good ice-cream truck plan while practicing handstands. How balanced can life be without free time? Not very. We understand this, but we also value productivity. Childhood and parenting are thoroughly examined now, much more than thirty years ago. Since childhood has become a "thing" (preparation for adulthood) and parenting has become a "thing" (what we do to *not* do things like our parents), we seek to control one with the other. Surely we can improve these "things." Surely we can add more choices. And there must be ways to increase productivity. (Handstands abandoned, she's lying down, splitting a blade of grass and blowing it like a kazoo.) This time—this afternoon, this childhood, this child—could be enriched! That's it! Enrichment. As parents, we've discovered fertilizer. And we're applying it by the ton to childhood.

Crop Rotation: Balanced Schedules

It was in the early 1950s, with the advent of chemical fertilizers, that farmers were able to bring greater control and productivity to their fields. They could enrich their fields, freed from the slow natural cycle of fertility. Fertilizer—fertility in bags—made it possible to dispense with livestock and manure, and with varied crops. Farmers were able to specialize, to plant acres and acres of densely packed monocultures. Miles of corn as far as the eye can see. Enriched soils meant greater outputs in shorter amounts of time.

The analogy has its limits, I agree. For example: Do three soccer practices a week equal one bag of fertilizer? But it provides some insights, and it can be a good guide to increasing balance in your children's schedules. What about motivation? Well, the farmer's motivation—to increase yield—is understandable, especially given the larger context. After all, the farmer is being pressured, too: How will his crops compare to those of the neighboring farms? In a fast-paced, competitive world, doesn't it make sense to seek an advantage? To try to exert some control?

Unfortunately, there are costs to applying industrial principles to nature. The price of overfertilizing is exhausted, depleted soil. Land stewardship involves time: it requires more trust than control. Sustainable farming involves rotating crops, balancing crop fields with fields that are completely fallow, and those with a legume cover crop. The same can be said about kids; there are costs to controlling their schedules, to "getting more out" of their childhood years. They are leading superphosphated lives, busy with activities from morning to night. Excess "enrichment" is not soaking in; it's running off, polluting their well-being. Activity without downtime is ultimately—like a plant without roots—unsustainable.

How does crop rotation apply to a "sustainable" childhood? Let's dig a little further into it, as a new way of looking at our kids' schedules so we can simplify them. Crop rotation is a model of balance and of interdependencies. The bounty of the crop depends on soil that has rested and soil that has been aerated and replenished by the nitrogen of long-rooted cover crops, or legumes. Rest nurtures creativity, which nurtures activity. Activity nurtures rest, which sustains creativity. Each draws from and contributes to the other.

In terms of our kids, the "fallow field" is leisure and rest. It is the much-lauded "downtime," kicking-around time, hanging out, mucking about. It is time for contemplation, for staring off, for trying to whistle a recognizable tune when you can only whistle blowing in, not out. It is time that exists beyond the school bell, beyond the long arm of homework. It may seem like parallel universe time, existing beyond piano practice, dance classes, and even washing up for dinner.

I think of the legume, or cover crop field, as deep play, losing oneself in the flow of something deeply engrossing. It is the type of involvement—whether with an art or construction project, or reading—when time stands still. Self-consciousness and frustration fall away; your child is focused and in control. They are connected with what they are doing, but also connecting with who they are. This is the deep-rooted quality of creativity.

In simplifying schedules, I suggest to parents that they create a visual image of their child in deep, creative play. Very often this image will have something to do with art or nature. When is your child completely focused? When do you and their larger surroundings disappear, as their attention is completely drawn to what they're doing? This time is not more or less important than leisure and activity; they are all interdependent. I emphasize it, though, because sometimes as parents, by not recognizing it, we haul our children right out of it. Like turning on the radio in church, we cut across it; don't honor it. This is some of the most valuable time for your child to process sensory stimulation, and children who don't experience it can be more nervous, less able to relax or sleep.

One more, small point about this deep play, or legume crop. As a parent I try to be mindful of when my children are fully involved in their play. It is something you can make space for and honor, but you can't "control" it. Trust trumps control. As Dr. Spock said, "Trust yourself. You know more than you think you do." It doesn't do to "instigate" deep play. You can't direct it; you can only leave time for it and trust that leisure and activity will nurture your child's creativity. It doesn't work to schedule scores of art classes for your child, to "boost" and "enrich" their creative output. Your vision of creativity may not be theirs. Their creativity, as with their identity, is evolving. But you can recognize and honor this crucial middle ground between "full on" and "full stop."

Activity—school, classes, sports, chores, socializing—is represented in the planted, or "crop field." This involves normal "daily life" busyness: activity and interaction. It also includes the "good stress," or slightly euphoric, elevated busyness of a class play, a sports competition or game, a musical performance, parties, even exams. A full and rich afternoon, or a day. On the go, and in-the-mix time.

Activity and interaction are crucial, in balance. Just as rest nourishes action, vigorous activity feeds sleep; it also feeds the imagination. But a schedule that is 90 percent activities is out of balance. As parents there is no need to get out the stopwatch, portioning your child's time into even thirds. But as we've seen in the past couple of decades, as a society we've "enriched" our kids' schedules, ironically, to the point of overuse and depletion. The overscheduled child is like soil that has been constantly and exclusively cropped. Without rest and replenishment, without the deep roots of legumes to aerate and pull nutrients down into the soil, it becomes compacted, a dust bowl.

QUITE SIMPLY:
Activity without downtime is ultimately—
like a plant without roots—unsustainable.

So how do we step off the "overscheduled" merry-go-round? How do we "oxygenate" our kids' schedules and simplify their daily lives? I'm going to assume that most parents today don't need help adding to their child's—or to their own—schedules. We've tipped the scales so far in that direction that many parents struggle to know how to slow down. They don't know how to simplify their own time, and they're increasingly at a loss about simplifying their child's.

Awareness is the first big step. We've worshipped at the altar of scheduled activities so dutifully that some parents only think of play in terms of playdates (a word that didn't exist twenty years ago). If we begin to recognize the value of leisure time and creative time, we'll make space for them. If we honor the importance of unscheduled time—of kids doing "nothing," but on their time and terms—then we're on our way. We'll open up their schedules, simplify. When we see a free afternoon as a glorious opportunity—the neighboring kids are out, Jed's frog eggs are turning into tadpoles, Mary's found an open spot behind the lilac bush where she can just squeeze in and not be seen at all—then the unexpected has a place. Pleasant surprises can take root. After all, it's not just what you make of your time, it's whether you have the time to make it your own. I hope to increase your awareness of balanced time in this chapter and suggest ways to make your children's schedules more sustainable, so there is time for them to *build* inner resources—energy, preferences, interests, resiliency—as well as expend them.

At each section of this book—simplifying toys, clothes, foods—I've mentioned that your life will also be simplified by simplifying your child's. I probably don't even have to mention that here, do I? I'm sure the thought has occurred to you by now. Here perhaps more than in any other facet of the process, it's true: the tenor of your family's daily life will change—will simplify—when you reduce the complexity of your child's schedule. After all, who is the "support staff," the drivers to all of these activities? If your child had fewer practices, club meetings, classes, test preparations, auditions, playdates, performances, practices, and meets, who else's schedule would open up? And as unscheduled time goes up, do tensions decrease proportionately? Balance benefits adults, too . . . even if they have to back into it by balancing their child's schedule first.

The Gift of Boredom

"I'm bored." I'm sure you've heard the expression. Numerous times, perhaps. In the span of a half hour. Here is a shift of awareness that will help you open up your child's schedule: Think of boredom as a "gift." Sigmund Freud thought of frustration as the precursor to learning. With apologies to Freud, I would like to shift that slightly to say that boredom is often the precursor to creativity. Think of a bridge between "doing nothing" and the sort of deep creative play we talked about. The bridge is almost always paved with (the frustration of) boredom. "I'm bored." Now *that* is when something interesting usually happens. (Don't bother explaining this to kids because they won't believe it, and they'll find the thought of it very annoying.)

In Chapter Three, when we were simplifying toys, we realized that nothing in the middle of a pile can be truly cherished. This principle holds true for activities, too. When a child is constantly busy, bouncing from one thing to another, it is hard for them to know what they "want to do." First of all, nobody's asking. Their schedule, responsibilities, plans, and parents are driving them. But scarcity—that frustrating, "nothing to do" state—is like a hush in the crowd. Silence. What whispered voice can begin to be heard? The child's inner voice. Stand back. Anything can happen. By reaching for something to do, instead of always being scheduled or entertained, children get creative. They begin building a world of their own making.

All right, the "gift" of boredom is hardly a gift for you, if your child continues their "I'm bored!" laments. My suggestion is to flatline it. Outbore their boredom with a single, flat response: "Something to do is right around the corner." "But Daddy, I'm bored!" Here you become a broken record. You become the most boring thing in the universe.

"Really? Something to do is right around the corner." "Huh?" "Something to do is right around the corner." Hmmm. It will become clear to them that not only are you *not* going to rescue them, you are also *not* going to entertain them, and you are *not* a bit interesting after all. You're boring. Off they'll go.

Some parents find this difficult to do. After all, as a society we parents have signed on to be our children's lifelong "entertainment committees." We're unpaid performers, that's for sure, but performers nonetheless. And we take it seriously. As such, we're accustomed to seeing our children's boredom as a personal failure. From their earliest days, we hung mobiles over their cribs and never stopped. A break in the festivities (or in the string of classes and playdates) and we are liable to jump up and dance. No wonder we're exhausted.

Let your kids be bored. Let them be. Sometimes in my lectures I write up a "prescription" for parents: "Boredom. To be allowed three times a day, preferably before meals." It's ridiculous, I know. But sometimes it's easier to make a leap with some sort of official "okay," and I am willing to offer the okay, even if somewhat humorously.

Once when I described my "flatline" approach to a child's "I'm bored" chant, a mom mentioned that she does something different. She grew up on a farm, where there was so much to do that being "bored" was a dangerous liability. If any of her siblings mentioned the word *bored,* they would have a chore to do within thirty seconds. "This tactic works in the city, too," she said. "If my kids are ever bored, they sure don't tell me!"

Arousing and Calming: Balanced Schedules

I am forever learning valuable lessons from the parents who come to my lectures and workshops. One mother, Sarah, showed me how she shifted her awareness about her daughter's schedule in a way that proved very beneficial. It has been helpful to countless others as well, and with her blessing, I'd like to share it with you. It began with the Jewish holiday of Passover. Holidays, Sarah realized, drove her daughter crazy.

Sarah's big, welcoming old farmhouse seemed to expand to accommodate however many people showed up. That was the good news: Family holidays, in all of their busy, messy, happy, and noisy glory, were always at Sarah's. The bad news was that Sarah's daughter, nine-year-old Emily, would invariably melt down at some point during these visits. There would be a lot scheduled, with places to go, people everywhere, big meals, and one thing stretching into the next.

Even though Emily claimed to love these gatherings, after the first full day her behavior would begin to disintegrate, going from naughty to aggressive; slamming doors and acting out. Embarrassment led Sarah to discover how she could make these holidays easier for Emily. One day during the long Passover weekend, when Emily was being quite disagreeable, Sarah wanted to get her out of the house, away from everyone's well-meaning questions and comments about her behavior. She took Emily out for a long bike ride, just the two of them. That break—an insertion of peace into the busy day—really made a difference for Emily. When they returned she was much calmer, her equilibrium restored. After that, Sarah made sure to build a break into each day. She and Emily would take the dog to the park for an hour, or take a walk on their own.

What Sarah realized was that these big family holidays were too crazy, too arousing for Emily if they weren't balanced with some more calming activities. As an only child, living a fairly predictable daily life, it took some getting used to having the house full of people and activity. Rather than adjusting, Emily acted out. With more balance, though, Emily did fine. She felt more in control, and she felt cared for rather than lost amid the hubbub.

QUITE SIMPLY:

Bringing more awareness and balance to a child's schedule can better serve his or her needs.

Sarah began to bring this awareness—the arousing/calming balance—more generally to Emily's schedule. She would look at the week ahead and, based on what was scheduled, decide whether each day looked to be either a very busy, active "A" day, or a fairly predictable, more laid-back, calming "C" kind of day. Her intention was not so much to control Emily's days as it was to build in a little balance when things got crazy. So if Friday was the big class play—a definite A on that day—Sarah would make a mental note to balance that with a quiet weekend, or two calming C days.

The idea is not to steer away from stimulation. The class play, with all of the buildup and the excitement of performing, is wonderful. Like the holidays, the class play is a big event. These events present wonderful counterpoints, or "high notes," to the normal melody or rhythm of a child's days. The purpose of being aware, or recognizing what is arousing and calming to your child, is to avoid the overstimulation that can string them out, or derail them in the same way that a big dose of sugar and caffeine derails them in the short-term. By working toward some balance in Emily's schedule, Sarah was not trying to avoid stimulation so much as overstimulation.

Here's a good example of this distinction. I received a funny letter from a mom, Eleanor, whose husband was a monster-truck fan. Now, Eleanor did not thrill to the racetrack: the noise, crowds, crazy promotions, the fast food. Her husband loved to take their eight-year-old son with him. This solved one problem for Eleanor—"If I never go to a monster truck rally again, I'll be a happy woman"—but created another: "Frankie comes home crazed! He 'crashes' all of his toys, and gives a blow-by-blow description of *everything* in this superloud announcer voice. He bounces off the walls!" Frankie loved these days with his dad, too, but honestly, Eleanor wondered, was it worth it? He seemed unrecognizable to her for at least a day afterward, and emotionally sidetracked for some time.

Based on the A and C balance, Eleanor made a deal with her husband: He could take Frankie to a rally, but that day would be considered a "Triple A" day, and it would need to be balanced (either afterward, or sandwiched) by three C days. Her husband agreed, and he saw, too, that the system worked. While he loved the rallies, he knew they were over-the-top, especially for an eight-year-old. By consciously building in some calmer days afterward, they both watched as Frankie settled down and came back to himself. The funny part was that Eleanor ended her letter saying there was a huge national, three-day super monster truck rally coming up in Atlanta. Her husband didn't even suggest bringing Frankie; he was going by himself. "As he said to me, looking with excitement at the website: There's *no way* we could possibly schedule enough 'C' days to balance *this* thing!"

Sabbath Moments

In terms of how kids spend their time, we've seen what a difference a generation can make. This has been brought home to me in another way. I sometimes ask parents whether they remember a Sabbath or Sunday feeling in their homes. Now, by this I don't mean whether they observed religious rituals or went to a religious service. Many of them did. But in posing the question, I was looking for whether there was a day of the week that felt "different" to them from the other days of the week. A day that seemed slower, quieter than the rest.

Is there a moment—not a day, but a moment—when you can't be reached? The very idea makes many of us nervous. Think of how communication methods have exploded in the past generation or two. The evolution from fixed to portable phones was a big change; and now with emails, pagers, and every possible phone gadget imaginable we are each a walking communication field, ever reachable, distractible, and available. However, given how reachable and distractible we are, you might question how "available" we really are at any moment. Surely if you're fully available to the person on the phone, you can't be to those you're with, and vice versa.

What has decreased, as the frequency and convenience of our communication has increased? Moments of Sabbath. As my friend and colleague at Antioch University, Torin Finser, points out, peaceful moments have been eroded as our various forms of communication and interruption have increased.

Sabbath obviously means different things to different people. But beyond the spiritual component, the Sabbath/Sunday "feeling" was usually one of increased quiet. It was very often a "family day," whether that meant the immediate family, or a bigger, extended family group sitting down for supper. Many people avoided commerce, and the work of the week was put aside. (That is, if you don't count cooking that family supper for four or twenty-four as *work*!)

However parents may feel when looking back on the days of their youth, most agree that those Sunday/Sabbath days had a quiet peacefulness to them that's hard to find today. Physicians are accustomed to being "on call," but now we all are: twenty-four hours a day, seven days a week. As a result, most of us are in a slightly anxious, arrested state most of the time. So when our cellphone rings just as we're trying to squeeze onto the off-ramp lane of the freeway ("It might be the school calling!"), physiologically we go from moderate to a hyperarousal state quite quickly. And we have a hard time returning to a calm state. Sorry to say, this is a symptom of high stress. We could all use more "moments of Sabbath" built into our lives.

Some parents feel that there's a separation—a safety zone—between their own lives and their children's. Some feel that their "reachability" is what affords their family some ease. But really, it's much more muddled than that, isn't it? Being reachable by cellphone may enable a mom to attend her daughter's soccer game, but it also means that she carries the office with her. An article in *The Wall Street Journal* detailed various ways some parents had to sneak their BlackBerries (hiding in the bathroom, slipping out for a walk) when spouses or children tried to limit their use at home.[5] Everyone is distracted when one member of the family is distracted. Even if the kids don't have their own cellphones or BlackBerries, they understand when they have someone's attention and when they don't.

Moments of Sabbath are "distraction-free zones." Not many families can set aside a whole day of the week for quiet family time, but we can still carve out some moments. Doing so adds balance to busy days and establishes boundaries. As you refuse to answer the phone during dinner the message your kids get is "Right now, we're together, sharing this meal." Some families can go further, setting aside a half day for a hike every week, or establishing a "no-drive Sunday" of staying home, a symbolic gesture for the family and the environment.

For others, a small start might take a lot of effort. One dad told me he turns down the answering machine as soon as he comes home in the evening. "For me that was a big step. And I did it as a conscious choice. I didn't want to be 'screening calls' with one ear as I'm hanging with my kids." A mom told me that she stopped checking her email after dinner. "I realized that just that stolen moment or two had a big impact. Without that interruption I could use the closeness we'd establish at dinner and segue right into the bedtime ritual. It was so smooth and easy. But if I left to check my email, and maybe return one or two, then by the time I returned, my little ones would be running around, involved in something. It was hard to get back into the bedtime flow."

If life is a run-on sentence, then these "moments of Sabbath" are the pauses, the punctuation. One mom mentioned that she was so busy, she realized that not only did she need to learn to relax, she needed to model "relaxation" to her kids. "I was modeling competency, and efficiency, but they hardly ever saw me sitting still!" She decided to read for twenty to thirty minutes in the evening, when and where her kids could see. Invariably one of her daughters would grab something to read and sit by her. They now have reading time together three nights a week. No interruptions, no television, completely unplugged reading time together. "I didn't have this in mind when I started, and I never would have thought I could do it. But now I love this time we have. I really look forward to it."

Anticipation

Most families have increased the speed of their lives and the number of their activities gradually—even unconsciously—over time. They realize that there are costs to a consistently fast-paced, hectic schedule, but they've adjusted. And looking around, there always seems to be another family that does everything you do, and more, managing to squeeze in skiing, or Space Camp, or French horn lessons on top of everything else. How do they do it?

They do it by never asking "Why?" Why do our kids need to be busy all of the time? Why does our son, at age twelve, need to explore the possibility of space travel? Why do we feel we must offer everything? Why must it all happen now? Why does tomorrow always seem a bit late? Why would we rather squeeze more things into our schedules than to see what happens over time? What happens when we stop, when we have free time?

Like engines that have been calibrated to a revved-up speed, we've adjusted to a high-stress "norm." As such, it may seem difficult to back off the all-activities-all-of-the-time treadmill. In Chapter Three, as you contemplated reducing the overgrown pile of toys in your children's rooms, it was hard at first to imagine what would actually be gained by getting rid of toys. Wouldn't it be a net loss? A loss that, at the very least, would be upsetting for the kids? We talked about the extraordinary power of less, how fewer toys allow a child to concentrate their attention, to engage rather than be overwhelmed.

Let's imagine that transformation as two simple gestures. In the first image we can't see the child; they're hidden behind a mountain of toys that they are gazing at, paralyzed. The second image is simple: Without the pile, it's a child, reaching for a toy.

There is something in the second image that's missing from the first. Even with that giant mountain of toys, there is something missing. And it's not the latest-and-greatest toy, the best ever, the one that will really please. If you back off the overscheduled merry-go-round, something has a chance to develop. It is the same thing that is missing from the first image and evident in the second: anticipation.

When we open up our child's schedules, we make room for anticipation. Just as it's hard to cherish a toy that's buried in the middle of a pile, it is hard to anticipate something when we're always busy, or when we're trying to do everything now.

Granted, as adults we're always looking for speed and convenience. Name anything—modems, cars, food, banking, commutes—and we'll take it faster, please, given the option. And we would also like what we want when we want it: on demand. We cram more in, in anticipation of the break that never comes, or the advantage that will allow us to maybe, one day, take a break.

When we allow this "on-demand" mentality to color our children's perspectives and schedules, then they lose the gift of anticipation. The joy of waiting. The passion of expectation. Do you remember yearning for summer? Literally counting down the days? When you back off the treadmill loop of planned activities, you make room for pauses, you make time for anticipation and reflection. In Chapter Four we discussed rhythm and rituals, and how they build consistency and a sense of security into a child's life. In their regularity, Sunday morning pancakes are familiar. But they're also special: a certain rich smell your child anticipates, but which still catches them by happy surprise as they throw back the covers and head for the kitchen. Unscheduled time has the same effect: It builds depth—layers of meaning and feeling—around activities.

"Here is the world!" we seem to offer as we drive our children from one activity to the next. Rather than creating excitement, overloading a child's schedule creates high expectations. "What's the next great thing?" they ask in return. If we pull back on scheduling, a child can see something coming up; they can literally "look forward" to it. This allows anticipation to build. And anticipation is more than a simple pleasure. It is identity building.

Anticipating gratification, rather than expecting or demanding it, strengthens a child's will. Impulsivity, wanting everything now, leaves the will weak, flaccid. As a child lives with anticipation, as it strengthens over time, so too does their sense of themselves, their ego. It's ironic, isn't it? In our on-demand culture it's easy to forget what tremendous power can develop through waiting. Let's look at what else builds with anticipation.

QUITE SIMPLY:
More than a simple pleasure, anticipation is identity-building.

When a child has time to look forward to something—a camping trip, for example—they bring their imagination to it. They begin to make mental pictures of the trip: what they know camping to be, what they imagine it to be, what they hope might happen, what they plan to make happen. They are making their own mental postcards in advance. "I bet when I'm roasting marshmallows around the campfire a bear will come and sit down next to me!" It doesn't matter that the reality of the trip will differ from their images. Richness is accruing. Already the camping trip is more than an event; it is becoming an experience, gathering layers of meaning and feeling for the child. You know the expression "This is what memories are made of"? These layers of meaning are what memories are made of, what anchors them in our minds.

Waiting for something with anticipation builds a child's character. It shows them that they have powers equal to the power of their own desires. It shows them their inner strength, the strength of powerful waiting. Unchecked, our wills are like weeds, threatening to take over our whole spirits; invasive vines of desire for what we want (everything) when we want it (now). Anticipation holds back the will; it counters instant gratification. It informs a child's development and growth and builds their inner life. A dad once listened to me say much of this and added, "Yes, plus, any activity your kid looks forward to automatically has more 'bang for the buck'!" More bang for the buck, exactly.

Seeds of Addiction

I believe there's something missing from our society's debate around overscheduled kids. The issue goes beyond parental motivation: Do parents act out of a desire to provide for their kids, or a desire to gain a competitive advantage for them? It goes beyond the obvious effects on kids: How much stress do they experience with their enrichment? These are certainly important questions, worthy of our consideration. Yet what concerns me most about overscheduling—as with other aspects of "too much, too early, and too fast"—are its effects on development, and on how a young child forms their identity.

Imagine a kid whose very busy schedule looks like a "cropped field," with rows of activities, classes and sports, places to go and things to do. I worry that such a daily life can sow unexpected seeds. It can establish patterns of behavior and expectation that become ingrained, difficult to alter. So much activity can create a reliance on outer stimulation, a culture of compulsion and instant gratification. What also grows in such a culture? Addictive behaviors. You can see the shadow of overscheduling in this definition of *addiction* given by my colleague Felicitas Vogt: "an increasing and compulsive tendency to avoid pain or boredom and replace inner development with outer stimulation."

I have seen it. I've seen how loading up a child's days with activities and events from morning to night can dig a developmental groove in their beings. It can establish a reliance, a favoring of external stimulation over emotional or inner activity. A child with a room full of toys has been set up to be dissatisfied. They've been programmed to imagine that pleasure depends on toys, and that the next one might be better than the rest. Likewise, a child who doesn't experience leisure—or better yet, boredom—will always be looking for external stimulation, activity, or entertainment.

What's next? The rhythm of their days will be mainly high notes, a rhythm that's difficult to sustain. Without pause they have little chance for inner activity, little chance to process their experiences. And little chance to deepen activity with what they bring to it: desire, imagination, or reflection. Without pause, there's no room for anticipation.

Ordinary Days

Aren't a good many of your days quite ordinary? It seems sacrilegious to admit it, especially when we're forever encouraged, and encouraging others to "Have a great day!" Yet I've found that embracing the beauty of an ordinary day is very helpful in simplifying our children's schedules.

There's a lot of pressure involved in "overscheduled days" for both kids and their parents. For kids there are the demands of participation, performing, and competing. And for the parent/driver there is all of that scheduling. The responsibility of getting to the cello lesson on time, with both the child *and* the cello, money for the lesson, and—miracle of miracles—the music book, too. But the biggest pressure involved in all of this enriching is the pressure of exceptionality.

Not everyone is going to be exceptional at everything they do. True enough, most parents would agree. We've been around long enough, and with plenty of personal experience to attest to that. Ballet dreams abandoned. A career path that has veered or doglegged; opportunities missed. Yet we tend to hedge our bets a bit with our kids. Who knows? Look at Tiger Woods. He was golfing at the age of two. Maybe with some extra lessons, or starting a bit younger, our child could be the exception to that rule? They might indeed be exceptional. Little League to the big leagues. It does happen. Isn't it aiming too low to imagine less?

But how many aspiring cellists will rival Yo-Yo Ma's artistry? If we hold on to the exceptional—if our children adopt that as their measure of success—most will fail, and almost all of them will feel like failures. There's freedom in embracing the ordinary: freedom, and possibilities. Because in most things, the exceptional is not really what we want for them anyways. What we want for our children, truly, is engagement. We want their love of the cello to grow, to evolve and endure throughout their lives, whether or not they perform . . . whether or not they are ever exceptional cellists.

After all, the ordinary allows for the exceptional, but not the reverse. Given ordinary opportunities and encouragement, a truly exceptional talent will surface. But interests—even strong interests and abilities—often burn out when they're pushed too hard, too fast, too young. The drive toward the exceptional leaves many loves and passions in its wake. Loving something for its own sake—not for its potential in fame, glory, or music scholarships—is far from ordinary. It's an extraordinary blessing—a strength of character any parent would wish for their child.

QUITE SIMPLY:

To fully appreciate "the ordinary" is an extraordinary gift.

There's another facet to the pressure of exceptionality, one that many parents willingly take on. It's the pressure to deliver exceptional days. We try our best, with so many activities, such on-demand stimulation and entertainment, to supply our children with a series of rainbow moments. Isn't this wonderful? How about this? Even better? We hope that these remarkable moments will come together, shimmering, into rainbow days, each fuller and more exciting than the last. A truly exceptional childhood.

I'm exaggerating a bit, for effect. But just a bit. This pressure is real, and it drives us. It drives us in ways large and small, and affects our children in ways we would rather not acknowledge. If we're exhausted by our daily "event planning" duties, surely they feel pressured, too, pressured to come through with increasingly enthusiastic and grateful responses. Yet when "rainbow moments" are the norm, children can grow accustomed to one peak experience after another. Their feelings and responses become muted. When every note is a high note, children lose the ability to fully engage in the present and to regulate their own time.

"How was your day?" When your child answers "Regular," or "Average," do you feel a sense of disappointment? Even if your day, too, was quite ordinary? Ordinary days are the sustaining notes of daily life. They are the notes that allow high notes to be high and low notes to be low; they provide tone and texture. If a child's happiness is not hinged on the high notes—not hinged on exceptional events or having exceptional talents—then they have a true gift. An exceptional character. They may be able to live their life with an appreciation for the moment, for the simple pleasures of an ordinary day. Can you imagine anything better?

Sports

Each year more than fifty-two million American children participate in organized sports leagues, according to the National Council of Youth Sports.[6] That number has risen significantly over the last decade or two. In just about every sport, there's been an increase. And children are starting younger than ever. The American Youth Soccer Organization, a nonprofit group that sponsors soccer programs, changed its starting age to four rather than five years old. Many organized sports programs—soccer, basketball, T-ball, and others—are now sponsoring teams and leagues for toddlers as young as eighteen months.[7]

With traveling, summer, and year-round leagues, organized sports for children are getting more complicated, competitive, and demanding. This is what's known as the "professionalization" of children's sports, and with it often comes premature specialization. It used to be that if children were athletic, they might do several sports, for a few months out of the year. Increasingly now, children concentrate on a single sport, working out and joining traveling leagues in the off-season, honing their skills in specialty camps and extra leagues in the summer.

"There's pretty good research out there that says that you need about 10 years and 10,000 hours of practice to become really expert at a sport," says Dan Gould, the director of the Michigan State University Institute for the Study of Youth Sports. "The trouble is, parents hear these kinds of things, and they try to get it all in the first two years."[8]

Across the country, pediatric doctors are seeing injuries they've never seen before in children. According to Dr. James Andrews, a nationally prominent sports orthopedist, "You get a kid on the operating table and you say to yourself, 'It's impossible for a 13-year-old to have this kind of wear and tear.' " *The New York Times* reported that in interviews with more than two dozen sports medicine doctors and researchers, the factor that was repeatedly mentioned as the primary cause for the sharp rise in overuse injuries among young athletes was "specialization in one sport at an early age and the year-round, almost manic, training for it that often follows."[9]

The understandable outcome of this push toward professionalism—or, the "too much, too fast, and too young" of sports—is burnout. Plenty of media attention has been given to the growing number of kids in organized sports, and the ways in which youth sports increasingly mimic professional sports. But there's been less notice of how many kids take an "early retirement" from organized sports. Data indicates that sports participation peaks at age eleven and is followed by steady decline through the remainder of the teen years. According to studies reported in the *Journal of Physical Education, Recreation & Dance,* 35 percent of participants withdraw each year from organized sports, while up to 67 percent of participants drop out of sports between the ages of seven and eighteen.[10] The *Journal of Sport Behavior* reported that by tenth grade, more than 90 percent of high school sophomores had dropped out of an organized sport they'd started.[11]

There is much to be concerned about here: from overscheduled kids to overzealous parents, from overuse injuries to the overemphasis on competition that leaves some kids sitting on the bench. The Josephson Institute of Ethics found in its Sportsmanship Survey that 72 percent of both boys and girls say they would rather play on a team with a losing record than sit on the bench for a winning team.[12]

Kids just want to play. It's simple, isn't it? It usually starts out that way, at least. Many families become involved in youth leagues—turning their schedules inside out, giving up family dinners, evening and weekend time—because they believe sports programs to be safe, regulated, refereed, and skill-building venues for play. But with so many adults involved, from coaches to refs to parents, play—active play for the sake of fun—can be benched, too, sitting out the game.

I want to clarify that I'm not against organized sports or martial arts for children; I am against the too-much-of-it, and far-too-young way we've embraced it. When I speak of the problems with early sport, I'm referring to children younger than ten or eleven years old who are playing formal team sports or engaged in martial arts and training more than twice a week. My concerns are compounded if the nature of the coaching is forceful or aggressive and if competition routs building friendships and fun.

Within this context—the too-much and too-young of it—I place martial arts right alongside organized sports. This is a very unpopular position to take, I understand, as I imagine thousands of white-uniform-clad children, elbows up and wide-stanced, arrayed before me. I am not against martial arts per se, just as I am not against sports . . . or toys for that matter. I am against the way that we've transposed adult endeavors—with an adult sense of competition, fanaticism, and consumerism—into children's lives. To do so we largely cut these disciplines off from their cultural and spiritual contexts. An art form designed to train an adolescent mentally, physically, and spiritually for adulthood becomes a hobby. Belts become trophies, and very young children are equipped with "skills" long before they have the maturity to use them wisely.

But clearly it's the developmental issues that concern me most about our love affair with organized sports and martial arts. Something is amiss at both ends of the age spectrum. When kids younger than ten or eleven become occupied with organized sports, especially to the exclusion of time for free, unstructured play, that involvement can cut crudely across their progression through a variety of play stages that are vitally important to their development. Equally disheartening is the fact that so many kids are quitting as they approach adolescence, just when the structure and rigors of organized sports and martial arts have so much to offer them in their quest for individuality, independence, and maturity.

Let's look at the fundamental differences between organized sports and play, differences that I'd like to address by turning our attention from one to the other, like a ball lobbing back and forth.

On one side of the net is organized sports (Little League, soccer leagues, etc.) or karate classes, and on the other is unstructured play (running around, or a pickup game in the neighborhood or at the park). First of all, I don't believe this is an either/or competition. I also don't think it's a game that's already been played. Some parents feel that sports have taken the place of unstructured play these days; that free play is no longer possible, a thing of the past. We'll talk a bit more in Chapter Six about "stranger danger" and other fears that are driving parents and kids into their cars and out of the neighborhood to formal games or classes. Keeping to our present focus on schedules, let's look at organized sports and unstructured play in terms of what they offer your child developmentally.

Three little guys, ages five to seven, are playing with small cars and an improvised ramp by the side of the driveway. There is a lot of arguing going on. "No, but, he said I could use the red car first and my turn includes four jumps, but on my last jump it fell off the side, so that doesn't count." In fact, the cars are often sidelined or in the shop while these important details are discussed, arranged, ignored, and rearranged. In play, children freely negotiate the rules, are actively involved in the social process, learning as they make their way. In sport, the rules already exist, and children instead learn how to play within predetermined boundaries.

With these elements—some space (a yard, or a park), some kids, and possibly some things to climb on or to hide behind—fun can develop when imaginations are exercised. "Whattayawannado?" may be the familiar starting point, but things develop from there. Today's progression to fun may be repeated, built on, or changed tomorrow, or it might be "archived" and resurrected another day. In sport, the picture of what is needed—in terms of equipment, and the nature of the game—is already determined. How the game plays out may vary, but the game itself is defined.

So much of imagination is mental picture making. Free play requires forming a "picture" of what's possible, a pictorial answer to the proverbial "Whattayawannado?" question. But in play there are also many possible outcomes. "We were going to have our beautiful tea party for the dolls, but then Emily slid down the hill by the rabbit hutch and then we all started sliding. At first it made me mad because of the tea party, but then we got cardboard and slid really fast on that, and then we made sleds for the dolls, too, and it was so funny to see them race down the hill!" This multiplicity of outcomes—beyond the win-or-lose of sports—builds an inner flexibility. In a general sense, kids learn, through the practice of play, not to be too attached to their vision of what to do or of what might happen.

QUITE SIMPLY:
The "messiness" of free play, with its many changes and possibilities, builds an inner flexibility.

In free play, children have to actively problem solve and to take one another's feelings into account if the play is to be successful. *Success* in free play means simply that the game continues, and continues to be fun. Sometimes this problem solving is external, sometimes internal. "What should I do if this is, like, the coolest game ever, but Alex doesn't want to crash the cars? It's no fun without him, and plus, he'd take the red car with him if he goes." When everyone has a stake in the play, feelings must be taken into account. In sport, the problem solving is largely extrinsic, facilitated by coaches, referees, or parents.

Because play is self-created and self-motivated it has great flexibility. There are roles and positions in play for whatever "type" a child believes himself to be, or wants to be. Why? Because kids make the play up as they go along, projecting themselves and their wishes into it. Because they create them, the roles and positions of the game serve their needs, whether those needs are deeply felt or of the moment. In sport, you are given a predetermined role or position to play. Ironically, that position may become even more restrictive ("But Mary *has* to be goalie!") the better you become at it.

Unstructured play is usually varied over the long haul, driven by the changing interests of the child and of his or her playmates. It provides a broad, multidimensional foundation of movement for later specialization. In sport, there is more of an emphasis on early specialization, with the physical risks inherent in a narrow set of repetitive movements. Speaking of repetitive motion, another difference is that play is portable; participation in organized sports, on the other hand, usually involves a committed, back-and-forth parental shuttle service.

Some believe that organized sports are vital preparation for an increasingly competitive world: kids should build skills and learn how to "play the game," the earlier the better. Yet, children construct their worldviews through play. Organized sports can present a "packaged world" of set rules and procedures to very young children, rather than a world of their own making. We've underestimated free, unstructured play. As a society we've discounted the developmental riches involved in what kids do naturally. Self-directed play builds multiple and emotional intelligences. It fosters the skills necessary to navigate an uncertain future, one that will demand increasing flexibility and creative problem solving. Play is not an old-fashioned thing of the past. Unstructured play—and plenty of it—is a developmental necessity for kids. Some might say now more than ever.

For families with kids younger than eight or nine years of age, schedules can be simplified tremendously just by emphasizing free play over organized sports and martial arts. First, consider how much time you spend each week, driving to and attending training, practices, meets, and games. Imagine devoting a similar amount of time at the park, or wherever kids gather to play near your home. Very often it is the same park you frequented a few years ago, when your kids were toddlers, before the mass exodus to tae kwon do and T-ball when the kids turned four and five. There may not be a lot of grade-school-age kids at the park now, but think of this as a resource—for your kids and the community—that you are helping to develop. The word will get out through the neighborhood grapevine, and kids will return. Plan to take the newspaper, or a book. Plan to get something done or read while being a benign parental presence: easy to ignore, but available should the need arise. The rest will evolve on its own in the democracy of the playground, with its ever-changing participants and games.

As a child reaches toward double digits—eight, nine, and ten—they're coming out of the "let's pretend" play stage and into "game playing." This is a sensitive time developmentally. Hopefully, they've made their way through the play stages of early childhood: solitary, parallel, and "let's pretend." They are letting go of imaginary roles and beginning to forge their own rules, make their own games. This period is a foundry for emotional intelligence; in dynamic social interaction a child learns much about impulse control and cooperation. Having had the time to fully explore the imaginary, a child can begin to bridge their view of what is possible with what is. Having been free to imagine, a child can begin to channel that power into more set constructs. At this age they really are beginning to be ready to learn how to "play the game."

The confines of organized sports can impose too much structure at too young an age, hindering a child's progress through the developmental stages of play. This is especially a shame if a child "swears off" sports as they're approaching and in adolescence, just when organized sports have so much to offer developmentally. Some people see it in these bottom-line terms: Wouldn't you rather your teenager be heavily involved in sports than heavily involved in other "popular" pursuits of adolescence? True enough. But beyond this either/or equation, organized sports offer teens an intensity that rivals their own at this age. Just as their emotional impulses turn inward, an external gesture like sports (or drama or community service) can be a deeply involving, excellent counterbalance to the very normal self-involvement of this period. With sports, kids can expand and deepen their sense of identity, seeing their own efforts within an individual role and within a group or team.

Nothing can complicate or railroad an entire family's schedule like a child's active participation in a sports league. Or two leagues. Or two siblings' involvement in two different leagues. During the same season. Or a child's involvement in two different sports at the same time. The permutations are endless, but the common result is a state of perpetual motion for the whole family. No matter what their sport of choice, a child's home team is their family. The home team can bend, it can accommodate, but it can't be sacrificed. Balance, where none exists, should be imposed.

I worked with a family of five kids, three of them very athletically inclined. There was quite a large age span between the siblings, the youngest being three years old, and the two oldest in high school. The mother of this beautiful group, Joelle, was feeling like a bus driver, but one who never quite arrived. The needs of her youngest children—for a close connection, with time to play and explore—were being strained to meet the needs of her oldest children—support and rides to various practices and meets. Joelle's husband traveled extensively for work, so he was often unavailable. Joelle contacted me when she realized that she had been thinking, "this is all going to let up next season," to no avail, for two years. I suggested she park the van, plan a family meeting, and work together on a schedule that would include more balance.

Balance, like the perfect swing, is elusive. You have to work at it. And very often, parents have to impose it. When Joelle realized that the whole family's schedule was revolving around sports, year-round, she knew it was too much. These are the guidelines her family adopted, scheduling—but not overscheduling—sports. The older kids, twelve and up, were able to choose two sports for the year: one "major" and one "minor." For example, David, the second-oldest son, chose to play soccer at school, but basketball, his first passion, was what he chose to do in a league. They each had to take one entire season—fall, winter, spring, or summer—off, with no sports involvement during that time. And each child was responsible for researching and networking car-pool possibilities for their sport's season.

Similar adjustments can be made with any involvement that threatens the needs of other family members, including the parent/chauffeurs. Or an involvement that threatens the overall balance that the family holds dear between scheduled and unscheduled time. Look at it from a number of perspectives—annual, seasonal, monthly, and weekly—to see where you can back off a level or two. The younger the child, the more free time he or she needs. These needs may not be felt by the kids themselves, especially by those who've grown accustomed to heavily scheduled days. But balance, like pace and endurance, are essential over the long run.

On some levels we recognize that young kids need help pacing themselves, balancing their time and energy. "Slow down!" we may caution them. "Don't forget the hill up ahead!" Or a child, excited about a sleepover that night, who is spinning like a mini-tornado before noon. We know they'll need a rest or they'll never make it in one piece to the evening. On the immediate level, it's easy to see when a child's energy and desires need to be reined in, conserved. Yet on the level of schedules—daily, weekly, monthly—many parents seem to have thrown up their hands, unable or unwilling to impose balance. "She loves it!" or "He loves it!" are the rallying cries of overscheduling. With kids and their enthusiasms we seem to feel that interest alone will protect them from the ill effects of too much, too soon, and too fast. Yet with sports participation peaking at age eleven, clearly some interests are being sacrificed rather than developed by being fostered at too young an age and too heavily.

QUITE SIMPLY:

A child's love of an activity is not enough to protect him or her from the effects of pursuing it too much, and too soon.

What about for older children who want to monitor their own schedules and involvements? Teens whose energy is more aligned with their interests? Certainly parental pacing is less important as children reach adolescence. Yet, as Joelle's oldest son learned, sometimes passions grow stronger in rocky soil. By and large, Joelle's family felt a sense of relief and ease with their new, less frenetic schedule. But not Tom, a junior in high school at the time. Every inch of Tom's room was covered with posters of Beckham and Ronaldo; every minute he could, Tom was either playing soccer or thinking about it. And he was quite talented, one of the star players in his traveling league. At this point in his development, Tom didn't really need more free, unscheduled time. He had a passion. Joelle relayed this quote, imitating the sarcasm in her son's voice: "By the way, Mom . . . passions aren't 'balanced.' "

True enough. But neither are they fragile. The rules imposed served as counterweights to Tom's desire, and as his will and resolve strengthened, so too did his passion. Unfortunate as it seemed to him then, Tom was still playing for the home team, his family. His passion was threatened and tested by the rules they adopted. His needs and desires were tempered by those of his other "team members," including the youngest rookies and the team managers. He had to work that much harder to play, scrounging up rides and "paying" for away games with family events. He had to take an entire season off, which seemed ridiculous at first, but his low-level recurring shin splints did finally heal. In the end, it turned out, Tom was a team player. And his passion—supported, but not indulged—survived. And grew.

Balance—like pace and endurance—is essential over the long run. It isn't just true for young children. It's true for adults (and teenagers) too. And especially true for athletes.

Balance is what we're after in simplifying our family's schedules. And once we cross our kids' names off the "Race of Childhood" sign-up form, time opens right up. Time for rest and creativity to balance activity; time for contemplation and stimulation, moments of calm in busy days, energies conserved and expended; time for free, unscheduled play, for ordinary days, for interests that deepen over time; time for boredom; and time for the joy and infinite passion of anticipation.

Rich, fertile soil takes time and balance to develop. The same is true of childhood. In fact, in simplifying your family's schedule it may be helpful to write a list of things that take time. Things that can't be rushed, things that deepen over time. (Such a list is ideally written while lying in a hammock, or sitting at the park, while your kids play.) But keep the list open, and keep it close at hand; you'll be adding to it over time. Your child's interests, their abilities, their sense of freedom, their sense of humor, and their sense of themselves will be on the list; these take time. The strength of your family's connectedness also takes time and balance. So start with balanced schedules. Sow the seeds of balanced childhoods. What will develop, over time, are strong and whole, resilient, balanced individuals.

Imagine . . .

- your child having time every day—unscheduled free time—to daydream and play.
- what your child could do with the occasional "gift" of boredom.
- what can develop when a child has time to dream: the joy of anticipation, and a greater depth of meaning and feeling.
- consciously balancing some of your child's crazier days with calmer ones.
- appreciating the pleasure of the ordinary.
- your child's worldview building from a deep well of unregulated, improvised, flexible free play.
- how well such years of general physical activity will serve your child as he/she moves into organized sports.
- appreciating that genuine interests and abilities take time to form and that those developed over time (not pushed or hurried) are more likely to become lifelong pleasures.
- what a lifelong gift you will bestow by gently insisting on, and modeling, the importance of downtime and balance in daily life.

SIX

Filtering Out the Adult World

Late summer afternoon sun was slanting in through my office window when I met with Annmarie. We had conversed for some time when I asked her to choose a word that best described her experience of motherhood. She looked at me quizzically, with an almost guilty smile. "Really?" she asked. "Just one word?" What a strange request, really, when every mother and father has a river of emotions about their role as parent, an ever-flowing current of thoughts and feelings about their connection to their offspring. Dip in, at any point along the bank, and you'll draw up a cascade of memories, sentiments, questions, and hopes. Annmarie was clearly devoted to her eight-year-old twins, Peter and Krista. I wanted to see which of her emotions would float to the surface, demanding to be acknowledged. Actually, it wasn't hard for her to choose.

"Worry."

The word hung in the air between us, clearly honest and deeply felt. Annmarie continued, saying she could speak for hours of her love for her two beautiful children. She could easily spend an afternoon trying to explain what a blessing they were, and how much they meant to her. But since I had asked her to describe the *experience* of motherhood in just one word, she said she had to acknowledge what she felt most of all, from day to day: worry. "Before I had kids, nobody ever mentioned this . . . how my heart would crack open, as a mother, and be filled with worry."

I think most parents can empathize with Annmarie. Worry and concern are with us in parenting from our children's first days. A baby's vulnerability is extraordinary. Nothing we are told, nothing we read prepares us for the feelings we have as a new parent holding our baby, and knowing that we also hold their life in the balance. Do you remember in those first weeks of parenthood, waking with a start from a dream in which you'd left your baby on the bus? Or in the garden, forgotten under the big green leaves of a summer squash? Nobody has to tell a new parent how completely vulnerable their baby is; we feel it keenly. But by attaching to you, the baby builds a ladder of relationships and attachments that will help them ascend to maturity. As a parent it may seem that *your* emotional vulnerability has just begun, and will only increase as your love does, over time. To love something so much: what a colossal risk!

When she came to see me, Annmarie was concerned about her children's third-grade teacher, who seemed to be more aware of Krista's abilities than of Peter's. Annmarie felt the teacher must "like Krista better than Peter," and she worried about the ramifications of this. She was also apprehensive about Peter's coach, who was clearly not giving him the chances he deserved to play and to shine. Peter needed to "feel good about" his athletic skills, and that wasn't going to happen with him sitting on the bench so much. She worried about their safety, about the fact that she simply couldn't "watch them both, all of the time." Annmarie was troubled about Peter. He and Krista were so close; what would happen if Krista pulled ahead of him academically, and maybe even socially, too? What kind of career would Peter have if he wasn't excelling now?

QUITE SIMPLY:

Worry is an aspect of parenthood, but it shouldn't define it.

Worry and concern are sewn into the cloth of parenting; they're integral parts of the experience. Our lives are rocked when we become parents, forever changed by the seismic shift we make clearing enough space in our hearts, intentions, and priorities to place another's well-being before our own. A large part of what we offer them is our care and concern until they can care for themselves. But in this moment with Annmarie (and many similar moments with other parents), what struck me most was the feeling of something being out of balance. Worry may be an aspect of parenthood, but it shouldn't define it. When it rises to the top of our emotions, coloring the waters of our relationship with our children, something is not right.

Raised in Michigan, Annmarie was one of eight children. Her twins shared her white-blond hair, testament to her Norwegian heritage. I asked her if she thought her mother had experienced the same worries about her and her siblings when they were young. "Not a chance!" Annmarie replied, with a laugh. "My parents are good people, and we never doubted their love. But there were so many of us kids, and my parents were so busy, that we were largely on our own. And things were different then. The house was never locked. There just wasn't so much to be worried about."

Was being a parent dramatically different just a generation ago? Is there really that much more to worry about today? Are there substantially more risks to children's safety and well-being? We'll look at the risks, and our perception of them, in a bit more detail. But what strikes me so often now is how our fears and concerns for our children have eclipsed our hopes for them, and our trust. Anxieties are often traded like currency. In the landscape of parenting today, fear has cast a long shadow over trust: trust in our children's evolving sense of self, in their world, their developmental path . . . and in our own instincts as parents.

I believe that simplifying a child's daily life is one of the best ways to restore a sense of balance in parenting. By simplifying their toys and environment, their schedules, and the sense of rhythm and regularity in the home, you allow them the grace to be a child. You allow your connection and your values to gain purchase, to rise above the noise of acceleration and excess, the drive for "the next big thing" to do, have, or attain. Simplifying acknowledges how a child comes to understand the world—through play and interaction, not through adult concerns and information. The pressure is off when childhood is no longer seen as an "enrichment opportunity" but instead as an unfolding experience—an ecology—with its own pace and natural systems. By consciously backing off the adult sense of "more!" and "faster!" and "earlier!" parents back out of a child's world, protecting it without trying to control it.

In this chapter we'll look at important ways to continue the process of simplifying by erecting filters to prevent a child's world from being deluged with adult information, pressures, and concerns. We'll learn the value of not sharing, of the freedom they gain when they're not privy to our fears, drives, ambitions, and the very fast pace of our lives. When anxiety is not allowed to pollute the atmosphere of our homes, we breathe easier as well. Our grip, as parents, relaxes. We'll consider the overall picture of our parental involvement with our children. We'll look at the enormous pressures society brings to bear on parents today, pressures that have turned parenting into a competitive sport. Pressures that have prompted many parents into "helicopters," to hover over their children, ever vigilant, held aloft by the fuel of anxiety.

I remember the silence of that late summer afternoon as Annmarie and I pondered what she had just said. As a parent, what she felt most of the time, and most keenly of all, was worry. She knew as well as I did that something was out of balance, that she needed to find more ease and joy, more flow in the waters of her day-to-day life with Krista and Peter. For our kids' sake, let's look at how to simplify further, how to filter out some of the pressures and anxieties of adult life that are pouring into our children's awareness. Let's consider how to simplify our involvement in their lives, how to build a "base camp" of security, one that allows *them* to venture forth to explore the world, and *us* to land that helicopter—to park it—permanently, out of gas.

Houseguests

Imagine that your spouse's brother, Andy, has just moved in with your family. He's very well liked, a good guy, but quite the monologist, so being with him tends to be a rather "passive" occupation. The kids love him! They find him riveting and spend as much time with him as possible. Because of this, they aren't getting out much, not playing with friends, reading, or riding bikes as much as they used to, but you figure that will even out over time.

Andy is entertaining, and since he knows a lot, he can also be informative. But honestly, he really goes too far sometimes, sharing stories and pictures with the kids that are scary, brutal, or even provocative. What's more, it seems like every time you turn around he's telling them about some cool new thing to eat or to play with . . . something they don't have but now want. Something you wish they had never even heard about. You can get him to knock it off; he really will change course, but it requires nearly constant vigilance on either your part, or your spouse's. Since he's always around now, and the kids are so taken with him, it's often easier (and you get more done) when you just let him be. You might as well accept the bad with the good; none of you can imagine life without Andy anymore.

When you add it up, your older kids are spending at least three hours a day with their uncle. Even your youngest (age two) has figured out how entertaining he is, and she now spends more time with him each day than she does outside. You're no exception. After a long day, you often sit back and let him entertain you, too. And he knows how to get your attention. Quite often you find yourself leaning forward, transfixed by the bad-news tales he tells—ranging from guilt-inducing to grisly—that pertain to kids. Where does he get them all? He knows they make you anxious, but he also knows that you'll listen; you won't make him stop.

You and your spouse have done so much to simplify life for your family, your kids. Andy definitely doesn't understand what you're trying to do. You've cleaned out your kids' rooms, so they're not overwhelmed by toys. (Now, because of him, they're constantly hearing about new ones.) You've streamlined your food, getting rid of a lot of the big-hit sugary snack foods that hijack your kids' nervous systems and everyone's waistlines. (Unfortunately, your brother-in-law is forever tempting them with some new pseudo-food. You hold the line, but it's an awful lot of work.) Your meals together used to be wonderful times for mutual sharing, but sometimes now the kids would rather hang with their uncle than eat. (And even when he eats with the family, he tends to dominate.) You've simplified your kids' schedules, cutting back on some of the classes and activities that were robbing them of free time. (Yet any spare time that they gained is now spent listening to their uncle.)

As far as simplifying goes, Andy doesn't "get it." He also doesn't see how often he's working at cross-purposes with you. He doesn't have kids, and, fun as he can be sometimes, he certainly isn't driven by your kids' best interests. Some of your friends don't see it, either; they're unsympathetic. "What's the problem? We have guests, too. Can't you just control him?" It's a never-ending argument; it seems unwinnable.

If you came to me with this problem, my advice would be unequivocal. Andy might be an okay guy, but I'd suggest that you kick him out, especially if your kids are under seven years of age.

Andy isn't an uncle, you see. "Andy" is a television. I would have said that from the beginning, making it clear that the black hole of a houseguest I was describing was really the almighty box. I would have, but I was concerned that you would read no further.

Simplifying Screens

The verbal expression of simplifying is "No, thanks. " One doesn't have to be an antitech Luddite to want some space and grace in a child's early years. To say no thanks to some of the societal pressures that push them—ready or not—into adulthood. Our dreams for them include success as adults, success in a technologically complex future that will surely be more advanced than our own era. Yet for many parents (and early childhood experts) there is a connection, not a contradiction, between that vision of future success and a less technology-oriented, more human-focused start to life.

A critical step in simplifying your children's daily lives is to simplify the "screens" in your home: television (the one that still monopolizes most of our free time), computers, video games, and handheld electronic devices. Because screens are so much a part of our lives, this step is not the place to start, especially if you are an inveterate news junkie or if screens are everywhere in your home. But once you've begun simplifying, once you've seen how your children relax into themselves when they're not overloaded, you'll be anxious to take this very effective and liberating step. It is one of the most critical changes you can make to safeguard their childhoods and ease your anxieties. And it is one of the most rewarding ways to simplify daily life.

When you simplify screens, you install valves to stop the all-day, every-day rush of information and stimulation pouring into your home. For your children, the importance of this step is fairly obvious, and I believe its effects will extend far beyond what you imagine or hope. If you've simplified in other ways successfully, you might think of this as an insurance policy for the work you've already done, and an expansion of the positive changes you've seen.

After all, television is a direct counterforce to simplifying, and it's stronger than the mightiest parent armed with good intentions. Television runs on commercials, the siren song of "stuff." An altar of commercialism, it is your home's most efficient conduit of clutter. And television can easily suck up any free, unstructured time you've gained by simplifying schedules. Between 1965 and 1995 Americans gained an average of six hours a week in leisure time; we then devoted all but a few minutes of it to watching TV.[1]

What's more, television seems to be the most influential media portal in the home. The Henry J. Kaiser Family Foundation, which has done several landmark studies on Americans' use of media, found that kids in "high TV orientation" homes (those with easy and unrestrained access to television) report almost two and a half hours more media exposure daily.[2] In other words, television seems to be the pivot point of a family's relationship to media in the home, and a predictor of how much overall media exposure a child will have throughout their childhood years. For this reason, I'll concentrate mainly on television in my recommendations for simplifying screens.

QUITE SIMPLY:
It is possible to say "No thanks," to minimize the effects of screens in our homes, at least while our children are young.

This is an old debate, one that will continue to be waged as ever more technological "screens" compete for our children's time and attention. It is also an issue that can divide the closest of couples. Do the risks of television outweigh the benefits? How much is too much? We know "the tube" doesn't have the best interests of our family or kids at heart—we do. Television is a media device, designed to entertain and to sell product. As such it is not an "uncle," not a friend or family member, but a stranger, and yet one whose place (usually in the center of the home) is unquestioned and seemingly irrevocable.

Simplifying screens will lighten your heart and bring more balance to your parenting, perhaps more than any of the earlier steps. Sensationalism, fearmongering, and violence sustain the profit margins of many media and entertainment industries. And given that their reach is omnipresent in our culture, it's liberating to know we can draw a small line in the sand: the line around our home. We can say no thanks to some of it, at least while our kids are very young.

To the question of television's risks versus rewards, neurodevelopmental science has provided some clear answers, at least in terms of very young children. The human brain is the least developed of our organ systems at birth. Most of its development, including its fundamental neural architecture, occurs during the first two years of life, in relation to and in interaction with environmental stimuli. Neurologists have identified three types of stimuli or interaction that optimize brain growth. (Any parent who's put in considerable lap or floor time with a baby can probably list these, too, in layman's terms.) Babies need interaction with parents and other humans; they need to manipulate their environment (to touch things, to feel and move them), and they need to do "problem-solving" activities (such as the eternal "where did it go?" problem-solving of peekaboo).[3]

Of these three critical forms of interaction, television provides none. For our littlest ones, neurodevelopmentally speaking, the "rewards" side of the television equation seems to be blank. Since 1999, the American Academy of Pediatrics (AAP) has recommended that children under two years of age watch no television, and that children over two limit their viewing.[4] In 2008, France banned its broadcasters from airing TV shows aimed at children under three years of age, stating: "Television viewing hurts the development of children under three years old and poses a certain number of risks, encouraging passivity, slow language acquisition, over-excitedness, troubles with sleep and concentration, as well as dependence on screens."[5]

Since only 6 percent of American parents are even aware of the AAP's recommendations,[6] companies such as Disney, Warner Bros., and Fisher-Price have not been hampered in marketing an explosion of so-called "educational" video programs—such as Baby Einstein and Brainy Baby—designed specifically for babies and toddlers. The promises implicit in the video titles, and outlined in the marketing campaigns—"Together we can help to make your child the next Baby Prodigy!"—are much more compelling than the AAP's conclusion that watching these videos is not helpful and may well be harmful to children preschool age and under. The science behind these marketing claims may be specious, but the emotional pull is strong: capitalizing on parents' aspirations for their children, and their fears that a child's intellectual "window of opportunity" slams shut after three years. Baby Einstein went on the market in 1997; by 2003, one out of three American children had watched a Baby Einstein video.[7] Multiple studies have now concluded that watching television, even such educational programming as *Sesame Street,* actually delays rather than promotes language development.[8]

Indeed, numerous studies before and since the AAP's recommendation have indicated that the youngest among us—infants and children below school age—may be the most vulnerable to television's negative effects.[9] Yet in 2006, researchers found that by three months, 40 percent of babies are regular viewers of DVDs, videos, or television; by two years of age, that percentage rises to 90 percent.[10] So, despite all the data on the "risks" side of the television equation, we continue to allow and even encourage our very young children to use electronic media, establishing habits and dependencies that can continue, and escalate, as they grow.

Kids and adolescents—ages eight to eighteen—spend an average of a little more than three hours a day watching television, though that doesn't include time spent watching videos or playing video games. When all media use (TV, computers, print, audio, videos or movies, and video games) is taken into account, the average is just under six and a half hours per day.[11] Television remains the largest component of that.

QUITE SIMPLY:

By the time the average person reaches age seventy, he or she will have spent the equivalent of seven to ten years watching television.[12]

Parents joke about how their kids appear "hypnotized" in front of the television. In *Scientific American,* Robert Kubey and Mihaly Csikszentmihalyi looked at the ways that "television addiction is no mere metaphor," noting that EEG studies show diminished mental activity during television viewing compared to other activities. Viewers describe themselves as "relaxed" and "passive" while watching, yet while the sense of relaxation ends when the set is turned off, the feelings of passivity and lowered alertness continue. Survey participants commonly reflected that television had "somehow absorbed or sucked out their energy, leaving them depleted," with "more difficulty concentrating after viewing than before." Kubey and Csikszentmihalyi equate this effect with the first law of physics: "A body at rest tends to stay at rest."[13] Further corroboration of this can be seen with studies linking the alarming rise in childhood obesity to increased time spent watching TV.

Researchers such as Dmitri Christakis of Children's Hospital in Seattle and Jane Healy, author of *Your Child's Growing Mind,* have questioned the effects of television programming techniques on brain chemistry. The "orienting reflex," or OR, is a technique used in children's shows to capture a child's attention. Essentially, if a child sees or hears something the brain doesn't recognize as correct or normal—flashing, animated figures, rapid zooms and pans, dancing letters—he or she will focus on it until the brain determines that it is not a threat. "We think that with continued exposure to high intensity, unrealistic action, you're conditioning the mind to expect that level of input," Christakis explains. In comparison to the high stimulation that television offers, real life can seem slow, and children can respond to it with boredom and inattentiveness.[14]

Television viewing's combination of neural hyperstimulation and complete physical passivity clearly doesn't stimulate the brain's development in the same way that interacting with the world does. While this is especially true in the first three years of life, it continues to be the case throughout the brain's period of growth, through adolescence. Michael Gurian, author of *The Minds of Boys,* has pointed out how the passivity of television is especially worrisome for young boys, whose brain growth is particularly dependent on physical movement.[15]

Also of great concern are the effects of television violence—and video game violence—on children. In 2000, at a bipartisan Capitol Hill conference, the American Medical Association, the American Psychological Association, the American Academy of Pediatrics, and the American Academy of Child and Adolescent Psychiatry issued this joint statement: "Viewing entertainment violence can lead to increases in aggressive attitudes, values and behavior, particularly in children. Its effects are measurable and long-lasting."[16]

Young children don't view violence in the same way adults do: Until the age of six or seven, children are developmentally and psychologically unable to differentiate between reality and fantasy.[17] So when they view brutal acts on television they see them as "real." What's more, by viewing violence—murder, rape, or assaults—from the comfort and safety of their home, snuggled up on the couch with loved ones, while perhaps eating snacks or a meal, children (and adults for that matter) become desensitized to violence, learning to equate it with pleasure.

The same disconnect between violence and reality exists with video games; playing violent video games can desensitize individuals to real violence, making it less shocking, and more acceptable.[18] The desensitization is further reinforced when the player is actually rewarded for violent acts. In a study titled "When I Die, I Feel Small," the seventh- and eighth-grade participants reported that the person they wanted to be "was very similar to their favorite video game character." Beyond the physiological and moral effects involved, beyond what a child feels or fails to feel in relation to the action of a game, when they identify so strongly with characters, their self-concept and identity are also affected.[19]

Have you ever wanted to read a book before you saw the film version of it? You chose to imagine what the characters would look like, to conjure a world mentally, as you read, before one was presented to you on the big screen. This internal imaging leads to creative imagination and higher forms of learning. In simplifying screens, you give children time to conjure their own worlds—not just through reading, but in terms of active and imaginary play—before they become passive consumers of entertainment "worlds" and their ancillary products.

The same argument can be made in terms of computers. A strong degree of computer literacy will be essential for children growing up today. Yet I feel strongly that computers, like any tool, are only helpful when age-appropriate. I don't believe they are meant for, or beneficial to, children under seven or eight years of age. And as any less-than-tech-savvy adult knows, most children come by computer proficiency quite quickly and naturally. In *Failure to Connect,* psychologist Jane Healy notes that kids who don't start using computers until adolescence gain competency within months equal to that of children who've used them since they were toddlers.[20]

The late MIT professor and pioneer of artificial intelligence Joseph Weizenbaum came to wonder about the appropriateness of computer technology for young children. He questioned whether we want to expose our young children to artificial minds without human values or even common sense. Weizenbaum believed that there are transcendent qualities of human interaction that can never be duplicated by machines; he used as an example "the wordless glance that a father and mother share over the bed of their sleeping child."[21]

Used too soon, does the two-dimensional screen of computers actually interfere with a young child's complex learning systems of relationships and sensory exploration? I question that as well. I don't believe that computers should be a part of a young child's (age seven and under) daily life. How curious will a child be, how mentally agile, creative, and persistent in seeking answers to their questions if, from a young age, they learn to Google first, and ask questions later (or not at all)?

"More!" "Faster!" and "Earlier!" is the bass beat of the tech, media, and entertainment industries. As adults, in our work and leisure, we may be keeping up with it all, ever mindful and appreciative of innovations. However, as parents, we can choose a slower, simpler path for our young children. Our relation to media and technology is not an "all or nothing" or "one size fits all" proposition, just as our needs—as children and adult—vary greatly. And as parents, we have control over media's place in our homes, and in our children's daily lives. We can do without; we can set and enforce limits. We can harness the power of less.

QUITE SIMPLY:

"Media saturation" characterizes our era, but it need not flood our kids' childhoods.

For families with children ages seven and under, I counsel doing without the television. I do so for three reasons: 1) Because I feel strongly that its negative, long-lasting effects far outweigh its benefits to young children; 2) its absence greatly supports the goals of simplification (less overwhelm, consumerism, and sense of entitlement); and 3) based on my experience, dispensing with television is not as hard as most families fear it will be.

The initial period of withdrawal is usually two or three weeks, during which the restlessness and "I'm bored!" complaints will gradually dissipate and a range of other activities will take the place of viewing. Most parents report that not having a television is much easier for their kids than they thought it would be, and for them it's considerably less work than constantly monitoring and limiting "tube time." (Families who've gone without television often report that the hardest part is dealing with the comments and unrequested "donations" of televisions made by friends and family.)

To say "No thanks" is not always the popular choice, either in our kids' eyes—"But Mom! *Everyone* else has one!"—or our peers'—"No TV?! Is this some sort of cult thing?" Choosing not to have a television, at least while your kids are young, does not say "Television is an unqualified evil" or "We want to go back to life in the 1940s." It says, simply, on balance, "No thanks." It is a choice for engagement (with people, and the three-dimensional world) over stimulation, and activity over passivity, especially while kids are young. By choosing to banish the tube, in one step you will greatly diminish your children's exposure to such hallmarks of adult life as violence and consumerism. Most of all, you will expand—almost doubling, on average—your family's free time.

The "babysitting" effect of television is important, I'll grant you, especially when it means the difference between a shower, or a load of laundry, that wouldn't otherwise get done. ("Yes! At *last* he's making some sense!" you may be saying.) But the long-term reality is this: The rich and diverse habits your children will develop without television will serve them well throughout their lives. It will also simplify your parenting enormously over the long haul. Without automatically "tuning in" for something to do (or Googling the answer to any question), your kids will find deep inner wells of creativity and resourcefulness. Better, more reliable babysitters don't exist.

Banishing the television ("Uncle Andy") while the kids are very young is the most controversial of my recommendations for simplifying screens. I have seen firsthand how remarkably effective it can be in honoring the tremendous growth and creativity of early childhood, as well as its simpler, slower pace. My experience has left me no doubt that for most families, the benefits of this step far outweigh its difficulty. I would also recommend that children under seven not spend their time on computers, video games, or handheld electronic devices. Further, I don't believe that television should be part of a child's bedroom. (Kids with a TV in their room spend almost ninety minutes more a day watching TV than those without a set in their room.)[22] After the age of seven, or school age, a child's primary focus moves beyond the home. As a result, their exposure to media, television, and computers will no doubt increase. As this happens, parents can begin to find a balanced role for screens in their children's lives.

I acknowledge that my recommendations won't work for everybody. One mom told me: "My husband doesn't think he can *live* without TV sports at home. I think he could, but I don't think I can live *with* him if he's denied!" On a "Top Ten" list of dangers to a developing child, "miserable parents" certainly has to be included. So, short of getting rid of the television, I suggest moving it (and the home computer[s]) out of children's bedrooms and communal rooms, and putting them into the parents' bedroom or a den or family office. This helps families equate the "family room" with shared activities other than television. It makes a real and symbolic difference, moving the television from the center, to the margins of daily life. Some families who limit television also report benefiting from intermittent television "holidays" of a week or a weekend. Such "breaks" help them simplify, and be more conscious of how much television they're actually watching. It also helps them develop new leisure habits.

However you choose to limit the use of television for your family (both in terms of time spent and the quality of shows watched), know that you are making a difference; it does help mediate some of TV's negative effects. Less than half of American children ages eight to eighteen report having any rules pertaining to their television viewing.[23] Yet studies corroborate what I have found: When parents do make and enforce rules to limit viewing, children spend more time reading and less time using and being exposed to electronic media of all kinds.[24] With limits on screen use a "given" in your home, the specifics that work best for your family will evolve as your children grow and their needs change. Simplifying screens and the use of media takes creativity and commitment. But then again, so does everything involved in being a family.

Involvement

Do you remember those grainy science class films of egg fertilization and cell division, as a fetus grows in the womb? Beyond all that is miraculous about new life, there is also a mathematical beauty to it: the coming together and splitting apart, how two makes one, how division first requires union. I sometimes imagine parenthood in the same way, as a series of coming together and pulling apart movements. There are geometrical shapes involved, too, like the ultimate oneness of a woman pregnant with child. I imagine a new father cradling his newborn, seen from above, as a sort of yin-yang symbol of connection. What's the counter image to the woman pregnant with child? Is it parents in a driveway, with their son or daughter, loading up the car for the big move to college? What are the ties that bind us, across time and distance? The ties that, like a membrane, must stretch without breaking, as a child circles out and back again, out and back again, on toward independence?

Biology informs the movement of life and the drive toward independence. As a fetus develops in the womb, cells are dividing in a complex dance choreographed by the infant's unique DNA. Fast-forward six years, and there is a pain in your back as you jog behind your daughter on her first two-wheeler. You've been up and down this stretch a good ten times, she's been wobbly, but now she is turning around, flushed and happy: "It's okay! You can let go!" And it is. It is okay; you can let go.

It's okay because she really wants to ride a two-wheeler, just like her friend Ellie. It's okay because there is no middle ground; a hand at the back of her seat is the same as a third wheel. No tricks and no help; in the end there is only her, balancing. It's okay because she is ready, and she is tough. It's okay because you've been there, for her and with her, so consistently that she has internalized your support. That's why she is ready. And why she is tough. That's why you can let go.

A child's first steps, first friends, the beginning of school—they are all driven by her need to explore, to know, and to master. With any luck, her biological push toward independence has been supported by *your* biological need to protect, nurture, and delight in her. Her successful, eventual division is dependent on the strength and support of your union. If the process were entirely biological and unconscious, perhaps it would be as smooth and geometrical as cells dividing in a petri dish. But the movements behind these two drives—yours to protect and nurture, hers to explore and separate—are not always smooth, not always in concert. In fact, they're often at cross-purposes, with many opportunities for missteps and bad timing. Luckily, it is not just biology that accompanies this parent-child dance. There is also the powerful force of love. Love may be messy ("What do you mean, you want to get your driver's permit?"), but it is the only force strong enough to contain and mediate these two biological forces with any sense of rhythm and beauty. With anything even approaching grace.

Let's look at this dance of parent-child involvement, and how to simplify it.

Base Camp

The security that we build for a child will be a "base camp" that will serve them, hopefully, throughout their lives. It is the hand at the back of the bike seat—at first real and essential, and eventually metaphorical—but always calming, supportive.

No parent needs to be convinced of the tremendous growth that takes place in the first three years of life. A baby usually achieves a weight four to five times that of their birth weight, and doubles in length. By the end of its second year, a baby's brain weighs three-quarters of an adult's brain weight, though it is twice as active as an adult's and will remain so until puberty. The baby's neurons become larger and more powerful, growing axons and dendrites, so by the time a child reaches three, each neuron has formed as many as ten thousand connections. That's about a quadrillion—give or take a few—or roughly double the number of connections that are seen in an adult brain.

As a baby is growing, in deep exploration of their sensory world, we are, hopefully, providing what they need for this remarkable growth: security and connection. A three-month-old baby grasps his mother's finger and takes in her scent as he nurses; she has him tucked in close, safe and free from too many distractions. As he explores, she protects; as he attaches to her, she bonds to him; the connection is strengthening, the dance is in full swing.

One way that we protect our children, especially in their first few years, is to act as a filter. For our small ones, so new to the world, we try to screen out some of the world's noise, its crazy sensory onslaughts. And we do so with good reason, biologically. The hippocampus, which regulates sensory input in the brain, acting as a sort of neurological filter, is quite slow to form. We do what the hippocampus can't yet. By mediating input, we reduce stress, allowing the baby to interact freely with its world. Erik Erikson called this critical period that of "trust versus mistrust." As we soothe the crying baby, as its hunger is met with food, trust wins over mistrust. Rudolf Steiner equated it with breath: the child "breathes" in the environment and "breathes" itself out into the world. If this "breathing," which is as critical as eating, is unimpeded, the child can continue to explore with security. Security and hope.

Even at three or four months, even firmly connected to the breast, a baby is exploring its world. With her attention, she leaves and returns to her mother; she watches the light play through the window and then returns her gaze, with comfort, to her mother's face. The toddler's first steps may be toward you, as you sit beckoning with outstretched arms. But as a semisturdy biped she'll quickly move away—off to see this, to touch that—and then back for a snuggle, or just back to safe proximity with you. With trust the explorations can continue; they can lengthen in time and distance. The security of your child's attachment, and the strength of your bond, will be their base camp for an entire childhood of exploration.

This struggle between trust and mistrust is central to a child's development. If a baby's needs are not responded to, if his primary attachment to a caregiver is weak or inconsistent—if mistrust wins—then he will have trouble forming attachments and empathizing with others. Clingy and anxious, he will respond to the world as though it were a platform laid on water: slippery, unstable. Without a firm attachment to a loving caregiver, a child can suffer from chronically elevated levels of the stress hormone cortisol. Cortisol is a neural hijacker, bullying out learning and other functions to make room for its floods.

However, when a child is able to explore from a foundation of loving connection and security—when trust wins—he gains the freedom to grow. Without high levels of cortisol he can regulate his emotions. Free of the stress-regress cycle, he is better able to learn. Secure in his attachment to his parents (or parent, or loving caregiver), he has a base camp. Unmoveable, it is the safe place he leaves to explore, and the safe place he circles back to, the foundation from which he ascends. He can develop his will, exploring and pushing his way toward a sense of self and independence.

This is a defining paradigm for us, too: trust versus mistrust. It is central to our development as parents, to our role in the parent-child dance. Yet for some of us, trust never wins. Still "spotting" a child who can walk and run, we remain stuck in a state of arrested development.

Our fears and worries overshadow our trust in the world, and our trust in them. Most of all, our fears eclipse our trust in our own instincts.

Remember Annmarie? When she felt that *worry* best described her experience as a mother, something was amiss. Her development as a parent was being hijacked. Stuck in a stress-regress cycle, Annmarie was caught in the deep primal urge to protect her children. They were saying, "It's okay! You can let go." But she just couldn't hear it.

When we let our fears overshadow our trust, we're abandoning the base camp, trying to "go with" our children. Picking up stakes, we're dismantling what they really need, and boarding the helicopter. But base camps aren't transient; they aren't portable.

Helicopter Parenting

Annmarie has plenty of company in her fears: 76 percent of American parents feel that raising kids today is "a lot harder" than it was when they were growing up, according to a 2002 Public Agenda survey. Only 20 percent of the parents polled felt that their job was "about the same" in difficulty as their parents'. What ranked highest of the added pressures parents feel today? "Trying to protect their child from negative societal influences." Fifty percent of parents polled said they worried "a lot" about someone kidnapping their child, with drugs and alcohol (55 percent) and negative messages in the media (39 percent) also ranking high on the list of worries.[25]

Have the threats to our children increased, compared to a generation or two ago? Have "negative social influences" grown, or is it the scope and influence of the media—in our homes and our lives—that has expanded dramatically? The lead story of any local news program—a missing child, a convicted child molester out of prison—will confirm that good news doesn't sell. Fanning parental anxieties, on the other hand, definitely does sell. Details at eleven. In 1985 the *Denver Post* won a Pulitzer Prize for a series of articles that took a closer look at the child abduction fears that were sweeping the country. The feature documented that 95 percent of missing children are runaways (most of whom come home within three days) and that of the rest, most are child custody disputes.[26]

Annmarie's mother, with her front door unlocked and eight children going in and out, probably didn't worry too much about potential kidnappers. What has changed? Fears for our children's physical safety have helped fuel the exodus from neighborhood yards and parks. According to one study, more than 90 percent of parents named safety as their biggest concern when making decisions about whether to allow their kids to play outside.[27] According to the Justice Department, the number of kidnappings of children by strangers has not increased for the past twenty years.[28] Yet a single incident can seem like a crime wave when it is parsed and sensationalized.

The media, pervasive and relentless, play a large part in parental anxieties. When graphic details of the same unfortunate story are broadcast through countless media outlets—from network and cable news to Internet and Palm Pilot news feeds—its emotional effect is exponential. A sense of danger becomes heightened and personal when horrors are delivered right into our living rooms, when they follow us throughout the day, wherever we go.

When a new mother is nursing, she begins to notice how her diet—yesterday's onion soup or very garlicky mashed potatoes—affects her milk. A morning spent with a fussy, colicky baby will make her think twice before pulling out leftovers for lunch. An emotional diet high in fear and sensationalism can be transmitted to our children, too. Long after babies are weaned from the breast or bottle, they continue to nurse from their parents' emotions. We sometimes increase our vigilance—sucking up every intimation of danger, feeding on every hint of concern—in a misguided belief that this increases our children's protection. Really, though, it only increases our anxiety. It not only pollutes our well-being as parents, it affects the way we see the world, and the way our kids do, too. It lengthens and broadens that shadow of fear, so we see danger first and foremost, before we see a situation's joy or possibilities.

QUITE SIMPLY:
Children feed off their parents' emotions.

Just as the flight attendant reminds parents to "secure your oxygen mask before you help your child with theirs," parents need to relax in order to convey ease to their children. I would like to make a recommendation directly to parents, especially those who, like Annmarie, are often fretful: Reduce your exposure to media, and particularly media news.

This may seem sacrilegious in our age of information, but let me clarify. I'm not suggesting parents crawl under media-proof rocks, avoiding news or any connection to the world. I have no problem with parents having what media access they need to be informed and connected. I am suggesting, however, that parents consciously say no thanks to media overexposure. Limit or cut your use of those media that alarm rather than inform. It can make a dramatic difference in your emotional life, and the emotional climate of your home, when you refuse to allow your fear to be provoked, stoked, and incited several times a day.

Yes, daily life in America (or any other country) involves risks and dangers to children. There are perhaps even more risks now than when we were growing up. I don't know. I do know that Annmarie and many other parents today are better "informed" than their parents were, but they're also much more nervous. Their emotional well-being is being eroded by media that, if allowed, can easily saturate their lives. Media that exploit our deepest, most primal urge to protect our children.

Yet, as parents, we need to be more than just our desire to protect, no matter how noble and important that is. We need to live with confidence, to parent with a sense of strength and openness, and perhaps most of all, a sense of humor. The primal urge to protect is our cortisol spigot; I'm suggesting we not invite it to be turned so easily and so often.

Lucy, a mother and teacher who attended one of my workshops, told me a story about a friendship that was affecting her well-being as a parent. Rena had a son the same age as Lucy's; the two women met through their sons' preschool. Yet, Lucy reported, she began to realize that she generally felt bad after speaking or spending time with Rena. Almost always Rena talked about something scary related to kids that she had read or seen on television. Rena talked a lot about the inadequacies of the schools, about how her son was doing in relation to other kids, about her concerns as to whether her son would get the opportunities he deserved. Lucy said that while she could understand and relate to Rena's concerns, she found the sheer unrelenting weight of them oppressive, unleavened by humor or joy. She realized that she needed fun, some inspiration and laughter with her friends, not just a stress bath. Lucy backed off her friendship with Rena a bit, with sadness, but with an even greater sense of relief.

We can't blame the media alone for making us more nervous as parents. There are many reasons we've taken to hovering. The term *helicopter parenting* was coined almost twenty years ago, in the early 1990s. It has since become so ubiquitous—as a term and a cultural phenomenon—that different degrees of hovering have been noted. (According to a study at the University of Texas at Austin, "Black Hawk parents" are the most angry and extreme.)[29] In the early 2000s, colleges began to decry the extent to which parents were exerting control over the decisions—from roommates to course teachers—of their young adult children. But that was the tip of the iceberg. Parental overinvolvement, or "hyperparenting," is not exclusive to parents of any particular income bracket, race, or level of education. It's also not exclusive to Americans. And kids of all ages—certainly not just college-age kids—feel its effects. Parental demands and anxieties can be heard in the preschool coatroom; they float above the eighth-grader being tutored for the SATs that she won't actually take for three years.

It makes sense that many parents today have managed to get their helicopter pilot's licenses. Compared with a generation or two ago, we're having fewer children, and becoming parents later in life. As a result, our parental attention, mental and physical energy, and our expectations are more concentrated on fewer kids, not dispersed among a larger brood. Frequently parents today, mothers as well as fathers, have considerable career experience before their first child is born, and are bringing the values of the corporate world—a work ethic and sense of competition—into their parenting.

QUITE SIMPLY:

Technology has helped to blur the lines between privacy and independence, involved and "overinvolved."

There's also a large "Because I can" element to why this generation of parents pays such extraordinary attention to their children's every move. With cellphones (the world's longest umbilical cords), email, instant messaging, GPS, and other navigational programs, we can be in nearly constant contact with our children. With some software, we can plot every fluctuation of our children's grade point average, monitor their chat room conversations, and have copies of their emails and instant messages sent directly to our computer. Technology has facilitated our overinvolvement in our children's lives to such an extent that the line between involved and overinvolved is easy to cross. For many parents, the accepted boundaries of privacy and independence, so obvious even a generation ago, seem to have been erased.

Some people point to the effects of 9/11 and such tragedies as the

Columbine High School shootings as contributing factors to increased parental hovering. Others equate it with a pendulum swing away from what Generation X (those born between 1965 and 1981) experienced when they were children. One in six of that generation (many of whom are parents today) grew up with a single parent, and more than 40 percent were latchkey kids.[30] Those factors in themselves are hardly indicators of abuse or hardship, but as a whole, the parenting style of the time was fairly hands-off. And so the pendulum has swung the other way.

Many factors combine to form a trend, a mode of thought and behavior characteristic of a particular era. Without a doubt, overinvolvement, in its many forms, is a parenting zeitgeist of our day. If the hovering parent is a descriptive image for the trend, I would point to anxiety and the pressures of competition as the fuels keeping our helicopters aloft. Parenting, education, and even childhood are now viewed as competitions. Parents feel tremendous pressure, both cultural and self-induced, to enrich, enhance, and escalate their children's early years. Under the guise of protecting and providing, we control and cater to our children. If childhood is a "window of opportunity" for growth, we assume that means it is a "limited-time opportunity." In a competitive vein, where more and faster are always better, our methods and our goal become clear: to "get more in" before the imaginary window closes.

Culture can be seen as the collaborative pool we draw from in our daily lives. We're influenced by what we see, the methods and experiences of others close to us. This is especially true among parents who compare notes on just about everything with other parents. Hyper-parenting is a large part of the cultural norm today, worldwide. It is part of the parenting waters we're swimming in. I'll share with you a few of the more common forms of overinvolvement that I commonly see, presenting a sort of "rogues gallery" in which most any parent will catch a glimpse or two of themselves. Most of us do some of these things, sometimes. Then, and most important, we'll look at how to back out of overinvolvement, how to bring that helicopter down.

In my work and travels I often see a parental type I think of as "Sportscasters." Basically, a "sportscasting" parent drowns a child in words. In real time (that is, blow-by-blow) they telecast everything the child touches, does, is wearing, or even what they may be thinking. "Would you look at this! Peter, darling, look at you! In your bright red shoes you're doing a wonderfully silly dance. Look at your arms! Like a windmill, you are! Or an elephant. And look, now! Look at you bend down all the way like a big, hairy baboon! Is that what you're being? Is that a baboon's dance, darling?" (This is an abbreviated version, actually . . . but you get the idea.)

The "corporate parent" holds a metaphorical image of their family as a corporation, or a corporate team. Decisions are made on the basis of a mythical "bottom line." What must be expended to get the desired results? And just what are the desired results? The ultimate goal is a "product launch": the launching of their child into the world. But until that point, life can seem like a series of "launch meetings." Corporate parents try to get kids excited about their own "packaging," about their "profile" and their advantages over other kids.

The "little buddy parent" (which morphs, as a child gets older, into the "best friend parent") sees no separation between their world—their adult conversations and activities—and their children's. They invite their children's involvement in decisions; they expend a lot of time and ever so many words on justifications mainly to avoid one word: *no.* Often this lack of boundaries speaks to a kind of loneliness. Some parents are so focused on their children, and isolated from adult friendships, that they seek a more equal, friendship-based relationship from their kids. The little buddy parents often want their children to be adults, or, better still, they themselves want to be children again. There is nothing new, and certainly nothing particular to parents about longing for "the fountain of youth." The only news is that there are now multibillion-dollar industries catering to these fantasies: selling rhinestone embellished thongs to seven-year-old tweeners and low-rise "gangsta" jeans to adults.

The "clown parent" feels the need to be "larger than life," an entertainer. They believe that childhood, in fact, needs to be "larger than life," a sort of ever-expanding carnival of delights. There is great love behind this image, but also exhaustion. My mental image of this parent ("Honk! Honk!") isn't one of them entertaining, and speaking with enthusiasm and animation. I imagine them later, depleted, like a puppet that has been set down. This kind of parenting often leads to disappointment—for the child, obviously, whose expectations are elevated daily, but also for the parent, who is left feeling that they can never do enough.

Here is a critical point: There is tremendous love behind all these forms of overinvolvement. Hyperparenting may stem from an overbearing love, one that doesn't fully respect (or sometimes acknowledge) a child's independence. Yet out of love we can also choose to *back off* from overinvolvement. Love is also the way out. We can change direction and vary the steps in our parent-child dance. We can learn to allow our children their own tasks, decisions, conflicts, relationships, and emotional lives. We can provide the kind of stability and security that they will internalize, a base camp that doesn't move. This archetypal base camp will be their own strength of character, their own resiliency.

Backing Off—Talk Less

Sometimes, when I give lectures and workshops to school communities, questions are solicited for me beforehand. So when I arrive, I'm handed a basket of questions that I then try to address during the course of the day, either in my lecture or in small groups afterward. I have an all-time favorite question, though when I first read it, it really threw me. Now I think of it as a lovely little symbol, or analogy, for what we must do to simplify parental overinvolvement.

Here's the question: "Why did Laura and Mary do what Pa said?"

If your children are seven or over, you may recognize the reference: Laura Ingalls Wilder's Little House on the Prairie books. This series, based on the author's own memories, tells the story of a family—Ma, Pa, Laura, Mary, and little Carrie—of homesteaders in Kansas. Theirs is a hard life, with monumental threats such as fire and failed crops, but also simple pleasures. The story, which extends over five books, has many ups and downs, but through all of these it can absolutely be said that yes, the girls really did do what Pa said. Without question.

Why did Laura and Mary do what Pa said? The short answer is this: Pa didn't say too much.

Discipline was really the focus of this question. But discipline and parental involvement are intertwined. This may surprise you, but several of the suggestions and tips that I offer to help parents back out of overinvolvement boil down to this: say less.

We often bathe our children in words. By keeping a running commentary on everything they do, we mean to assure them that we're noticing. Yet the more we're talking, the less we are really noticing. My youngest daughter and I were walking recently in a meadow, and she pointed to a single wheat stalk that was taller than the rest, and arched over beautifully. "Look, Daddy, see that?" she asked, tugging my sleeve and pointing. "Yes," I said, and we both stopped and looked at it for a moment or two before continuing on.

Now, I'm a garrulous fellow. I offer this snapshot not to suggest that I am always a master of Zen calm and silence. I'm using it to show the golden possibilities in an ordinary moment. I could have responded to my daughter with a lively little talk about native plants, about the symmetry of the wheat's kernels, and why this particular stalk had pushed up higher than the rest. I could have praised her for her lovely vision, her insight and recognition of beauty in its purest form. In fact, I could be there still, talking . . . though she wouldn't still be listening.

QUITE SIMPLY:
The more you say, the less you are listening.

My daughter made a simple observation. She pointed out something that struck her in some way, something she wanted to share. I did not need to take that moment and "make it into something" of my own design. I didn't need to enrich her observation, to repackage it with a lot of information or praise or verbiage, and hand it back to her, with my stamp on it, or ribbons attached. As her father, I don't have to make every moment a "teaching moment," or even a "special moment." I can often just notice.

When we talk over and under and around a child—when we talk too much—there's less space for their thoughts, for what they have to say. A child's curiosity and creativity are stifled when they believe that something is not "real" unless, or until, you talk about it. It's hard for a child to go down deeply into their play when someone is telecasting their every move. Processed information is like processed food: quick and easy. We often fly into soliloquies, overexplaining, and predigesting every experience for our kids.

Must we all emulate Pa, then, a hard-bitten, rugged man of the plains, who worked endlessly and said almost nothing? I don't think so. But when we're overinvolved, when we're hyperparenting, we're usually talking too much. We're usually jumping into most experiences, and almost any silence, with a verbal offering. Our intention may be to acknowledge something, but very often we describe, praise, instruct, and embellish it as well. Like a dancer who is leading too much, we lose the chance to see how the other person was going to move. After a while, he or she may simply let us carry them along, their little feet never touching the floor.

Imagine that your five-year-old runs over to show you the drawing he has just made of you. Can you acknowledge it, without talking? Can you take it in—really look at it—and give it back? Or, if you must talk, can you make an observation, without judgment or praise? "Hmmm, yes, you used a lot of red." Or can you ask a simple question? "How did you get Daddy's foot like that?" Off they'll go, telling you about the red, or the foot, or the way that they love how they made your head look just like a melon, or how they want to try again, this time drawing with their left hand. They are in the midst of a creative process, their attention is fully engaged, and what they need from you is usually just a quick connection, rather than a critique or complement.

As we multitask, this might be one of our most difficult tasks: to just notice, to quietly bear witness. To be a parent is to have one's attention split several ways in any given situation, and we often try to bridge our fractured focus with words. As a result, it is very powerful when we are able to acknowledge something quietly, to not fill the space with words; to not bend, bolster, or embellish. To turn away from the email, the phone, or the next important thing, and to offer—even briefly—our full and silent attention.

Should we do this every time? That would be unrealistic and unnecessary. I am not suggesting that parents stop talking to their children. I am suggesting that parents talk less. In a noisy world, quiet attentiveness speaks louder than words, and it gives a child more space for their own thoughts and feelings to develop. Talking less is a fundamental way to simplify our involvement with our children. Here are some conversational filters you can use to help you limit verbal clutter.

Adult Topics

In his book and monologues about Lake Wobegon, Garrison Keillor mentions the Lutheran suppers and church gatherings he attended as a child. His recollections capture the sense of two separate social worlds existing in one room: the adult world with the drone of their conversations on top, and the kids' world swirling and circulating below, ever poised for escape and play. In that setting what the kids noticed most about the adults, according to Keillor, was how big their feet were. The children weren't looking up, trying to be involved in their parents' conversations (that would only prolong their "displacement" in the adult world). They much preferred their own world of doing over the dull adult world of talking.

One of the ways to "talk less," is to be more conscious of the sanctity of these two worlds—the adult world and the world of kids—in conversation. That doesn't mean that the two worlds never intersect, but it does mean that there are, and should be, conversations and topics that are for adults only. There are several points here. The most obvious form of "adult topic" is a subject that isn't suitable for young or immature ears. Mom and Dad don't discuss their sex lives with their kids, and Mom's conversations with her sister, detailing the ins and outs of her sister's divorce, is one that Mom has in private. These are straightforward examples of clear conversational boundaries.

Those lines can get very fuzzy, though, often disappearing entirely. Many parents "flashbulb" their children with too much of their own adult concerns, their own unprocessed thoughts and feelings. I worry sometimes that we've let our guards down as a society, talking to children too openly about too much. When we let children in on too much information—adult verbal and emotional clutter—it rushes them along, pushing them ahead without a foundation. "With any luck, little buddy, I'll be able to make this trip without Jasper, the sales manager, coming along!" "We're going to switch car pools, love, because I just can't take any more of Lizzie's mom being late all of the time." "A trampoline? Sweetie, we are barely making ends meet unless Mommy gets her promotion." "Oh, I wish we didn't have to always go to your grandparents for the holidays . . . but don't repeat that to Nana!"

Some parents want to be an open book to their children; they equate honesty with full disclosure. By its very nature, though, respect requires some distance and separation. We all slip and slide into boundary bending occasionally. This can be a real difficulty for single parents, especially those who don't have many outlets for the kind of verbal processing that is a necessary part of daily life. Very often when we're tired, when our physical or emotional reserves are low, we can mistake our child for a sort of sounding board or sympathetic ear for whatever issue or quandary is on our mind.

Yet despite their questions and curiosity, children need boundaries to feel secure and free. They need to know, and to be reminded, that some things are for adults to discuss; they are not for kids to hear, or to comment on. Children need to see your self-restraint, your confidence in meeting your own world. With security and freedom they can begin to find their own inner voice. They can begin to develop their own ability to self-direct, to work things out internally. This is the genesis of self and morality: the development of an inner voice. And in order to develop—to strengthen and be heard—a child's inner voice cannot be drowned out by unprocessed adult thoughts, feelings, and concerns.

QUITE SIMPLY:

One way to "talk less" is not to include children in adult concerns and topics of conversation.

Do you have any childhood memories of being in the backseat of the car at night, perhaps dozing, while your parents drove through rain or snow, talking quietly in the front seat? Maybe you were on vacation, maybe just driving home from a late dinner, but the feeling was one of safety, of being cocooned and watched over in the darkness. There were distant concerns in the darkness and the weather, concerns perhaps even in whatever they were talking about, but all was well. How wonderful that they knew where to go and how to get there. How comforting that they would deliver you through the dark night, whatever it might bring. And when you got home (if they thought you were asleep) they might even carry you all the way to bed.

It's a misnomer to think that we are "sharing" with our children when we include them in adult conversations about adult concerns. Sharing suggests an equal and mutual exchange, one that is impossible for a child to offer and unfair for an adult to expect. The child in the backseat feels a great sense of security partly because they know their mom or dad is not going to turn around and ask them to drive. By accepting the responsibilities, and respecting the boundaries of your adult world, you give your children the gift of freedom in their own world. And there is "sharing" involved: Both worlds thrive in the shared atmosphere of family, and of love.

There is one more point. When there are topics that you don't address with your child, they carry an image of you, and of adulthood, that retains an element of mystery. When you have an inner life, your children have a model of self that is both loving and unique, an individual. They'll come to realize that there are things about you they don't know, things that they may learn over time.

Do You Love the Times You Live In?

As adults our answer to this question would be complicated, and could easily depend on the day we were asked. We might have a thing or two to say about the current administration, and the state of the economy. Like Annmarie, we may feel that raising children is harder (or at least different) today than it was for earlier generations. But just as our answer might be complex and nuanced, so too are our powers of analysis. We've seen issues evolve and resolve; we've seen how history reshapes the social and political landscape. As adults we have ways of prioritizing our concerns, of seeing "the times we live in" in various lights, and through various contexts.

Children don't have the mental faculties to process a lot of information that way, especially information about issues and things far beyond their scope of reference. Too much information does not "prepare" a child for a complicated world; it paralyzes them. Remember the earliest developmental stage that Erik Erikson termed the struggle of "trust versus mistrust"? When trust "wins," when a baby's needs are consistently met by a loving caregiver, a foundation of safety is established that makes further exploration possible. In a fundamental sense, this continues to be the case—trust should win—throughout childhood.

QUITE SIMPLY:

Children need to know that they have a place in a good world, and a future of promise.

This doesn't mean we should fit our children with rose-colored glasses. I am not saying we should avoid any discussion of the challenges of our time. Nor does it mean that children can't recover, and grow in strength and resiliency, from hardships they experience in their early years. But our adult anxieties and concerns should not be the atmosphere, a haze of too much information, that they breathe. Children need to know that theirs is a good world. They need to feel that, sheltered by those they love, they are where they should be. They have a place, in a time and a world of hope and promise.

Kids as young as kindergarten age are hearing, over juice and crackers, about shrinking rainforests and oil reserves. In their concern, and remarkable ability to drink in information, many very young kids hold a precocious awareness of huge issues. But is that helpful, to them or the environment? This kind of information needs to be balanced with doing. A child is preparing for world issues in their own ways, in vigorous interaction with their immediate sensory environment, their childhood world. Through play, with its engineering and problem solving, they are gathering the mental flexibility they'll need to make a difference in the larger world.

I'm reminded of the road sign: CAUTION: BRIDGE FREEZES BEFORE ROAD. The bridge is more vulnerable to frost because it lacks a foundation. The earth below the road provides grounding and warmth. In the same way, too much information can freeze a child. Not only do they lack context for the information, they lack the foundation that childhood slowly provides: the foundation of years of relatively safe observation, interaction, and exploration.

My friend Kathy mentioned that her nine-year-old son, Sam, was having some trouble at school. Casually she described a phone call from Sam's teacher, but her voice betrayed more emotion than her words. Evidently Sam was questioning his teacher's authority, making sarcastic comments out loud or under his breath, and rolling his eyes in response to things that she said. "That's just not Sam," Kathy said. Maybe not, I thought, at least not entirely, not yet. But it sounded very much like Eddie, Sam's father.

A financial analyst by trade, Eddie's passion is politics. He is one of the brightest, funniest men I know. But his wit is biting and acerbic, and he spares no verbal punches for some of the politicians in office. The target of Eddie's most caustic and cynical comments was an American president whose term began the twenty-first century and extended for most of Sam's life. It seemed to me quite understandable that Sam was having trouble respecting an authority figure in his own life, after years of hearing his dad call the president a variety of names (with *idiot* on the top of the list). Sam didn't hear the reasoning or policies behind his dad's opinions, but he did hear the derision. He didn't understand party politics or campaign promises, but he picked right up on his dad's cynicism and disrespect. Sam's nine-year-old versions of the same things—sarcasm and disrespect—were not serving him well in the fourth grade, not in the least.

One aspect of talking less is realizing that what children mainly hear, in your wash of words, is the current of emotion running through them. And what they understand, more than the details, or any words we could possibly use, are our actions. When we speak of others with respect—whether it's our mother, bus driver, the president, or the man at the checkout stand—no explanations or distinctions are necessary.

Do you love the times you live in? We project a general sense of optimism to children when we talk less (with them) about things they may not understand and definitely have no power to affect. The details are often lost on them, but the way we move in the world determines their view. We may not be crazy about this or that politician, or the politics in our workplace, but as adults we know things change. We know we have the recourse of our actions and our vote.

When we talk less, we convey a sense of confidence and competence in the world, a world where people strive to be just. There's less need to explain, expound, justify, clarify, or qualify—and our meaning is clearer—when we pay more attention (as children do) to the tone of our words and our actions. When I remind myself about "talking less," I sometimes think of the character Atticus Finch in *To Kill a Mockingbird.* In the midst of a difficult, even scary situation, it was his calm and consistent manner more than his words that spoke to his children. Such security is priceless. It is a solid foundation. It helps a child through those dark nights when, in your ham costume, you can't see clearly.

It points ahead to the promise of a better day.

True, Kind, Necessary

Most every wisdom tradition cautions for the wise use of words, acknowledging their tremendous power to inspire *and* to wound. This might be most obvious on the world stage, where the words of someone like Martin Luther King Jr., can echo through history, capturing an era and galvanizing change. But I see the power so much more commonly wielded in the family. Through the noise and bustle of daily life, a parent's words can help shape the way a child sees the world, and, most important, sees themselves. In our era of spin and counterspin, when words are parsed and split, where news stands beside opinion and embraces blogs, meaning is often drowned out. Just as it's hard to cherish a toy lost in the middle of a mountain of playthings, when we say less, our words mean more.

One of the best filters I know for talking less has been attributed to (among others) the nineteenth-century guru Sai Baba, Socrates, the Bible, Quakers, Rotarians, the poet Beth Day, the Sufis, and an early-twentieth-century Unitarian sermon. Known by various names, including the Threefold Filter, it forms the basis of "Right Speech," one of the pillars of the Buddhist Eightfold Noble Path. You could probably find an echo of it in every religion and culture, and like most basic truths, it's easier to remember than it is to put into practice. I find that this filter works wonders for parents, wherever and whenever they remember to use it, in helping them speak less, and more consciously.

Before you say something, ask yourself these three questions: Is it true? Is it kind? Is it necessary?

True. Gossip and hearsay will fail the first filter every time. This filter alone is worth its weight in gold. By asking ourselves if something is true before we say it, we also notice how often we pass off exaggeration, opinion, and supposition as truth. Imagine the "verbal load" of your home—all the words that swirl around, whether they come directly from family members or are brought in from outside. Now imagine a basket at the front door for the rejects, the words that can't come in; in it are all of the unsubstantiated, nasty, hurtful, mean things that people say about one another. With the filter in place, is there more air, more quiet in the home? By filtering your own speech you lead by example, but you can use this as a guide for what you will listen to as well. "Hey Mom, did you hear about the Andersons, and what their mom did?" "No, but first, Kiki, is it true?" "I think so . . . Amy told me, and I think her dad is maybe their accountant or something like that, or at least he used to be, so he would probably know." "No, darling, that doesn't sound like truth to me. I don't want to hear it."

Kind. Is it kind? If what you are about to say has passed the first filter—it is true—it must still pass a test of compassion: Is it kind? Some things that are true still do not need to be said, if doing so would be hurtful. Bullying wouldn't exist if kids used this filter, but adults have to model and reinforce it first. If a bully's most common weapons are put-downs—taunts or criticisms—parents sometimes engage in the same behavior—through words and body language—under the guise of instructing or motivating a child. Where I see parental overinvolvement, I very often see put-downs.

Sometimes in my work, whether in family therapy or in a school setting where there are bullying issues, I challenge parents to go on a three-week, self-imposed put-down diet. By being more conscious of the put-downs they use with their children—the judgments, the names, and the characterizations ("You always . . ." and "You are so . . .")—they begin to see how "admonishing" and "challenging" can feel a lot like bullying. "Is it kind?" is a critical filter, and home is a wonderful place to put it into practice. What better place to set a standard of kindness to others and to one another? When we have to instruct our children, as parents, it helps to remember that even difficult truths can be said with kindness. Is it kind?

Necessary. I think of this as the verbal "clutter" filter. Is what I am about to say necessary? Is this now my sixth pass at an explanation, and my kids stopped listening during my third? I don't take *necessary* to mean that everything we say has to be instructive, or have some larger educational or inspirational purpose. Instead, I take *necessary* to mean "more important than silence." What enables us to read a word is the white space all around it, and without some intervening quiet we couldn't hear a thing. Silence is important, especially in a noisy family in a noisy world. And noise is self-perpetuating, so if your kids grow accustomed to a "noisy norm" they will always try to create and maintain that level of clamor. There, I've scared you. Let's agree to the obvious: that silence is important, wherever and whenever we can find it. Given the importance of silence, the clutter filter, "Is what I am going to say necessary?" should clear the air in your home even further.

"Is it necessary?" will be most helpful in guiding your own speech. As your kids begin to notice that you are saying less, they will listen more. But it is tough to use this one as a filter for what you will listen to from your kids. Necessary? "Dad, I was thinking about space travel and I realized that jet packs might work even better on your shoes than on your back." "Mom! Quick! There's a ladybug in the bathroom and it's the same one I saw when I was five! It is in the *exact* same spot, only now I can't remember its name!" Necessary? Yes, actually, these probably are "necessary." "Please, please Dad, can I have it?" "Mitch, I said no. You've already asked me twice; a third time is unnecessary."

This three-part filter is beautiful in its simplicity. I sometimes jot down the words—*true.kind.necessary*—on my calendar or notebooks, just so I can carry them through the day. Like everything worthwhile, it takes practice to consciously erect these filters somewhere between our minds and our mouths. Luckily, as parents, we have many opportunities a day, every day, to practice.

Backing Off—Work Together

Here's another "mathematical equation" I've noticed in the parent-child dance of involvement. Very often, in two-parent households, when one parent is overinvolved in their child's life, the other parent is under-involved. I need to reiterate that this isn't always the case. Sometimes both parents are equally overinvolved. Like a shared hobby, they both insert themselves into every aspect of their child's life.

However, from what I have seen working with families for the past twenty years, the scale of involvement is often tipped toward mothers. Hyperparenting dads tend to be more achievement focused, overly involved in their child's academics or athletics, or both. More often however, it is the mother who is overinvolved, and her concerns for her child are often generalized, perhaps orbiting more around issues of social adjustment. Worry often overshadows joy, as was the case for Annmarie, when a couple's involvement with the tasks and concerns of child rearing becomes increasingly imbalanced.

What might Annmarie's husband say about his experience of fatherhood? The word I often hear from dads is *calm.* A sense of calm is what they strive to provide to the joint task of child rearing. Stepping back, being "laid-back," trying to "take the long view"; these expressions come up frequently as men explain what they perceive to be their role in the parenting dynamic. Their goal is a sense of balance, but very often the result is a lack of involvement, and increased isolation and anxiety for their spouse.

Numerous books have been written about gender roles in parenting today. For all of the differences between Annmarie's and her mother's child-rearing experiences, the biggest is often not even mentioned, given how widespread the change has become. In addition to shouldering primary responsibility for child care, Annmarie also has a job, while her mother did not. With such a seismic shift between then and now, there have been numerous aftershocks in gender relations, and the division of labor in child rearing.

These issues are well beyond the scope of this book. Sociological theories are being developed while, in almost any setting where parents get together, experiences and ideas are being exchanged, compared. The balance of power and responsibility within the home is in a great state of flux and adjustment.

What I have noticed, and what I feel compelled to mention, is that the experiential scale of parenting—anxiety versus joy—is tied to the "scale of involvement" between the spouses. In my experience, it is more commonly the case that the mother is overinvolved. What I have seen, though, is that when the father steps up, many mothers are able to take a welcome step back. These adjustments take time, as habits of work and responsibilities are ingrained, but the results are usually well worth the effort. A better balance of involvement benefits the partnership. It also simplifies parental involvement in the children's lives, reducing anxiety as the duties and concerns of parenting are spread on a wider, stronger base.

QUITE SIMPLY:
A partnership that is more balanced in terms of parenting yields benefits for all: a strengthened partnership and much less hovering.

I have found that the most effective adjustments to a parenting balance of involvement are made in small, practical steps. Debates can be waged, and philosophical manifestos can be drawn up, but they very often wind up wedged behind the dirty clothes hamper; a hard-won document now covered in dust bunnies. Where positive, lasting changes have been made I've noticed the beginning was often the kitchen counter, or the bathtub. Of the many parenting tasks that must happen every day, dads need to move some to their side of the "full responsibility" list.

Every day, if a lunch is to be packed, it will be Dad packing it. Bath time is Dad time. And where the child or children's lives intersect with other groups (a babysitter, school, a playgroup), Dad should find a consistent role. Exclusive provinces (or nearly exclusive) need to become Dad's, so his efforts are part of "doing," not "helping." So that, in the child's eyes, Dad is the "go-to" person for that slice of daily life, not the occasional "substitute." So that, for Mom, trust and ease make inroads into every day. Her grip loosens.

Some couples strive for a fifty/fifty split; for most the percentages change according to a number of factors. What has struck me over time, however, is the importance, for couples and children, of each parent taking fairly exclusive responsibility for several aspects of daily life. That doesn't mean that parents shouldn't have some areas of shared responsibility, and spend time together with daily life tasks. But the work of child care can expand to fill most every crevice. And for one person to really get a break, to really let go of a task mentally and physically, the other must do it consistently, with no need for requests or reminders.

When a partner takes a role in various aspects of a child's life, their understanding of the child broadens and deepens. With consistency and exclusivity from each, there is much greater rhythm in the household. There are anchors established, guaranteed opportunities for connection.

Men often feel that when they take over a responsibility previously held by their wives, their efforts are doomed to inadequacy. They feel as though they are speaking a common language—whether the dialect of baths, bedtime, dressing or school meetings, car pool or breakfasts—but with a foreign accent. Their versions of the task are perceived as "less than" in addition to being "different." Success involves effort and some level of short-term discomfort from both partners. Until the change feels natural, accommodations have to be made, methods changed, and standards realigned. For most women, as an alternative to doing *everything,* doing things *differently* becomes a welcome transformation. As with partner dancing, a person can't step forward unless his partner steps back. I've found that exclusive domains help both partners move away from the extremes of over- or underinvolvement, and toward each other.

Backing Off—Less Emotional Monitoring

It's not often that you ponder the merits of your driveway, but you do once your child learns how to ride a two-wheeler. Back and forth, back and forth my daughter rode, the summer she was seven. Fairly long and fairly straight, our driveway is safe, but not long enough. Walking down to get the mail, I could see that just as she worked up some speed it was time to turn around. One hot day that summer, she was singing a song as she rode, back and forth, back and forth, her brow furrowed. The song went something like this: "I'm as afraid as a 'fraidy cat."

Coming in for a snack, she announced that she was going on an adventure. Grabbing a backpack, she stuffed in a hat, a book, and a bottle of water. The screen door slammed, resolutely, on her way out. And yet, twenty-five minutes later, she was still riding up and down the driveway, singing "I'm as brave as a great big lion" as she rode away from the house, and "I'm as afraid as a 'fraidy cat" on her way back.

The issue clearly wasn't just the length of the driveway. She wanted, and didn't want, and really wanted to move beyond the circle of home. Her backpack ready, her sights on the country road outside our fence, she longed to go. When she wasn't also longing to stay. We heard the bike fall onto the ground and in she came, this time in tears. Her mother leaned down and asked, "What do you need to do it?" Mid-blubber, our daughter looked up, surprised and hopeful, and said, "Do you think you could ride with me, just as far as the cow barn?"

So Katharine got on her bike and they rode down the road, cutting in on the dirt road next to the barn. When that doglegged back toward the stream, Katharine gave our daughter a kiss and turned toward home. I remember when she got back, Katharine and I shared a little laugh, relieved and pleased that our sweet child had been able to cross this stormy threshold, so clearly important to her. I should also note, though, that an hour and fifteen minutes later, when she still wasn't back, her mom and I did share a few less cheerful, more nervous moments. We managed—I hope—an air of calm confidence when our daughter did walk through the door, a triumphant smile on her face. It turns out the threshold was a bit stormy for the couple of adult 'fraidy cats as well.

Remember what a relief it was when your toddler was first able to tell you where it hurt when they were ill? When they're babies, we sometimes feel like cryptologists, looking for various clues—Do they have a fever? Are they pulling on their ears? Are they flushed?—to crack the code of how they're feeling. Still, our instincts became well honed. We learned to recognize the signs: variations in how they looked, sounded, or behaved, to determine when something was up. Such instincts are important and can continue to serve us well throughout our children's early years. In terms of your child's emotional life, and their soul fevers, those parental instincts are more important than words.

QUITE SIMPLY:

Don't talk too much to kids nine or younger about their feelings.

Many of us parents take our children's "emotional temperature" several times a day. We monitor their feelings, asking them to describe those feelings, to express them, to talk about them. We expect our children to have a complex awareness of their own emotions, with the insight and vocabulary to convey that awareness. While our intentions are well-meaning—"Honey, do you think your anger at your sister might also be a little jealousy? Can you tell her how you feel inside?"—this emotional monitoring has an unexpected effect. It rushes kids along, pushing them into a premature adolescence.

Children under nine certainly have feelings, but much of the time those feelings are unconscious, undifferentiated. In any kind of conflict or upset, if asked how they feel, most kids will say, very honestly, "Bad." They feel bad. To dissect and parse that, to push and push, imagining that they are hiding a much more subtle and nuanced feeling or reply, is invasive. It is also usually unproductive, except perhaps in making a child nervous. While young children have feelings, they only slowly become aware of them. Until the age of ten or so, their emotional consciousness and vocabulary are too premature to stand up to what we ask of them in our emotional monitoring and hovering.

Thanks in part to the pioneering work of Howard Gardner, Daniel Goleman, and others, our view of what constitutes intelligence has expanded in the past few decades to include emotional intelligence. Clearly a person's success and happiness in life depend on more than their penmanship, their mastery of foreign languages, or their ability to plot complex algorithms. What makes a huge difference in whether a person will achieve their goals and connect with others is a set of skills, insights, and abilities that Goleman termed "emotional intelligence." Emotional intelligence includes a self-awareness that allows one to recognize and manage one's moods, and to motivate oneself toward a goal. It involves feeling empathy toward others, being aware of their feelings, and being able to relate to others through interaction, conflict resolution, and negotiations.

As we mature, we certainly become more cognizant of how people with high emotional intelligence stand out—in business and personal relations, and even in mundane, everyday transactions. How delightful it is to meet someone who smiles at you, and offers their help with a genuine sense of caring. How frequently we realize that a conflict could have been avoided had we been more aware of another's feelings, or more in control of our own.

In our hopes and our dreams for our children, emotional intelligence should probably elbow out that football scholarship, or the viola concert tour, even the stellar report card. Emotional intelligence would serve them every day, and in every social setting they encounter as an adult. A GPS system of the heart, emotional intelligence is what we strive for in our own lives, and what we want for our children.

Yet emotional intelligence can't be bought or rushed. It develops with the slow emergence of identity, and the gradual accumulation of life experiences. When we push a young child toward an awareness they don't yet have, we transpose our own emotions, and our own voice, on theirs. We overwhelm them. For the first nine or ten years children learn mainly through imitation. Your emotions, and the way that you manage them, is the model they "imprint," more than what you say or instruct about emotions.

One way to back off from parental overinvolvement is to allow a child more leeway and privacy with their own feelings. By imposing our emotions on them less, we allow our children to develop their own emotions, and their awareness of them. Rather than taking their emotional temperature frequently with probing questions, we can allow our instincts to guide us more when they are quite young. We can be available, and willing, to listen. Follow their lead as to what and how much they want to express. Trust that our instincts will tell us when there is much more involved emotionally than they are able or willing to say. Usually, your consistent willingness to listen is what they need. It offers both the help and the trust they need to *feel* their emotions, and to slowly become aware of them. To begin to recognize them. As a part of themselves. The selves they are slowly (with freedom and grace) becoming.

When your children are young, let the world of *doing* be their domain. There was no real help for Sophia's dilemma except to let the lion leave the 'fraidy cat behind on the driveway. That bike had to be ridden; words would not have helped. Often when young kids feel emotional about something—when they're angry or hurt or sad—they need to put it right by doing. They need to have a hug or give one, to dig a hole or find the dog, they need to draw a picture with a lot of green in it, or make something. They need to work it out by doing. If they need to talk, it helps to know you will listen. They might need to throw something (hopefully not at their sister), to throw it again and maybe again until they've made a game where one bounce is a win but two means you've fallen into molten lava. They need to engage in the world, to put the feeling to right in some physical way. And with that, sometimes, they may need a bit of help.

Backing Off—Into Sleep

Is there a standardized test for unexpected, remarkable moments? A ratio, a guideline of how many ordinary moments in a day should shimmer and stand apart? A number that we are allotted, depending on the age or the height or the birthday of each child? Look at your daughter's eyes, astonished and joyful, as she sees the pale blue robin's eggs in the nest she's found. Or your three-year-old son, as bright and bold as the summer sun, who seems determined to greet absolutely everyone he passes on a crowded beach. Thankfully, there is no way to quantify these moments, no graph to plot their frequency, quality, or duration. No way to compare or qualify them.

QUITE SIMPLY:

The heart of being a parent—the joy of it—is still unpredictable. Absolutely remarkable and unexpected.

When Annmarie's mother was raising children, "parenthood" was not yet a "science." It had not yet been studied from every angle, every possible academic lens, nor was it the subject of countless books and theories. "Parenting" was not the most crowded shelf at the bookstore; before Benjamin Spock, there were no parenting gurus. Annmarie's mother probably knew how Annmarie compared to her brother as a baby, but she wouldn't have been able to say that at eighteen months Annmarie fell into the 90th percentile for height and the 95th percentile for weight compared with all babies her age.

For better or worse, ours is an era of conscious—some might say hyperconscious—parenting. Of course it is helpful to know when children should reach developmental milestones; guidelines are important in determining when a child might need help or intervention. But too often anxiety is the result of all of the graphing and comparing we do, the percentages, benchmarks, standards, and criteria that now influence our view of our children. As a parent, Annmarie may have more information than her mother did, but does she enjoy, or worry about, her children more as a result? For all of the measures we now have at our fingertips, by and large children defy them by being both more "normal" and more extraordinary than any scientific measure, or means of quantifying them.

If one image of overinvolvement is the helicopter or hovering parent, another image—one that occurs to me often—is that of a parent looking at their child through a magnifying glass. Armed with this study or that, this criterion for achievement or that measure of normalcy or "giftedness," we monitor their behavior closely. But the magnifying lens is not helpful; its view is too close to be pretty, or even representative of the child.

My last suggestion for backing off from overinvolvement is a simple one. I've seen it make a profound difference, however, in some parents' attitudes, and the emotional climate of their parenting. It is a meditation, a mental exercise for the end of the day that will take just a minute or two. Before falling into sleep, remember the ordinary moments of the day, the moments with your children that meant something to you. This simple exercise is like a spiritual corrective lens. In your vision of your kids, it helps restore the prominence of "who they are" over "what they need to do" or "what they need to work on."

Review the images; revisit the funny yet strangely insightful thing your daughter said, the gesture your son made that surprised you. Think about how your little one climbed up on the bench by the window at three o'clock, somehow sensing that her sister's bus would arrive soon. Remember how your twins looked at the park; the newly minted freckles on their cheeks; their pride in mastering the jungle gym rings. Remember the way your daughter looked minutes ago when you checked on her: horizontal on the bed with her arm flung back over her head, as though she had tried to outrun sleep. Relive those moments, and give them their due. Let the images rise to the surface of your day. Let them fill the emotional waters that will lull you, in waves of appreciation and wonder, into sleep.

Imagine . . .

- feeling calmer, safer, and less anxious as a parent.
- maintaining your emotional well-being as a goal, and taking steps to reduce your exposure to media that profit from fear and sensationalism.
- your child's early years, without television.
- how engagement and connection—rather than passive "entertainment"—will feed your child's imagination, enrich their play.
- your child *not* being exposed to thousands of commercials and violent TV shows while they are young.
- your child not being privy to, or involved in, adult issues and problems.
- the sense of calm increasing in your home.
- that by emphasizing connection and increasing the regularity of daily life while your child is young, you are building a "base camp" of security that will serve them into adulthood.
- that you increase your chances of being heard when you talk less.
- being able to back off overinvolvement as your partner increases their involvement in the daily tasks of parenting; or
- stepping up and becoming more involved, so your partner can experience and project more ease as a parent.
- what is said at home becoming kinder, truer, and more necessary.
- feeding your dreams with a rich appreciation of the present.

EPILOGUE

Simplicity Parenting to Go

When I first met Carla, there was great mistrust in her eyes. I had come for a visit, unexpectedly, and as her mother introduced us, Carla turned a steely gaze my way. She was sitting on the floor, a large pile of wrapping paper and shiny fabric in a pile next to her. As we chatted I could see that this bright almost-six-year-old was very much in control of the home. Just what, her eyes demanded, was I doing there, anyway?

Carla's mother, Michelle, had come to see me a week or so before, to share her concerns about Carla's behavior. Michelle and Clark Adams were expecting a baby in a few months, and Carla had been acting out at home, school, and day care. "I know this is very common," Michelle had said. "Carla is not at all happy about the baby. But her behavior, on top of all that we have going on right now, is more than we can take!" She explained that Carla had recently become quite aggressive—hitting and kicking—and they were concerned about how she might be with the baby. "Carla has a flair for the dramatic," Michelle had said, "and we're trying our best to support that, while doing everything we can to reassure her of our love." Michelle felt they needed help—"and quickly!"—to get Carla excited about the baby.

From our conversation, I could see that Michelle and her husband really did lead busy, stressful lives. Both had demanding jobs, and Clark, as the manager of a professional sports team, had work hours that were anything but regular. Neither parent had family in the area, and their friends were more connected to work than the neighborhood or community. Michelle and Clark were short on time, and media "babysitters" were often used to bridge the gaps, but there was no end to their love for their daughter. In fact, they had taken years to consider another child because they both harbored doubts they could possibly love anyone as much as they did Carla. These two were doing their best, but generally flying without any net of connection or support. And Carla was smart enough to see that her already unpredictable time with her parents was headed for a reduction. With new and more frequent episodes of naughtiness she was testing the age-old theory: Isn't *any* kind of attention better than none?

"This is a child who knows her own mind!" Michelle had said when we met. I remember that expression clearly, because it didn't begin to explain the controlling behavior she went on to describe. Carla had sworn off all but her three favorite foods: bread, pasta, and apples. ("Luckily, I've learned to be creative with those," Michelle said.) There were many things Carla insisted on: her meals had to be on a certain Wonder Woman place mat, her pink sweater with the appliquéd pony was the only sweater that would do, and she was very particular about how she was driven to places. She hated when her parents varied from their standard routes. She had recently made an "off-limits" corner of her bedroom. Nobody was allowed to touch anything in that area. ("I think she's anxious about the baby getting into her things.") Carla would not go to bed until she felt "really tired," and that magic moment seemed to vary nightly. ("I'm the same way," Michelle reported. "I can't sleep until I'm dog-tired.")

Just before my visit—perhaps because of it—Michelle had given Carla a beautiful gown made of yellow and blue satin. "It's Beauty's dress," Michelle explained as she picked it up to show me, "from *Beauty and the Beast.*" The dress was lovely, but Carla could not be coaxed to try it on. She left it on the floor and insisted that she be the one to give me a tour of the house.

Carla's room looked like the dressing room for a national theater company after opening night. There were mounds of costumes and accessories everywhere, a jumble of sequined shoes and feather boas strewn on top of furniture and wadded among heaps of toys and books. When I asked her where her "off-limits" area was, she pointed vaguely to a corner of the room. It wasn't very easy to distinguish, I told her; wasn't that dangerous for those who wandered into it by mistake? She looked at me quizzically, amused but surprised. "No, silly! I know where it is . . . and besides, I can change it whenever I want!"

The baby's room was jam-packed, too, but the clutter was of a different sort. Unopened boxes and shopping bags were stacked up the walls, and in the center, covered in plastic, was a brand-new crib.

Michelle's plan was to work until a week before her due date ("I should be fine; Carla was late . . .") and use that week to get the room ready. After the baby was born she would take off her allotted six weeks and then go back to work; Carla's day care would accept the baby. It could work. Time was tight—it always was—but both Michelle and Clark felt that things could possibly fall into place if only they could "get Carla excited about this baby, too."

If only. If only you had seen Carla's suspicious appraisal of me, you would understand my concerns at the outset of this work. How much would this family really commit to change, if their sights were limited to their immediate dilemma? Carla and her parents shared a deadline—the baby's birth—but had very different goals to accomplish by then. Michelle and Clark wanted to please and appease Carla; Carla wanted (it may sound crazy, but she was well on her way) to gain total control of the home. The clock was ticking.

When I think back to this family I remember my doubts. If the Beauty dress had limited appeal to Carla, I clearly had less. And Michelle and Clark seemed less interested in the work than in squeezing it in before their first Lamaze class. I was not hopeful. Yet I'm telling the Adamses' story because it was ultimately very moving—for them and for me—and illustrative of a number of things. There is no "ideal candidate" for this work; no prerequisites or credentials are required. Any family can bring fresh inspiration and attention into their daily lives. And despite my doubts, the Adamses did exactly that. Any family can, by limiting distractions, take a new measure of what is important to them. The Adamses' illustrated what is possibly the most important thing I've realized about this process: When a family simplifies, what happens is usually more far-reaching and powerful than what they imagined when they started.

Having read to this point, you know that simplification is not a quick fix. But as Carla showed me around, I realized that her family needed to move quickly. They needed to make some space—not only in their cluttered home and busy lives—but also in their hearts. To make room for one another, and to carve out a center in their family, from which they could begin to look forward together. Michelle and Clark wanted Carla to be more excited, yet what seemed lacking in their home was harmony, not excitement. I also felt that Carla was not alone in her anxiety about this baby; she was just the dramatic flag bearer for everyone's concern. Before they could move forward, the Adamses' needed to take a big step back to pick up some things they had dispensed with along the way. Only then could they dream this baby into existence before its arrival.

This was a tall order. I decided to ignore the impending birth date as a deadline but use it as a hinge. Would Michelle and Clark agree to fully commit to the process, to make perhaps more and faster changes than I might otherwise suggest, at least until the baby was born?

My first request was for Michelle and Clark to stop giving Carla presents (a sign of their anxiousness) as we began to simplify the clutter in the house. All but one or two of Carla's costumes were removed to a hanging rack in the attic. This would serve as a lending library so she could periodically discover each dress anew. Her room seemed much more spacious after it was dramatically decluttered. There was a special area with the room's long-buried comfy chair, a wool rug, and a lamp, which Carla instantly proclaimed "Carla's corner." It seemed to me this was the general area that had been off-limits, but we didn't press the point.

As part of this process, Michelle and Clark set up the baby's room, but they backed away from the instant clutter they had gathered and planned for the room. Instead of multiple mobiles, pictures, and stuffed animals, they decided on a simpler but welcoming look: the crib and a changing table, and two rockers, with a smaller one for Carla. Having just done the work of simplifying Carla's room, neither parent had any desire to overload the baby's room. They both felt excited about this new aesthetic—a more spacious and less cluttered look—and about expanding it throughout the home. They felt they had discovered it, and earned it, together.

We moved on to our primary focus: increasing the rhythm and consistency of daily life. Clark, who was generally a walking force field, was willing—just barely at first—to turn off his cellphones and pager when he was home. A family dinnertime was set and he agreed to make it home for dinner at least four times a week, marking those nights on the calendar. Sometimes Michelle could just manage picking up takeout in time for dinner, and sometimes Clark had to work afterward, but a groove was slowly being dug in the procession of days. Dinner was not pasta and applesauce, as you might think, given Carla's diet. No, dinner was a well-balanced meal, and they all ate it—even (after a few days of fussing) Carla. Small rituals were established—bath, reading, talking about the day and what might happen tomorrow—as a platform was built toward a set bedtime.

What was Carla gaining with all of these changes, you might ask? She had less "stuff," less power, and it looked like her parents were still going to have "that baby" (as she liked to say). She had to set the table each night and go to bed at a regular time. Her television viewing was being severely curtailed, and her menu horribly expanded. Carla was suspicious; wasn't she in charge here? She definitely felt the shift. But the new rituals didn't go away, and not a lot of fuss was made of them. In their regularity ("Carla, time to set the table!") they seemed, at least, reliable. What did she gain? This is the point when I'd love to pull a rabbit out of my hat, but the answer is less surprising, though still magical. She gained time and connection, security and ease.

When Michelle and Clark decluttered the house, they reclaimed the dining room table. It had become a depository for all manner of things: papers, junk mail, little toys, old golf scorecards, misplaced piano books. I suggested that Michelle make this table not a workbench, but a place for building. What exactly they would build remained to be seen. But what they needed were things that lasted. So often in the rush of days, home becomes a sort of way station, with people coming in and out, meals on the run, and schedules in a state of flux. Even with the best of intentions, when busyness rules the day, life can seem hurried and transient. Consistency in the home sends down roots, and the family begins to anchor their days. But with no sense of inner calm, even consistent rituals can be treated like items on a checklist, instead of invitations to slow down. Both Michelle and Clark were constantly in motion, and Carla was having her own troubles with stillness and focus. Michelle and I talked about a change, one that might begin at the old dining room table.

It took a while to get started. It felt strange at first: awkward and sometimes pointless. But Michelle's simple goal was to commit to time each day with Carla, and for them to make something together. They began with clay. Paints. One day they started a "get more mail" campaign, with each working on postcards to friends and relatives. They got a beeswax candle for the table and experimented with relaxing background music. Michelle sometimes brought something—a picture, poem, or joke—to share before they started. Carla opened up, talking about school and friends. Before too long they hit their stride, with a project that seemed to flow directly from their hearts and needs at the time. Michelle hauled out the boxes of photos from the office closet, and together they made three beautiful family albums, with one exclusively of Carla's baby years. It took weeks, and it brought back so many memories, so many funny stories and forgotten moments. (Even of stories from her birth, Carla would claim in the retelling, "Oh yeah! I think I really do remember that too, Mama!")

The building that happened at that table—which turned out to be relationship building—was perhaps the hardest work of the process for Michelle. I have to think Carla knew that on some level. Seeing her mother sitting quietly opposite her, and not as a body in motion on her way to another room, sharpened Carla's attention from the very beginning. Something was up. It may have taken a while for that something to feel natural, but believe me, it did. It began to feel natural *and* essential. Michelle and Carla slid into each other's company, discovering with surprise and delight that they could build something lasting. Not just for the photo album, but an ease with each other. A trust that would carry them forward.

At first Clark had been relieved when Michelle took on this part of the process. It was something that he was happy not to be involved in. But as he saw what was happening—how Carla and her mom looked forward to this time—he felt increasingly outside a circle he wanted to join. He had been putting Carla on the bus each day, but since his and Carla's schedules coincided in the morning, he decided to drive her instead. This seemed like a windfall to Carla. "Guess what?" Carla asked her mom. "Dad is really funny in the morning!" I suggested Clark assume responsibility for piano practice, too, because I knew he played. "But Carla hates practicing the piano! I hated practicing, too." There it was. A perfect opportunity for them to find their way in, and out, of the piano-playing knot together. And they did. They allowed repetition, quiet insistence, and some necessary silliness to carry them through the beginning until practicing became a pattern and playing piano became something Carla could do and be proud of. Until they had something, together.

Before long, Michelle and Clark were on their own path. Carla's little brother, Alex, arrived six months after our work began. Was Carla excited? That isn't what would strike you first about her. I think you, as her parents and teachers did, would notice how much calmer she was. She had really settled down in her behavior. She was doing well at school, had a number of interests, and she was happier than she had been since we met.

I remember her steely gaze that first day, and I would imagine there was a bit of suspicion in her eyes when she first met Alex, too. But for different reasons. She was no longer in control of the house, but her family had a new closeness she would have to learn to share with him.

Simplification is a process; a pebble dropped in the waters of a family's daily life. It inspires changes that expand throughout the home, touching each member of the family and their relationships. Let's look at some of those ripples of change, and how a family finds its own depth, its new equilibrium. In two decades of helping families with this work, I've been fortunate to gain a wide and long perspective. I've kept in touch with, and heard back from families with kids of all ages, on three different continents. Often I've seen that the work we did together was just the beginning, a small part of the overall transformation they went on to achieve.

It takes time to reduce, to say "no thanks" and mean it, to the distractions and excesses that have overwhelmed our daily lives. And changing a family's direction isn't easy, especially when life feels like a cyclone. Yet perhaps the strongest force on earth can be harnessed for this work: a parent's love for their children. The process of simplification—a shifting of a family's core axis—is usually driven by a parent's simple desire to protect the ease and wonder of their child's early years. I've seen the wisdom of starting small, of beginning with the possible, relishing the results, and allowing success to then fuel the process. I've found that what works best is to simplify the child's life first: to declutter their overloaded rooms, diets, and schedules, and to increase the rhythm and regularity of the home.

There is a period of adjustment to a more rhythmic, less frenzied lifestyle, which will be longer the older your kids are. Children under four or five probably won't even register the changes consciously, though you'll notice a difference—a lightening and ease—in their play, moods, and sleep. Teenagers will resist the changes—without a doubt—out of sheer developmental necessity, if nothing else. Your quiet unwillingness to back down will help ease this transition toward a new and usually appreciated family norm.

As distractions fall away, a sense of ease takes hold and expands. There's more time for connection, room for contemplation and play. Boredom, once feared and banished from the home, will be allowed in again, appreciated for how often it precedes inspiration. Contrary to what you might think, regularity is more liberating than "boring" to most children. Rituals that can be counted on throughout the day and week act as powerful affirmations. For teenagers rhythms provide a steady, reassuring counterweight to the volatility and strong emotions that define the territory of adolescence. Rituals loosen a younger child's grip, relaxing their need to control small and seemingly random aspects of their day. Remember Carla's place mat, without which there could be no eating? As the family's dinners became more regular, and as Carla assumed the mantle of table setting, she was swept up in something bigger than her need for control. She quietly dispensed with the place mat, leaving it shoved in the back of a drawer. Wonder Woman's power had been eclipsed.

Such islands of consistency assure a child that all is right with the world, freeing them to relax into their play and their imaginations. Time, which can seem like an unpredictable tyrant, pulling and pushing a child through the day, is tamed and tied down with family dinners, reading before bed, with chores and unscheduled play, and the "compass kisses" (north, south, east, and west) bestowed before they head out the door. Only with regularity can the joy of the unexpected and the luxury of the unplanned find a place in the home, too.

Parents are often surprised by the power of less as it relates to everyday choices. We live in a country and era that equate "choice" with "freedom." Yet for young children, "freedom of choice" about every small detail in their day—everything they eat, wear, or do—can be a paralyzing burden. You've seen this at work; I recently did at the community pool. A dad with a suitcase on wheels attached to the back of his stroller found a few free lounge chairs. "Here, boys? Or do you wanna sit here? Sun or shade?" Settling in with his twins (who looked to be about four years old), he started to unpack, keeping up a steady stream of questions. "Nathan, Liam, do you boys want to swim now, or eat a snack? Swim? Okay, Nathan, now look at this . . . What do you want to swim with? The rubber shark, the missiles, or the mask? Snack, Liam? Crackers, grapes, or cheese? Liam, buddy, do you want your crackers on a napkin, or do you want a little bag you can walk around with? Nathan, you can swim while Liam eats, or wait, Liam, will you swim with Nathan and have a snack after? Your mom packed some juice but they have tea here, too. How long do you boys want to stay? Should we swim for an hour, maybe, and go home for your nap?" My unspoken question was whether these little guys would ever manage to get wet. This is a fairly extreme example, I'll grant you. But in general, we offer our children more choices than they need, or want.

As choices are reduced, pressure is lifted. A child has the time and freedom to have their own thoughts. They can find the ease to slowly forge an identity, an identity that is more than the sum of their choices, preferences, or purchases. More than a "brand identity."

Imagine your own version of "choice overload." Perhaps you are trying to find a health plan, or shopping for a car; maybe you've stopped to rent a movie on the way home from errands. The options are dizzying. Scan up and down the aisles, and suddenly a nice idea seems like an overwhelming task. At that moment—glancing back at the exit, considering an escape—success doesn't seem too likely, either. What if, ironically, the movie that would really hit the spot isn't at the Super-Mega Movie Store? Just the sight of so many movies raises your expectations. What's the point of watching a movie if it isn't one of the best? And with so many to choose from, how would you find it? How could you possibly know that you've made the right choice? And at this rate, what if you're still in the middle of the store, glued to this spot, at closing time?

Movie stores may not plunge you into a black hole of Woody Allen–esque indecision. But I trust you can relate in some fashion to my description, since "choice overload" is increasingly a part of our daily lives. Several things happen when you have too much stuff and too many options: Decisions are more difficult, and expectations rise. If I have all of this, what *else* might I have? Or, more commonly, "What's next?" Unwittingly we are passing on this surfeit of choices—and its consequences—to our children. What's next?

Let's back up a moment. In simplifying we are trying to move away from excess and toward balance. Sadly, many children need more—not less—to lead healthy and comfortable lives. There is nothing uplifting or expansive about hunger. "The power of less" is meaningless for those in real need, for a child whose refrigerator is empty. No, simplification is for those of us whose lives are characterized less by need than by want. It's not just the affluent: Very often children who are overwhelmed by material possessions and choices come from decidedly middle-class homes. And sometimes parents of relatively modest means still try to shower their kids with largesse and a sense of limitless options. But a refrigerator that is always crammed with everything imaginable is, ironically, not satisfying. It usually sets you dreaming about the one or two things that may not be in there.

Only with less can a child learn what it is that they do like, and what speaks to them. When their expectations are always met—even anticipated—their will is left flaccid and weak. I know that crammed refrigerator may sound lovely; it is a rare image for most of us ("Whose turn was it to go to market anyways?"). But when a child grows up with a metaphorical refrigerator that is always overflowing, the results, in terms of their happiness *and* their behavior, are rarely lovely.

What happens then, as we continue to deliver "everything their hearts desire"? For one thing, like well-exercised muscles, their little hearts keep desiring. But also, as all of this largesse pours in the front door, anticipation quietly slips out the back. It is one of the first victims of overload. There's no room for anticipation when expectations are always met. The possibility of happy surprises? That will tiptoe out the back, too. Sometimes parents only notice it's gone when their six-year-old greets each new thing with a kind of world-weary ennui.

When it isn't governed by the drumbeat of "More!" your home will be a calmer place. It will be a testament to "Enough." But surely "enough" is disappointing, and just plain boring compared to the abundance of "More"? The question is fair, and it's the most common reaction parents have as they ponder a mountain of toys they need to reduce to a molehill of beloved keepers. Won't the kids be devastated? Generally, no. With fewer choices, there is freedom to appreciate things—and one another—more deeply.

I sometimes think of simplification as a powerful anti-inflammatory for families. Inflammation is our body's "red alert," its way of responding to harmful stimuli or irritants. It can be acute, or low level and chronic, an imbalance that begins to seem "normal." So often I've seen how simplification can break the cycle of inflammation—the itch for "More," and craving for greater and greater stimulation—that threatens to overwhelm a family's "system."

A mother emailed me about her eleven-year-old boy: "Between his iPod, computer and Game Boy, there isn't a moment of the day now when Todd isn't 'plugged in' now. I've begun leaving him little notes because he always has some sort of earplugs in. Maybe it's just the way things are? I see the same thing all over, with all sorts of kids. But I just can't stop wondering if my days of talking to Todd are pretty much over."

What an excellent example of inflammation. This mom was recounting a change that had happened gradually. Looking around, she saw plenty of examples of "plugged-in kids," almost enough to convince her that what she was experiencing was "normal." Yet it didn't feel right. It pained her to be leaving notes for a son she no longer talked to, and who no longer talked to her. What she felt was an imbalance. An imbalance that could worsen if left unattended, its effects spreading systemically, throughout the family. Part of the process of simplification for Todd's family was to increase time spent together, to make Todd's access to media and electronics privilege-based rather than limitless, and to dramatically unplug as a family.

The process of simplification removes some of the major stressors of daily life, reducing swollen expectations and sensory irritants. It closes down the "red alert" or triage approach to daily life, so parents can restore a more natural balance, one where the "everyday" has a place, and time expands. Where distractions don't overwhelm connection, and the rituals we share are small promises made and kept, every day.

What I have seen, clearly and often, is that a parent's love for their children inspires the first difficult changes of simplification. Excess is removed, and limits are imposed to protect the space and grace of childhood years. What Michelle and Clark noticed is that those limits began to carve a path, not just for Carla, but for the whole family. This is another paradox of the extraordinary power of less. Limits may define that path at first, and provide direction where none existed. But not for long: The path becomes something else, something of your own making, something you have a stake in.

When you act to limit what you *don't* want for your family, you clarify what you really *do* need, what is important to you. Your values clarify. Simplification is a path of self-definition for the family.

It is quieter when the insistent noise of popular culture, competition, and consumerism are turned down several notches. Just as a singer has to shut out ambient noises to hear their own voice, simplification allows a family to "tune in" to their values, to what works for them, what defines them. The voice that can be heard, as the noise diminishes, is your own, your own true voice as a parent. With distractions increasingly in the background, what develops is a foreground, a center. A family center emerges and strengthens.

"Mom, the girl who sits next to me in class, Marietta, is so stupid. Yesterday, she . . ." "We don't use the word *stupid* in our family." "But everyone uses the word *stupid.* It's just a word!" "Some people do, and some don't; but we don't. When you grow up and have a family, you can decide whether your family will or not."

As clutter and overwhelm find their way out the door and a less frenetic pace takes hold, your parenting will become less inflamed, too. Greater consistency gives parents the space and grace that we need, too. The family center that is built with consistency—what we do and don't do, how we behave, and the connection we have, together—helps parents become more centered in their discipline. It builds a trust that makes a child a willing "disciple," and the parent worthy of being followed. As Michelle and Clark lost their tentativeness with Carla, as their behavior and expectations of her became more consistent, Carla lost a lot of her nervousness and controlling behaviors. It seems Carla didn't really want to coparent herself; she wanted parents. When Michelle and Clark provided more direction, Carla was able to hop back into the passenger seat, where she belonged.

There's more to the subject of discipline than I was able to cover in this book. But the simple truth is this: More effective discipline is invariably an outgrowth of the simplification process. I worked further with Michelle and Clark to shift the balance of their communication with Carla from a vast majority of requests with a few instructions to mainly straightforward instructions with a few requests. When everything is a request, you have another form of verbal clutter: "Taylor, howya doing? Would you like to get in the car now? What do you think? Can you buckle up that seat belt? Will you shut the door? Sweetie, is that you throwing those toys up to the front? Would you please stop?" Directions can and should be direct. "Taylor, time to get in the car and buckle up. Shut that door, please." "I can't drive with distractions. We don't throw anything while the car is in motion." Requests may seem like "gentler" forms of communication, but with so many of them they're very easy to ignore, and their uniformity make it hard for a child to know what's really important. They invite response, but not really, so the overall effect is one of background noise. "So Ben, what do you think? Wanna get ready for bed now? Brush your teeth, buddy, okay?" "Bedtime, Ben. You know what to do." By simplifying the requests you make of your child—asking fewer, but meaning those more—you can begin to "stand inside" each one.

Our instincts strengthen with regular moments of connection with our kids; we're more responsive, less reactive. We can become a better judge of when there is cause for concern. Our hair trigger relaxes. We can hear about something that happened at school—hear the whole story—without reaching to dial the teacher's home number (if it isn't already programmed into speed dial). And when kids know that you won't go off like fireworks at the slightest thing they mention, they ease up as well. They feel free to talk more.

The effects of simplification extend beyond the parent-child relationship. I'm no longer surprised when a dad who may have begun the process reluctantly for his kids tells me that it has had a profound effect on his marriage, and his intimacy with his wife. When a family slows down, and dramatically limits their distractions and clutter, it won't just be the kids' attention that deepens. With less emphasis on stuff and speed, and more consistent opportunities for connection, Dad may very well catch Mom's eye across the table. When such filters as "Is it true?" Is it kind? Is it necessary?" are being practiced, more respect is felt all around. Simplification offers a new way forward for parents; it aligns their daily lives with the dreams they originally held for their family. Before things got so crazy.

Having children is supposed to be the ultimate shared journey, isn't it? But a baby's arrival has all of the subtlety of an earthquake. Very often a couple will only look up several years (and perhaps another baby) later to see how altered their relationship has become. Adjustments have been made, contortions have been adopted, almost all for the sake of the baby; not for each other, or the marriage. Simplification holds the promise of a shared journey. Not a week in Paris, no. This is a longer path, but one with benefits that expand and multiply. And as a midcourse correction for the family, it can be something you and your spouse both embrace and commit to. Couples have reported that through the unexpected triumphs of this process, they regain a mutual sense of purpose and accomplishment. They have feelings that remind them of the emotional wellspring they shared in the delivery room. Feelings they may not have experienced much since.

Does simplification mean that as a parent, all of your decisions will be made? Your way always clear, your instructions always adhered to? To put it simply: no. But as you define the center of your family you will be far less reactive. You won't be buffeted as much, and blown off course by every new distraction that presents itself. You'll recognize the societal pressures of "More! Faster! Earlier!" as a centrifugal force that may threaten, but will no longer pull your family apart. Having done the hard work of simplifying, you'll see when "must-have" things or activities are really just new variations of "More!," bound to be quickly forgotten or discarded. When your child's best self is more frequently at home, you'll have no trouble protecting their time. You'll instinctively guard the leisure that unfurrows their brow and allows them to follow their curiosity.

After all, they do the same for you all of the time. What better reminder do we have than our kids of our own best selves, our less stressed and more carefree selves? In their silliness we see the echo of the way we used to be: when we were kids, yes, but also before we had kids, or even two weeks ago, before all of the stress of these year-end corporate meetings. Their joy, their infectious enthusiasm, their sense of "mission" as the poor dog is dressed in boxer shorts, cannot help but cajole you, and beckon you, to lighten up. My point is this: Rescue their childhood from stress, and they will inevitably, remarkably, day by day, rescue you right back.

Life will remain unpredictable after you simplify, of course. "Things happen," as they say. And when you have kids, "things happen" with regularity (and truly remarkable variety). But "things" become far less threatening when viewed from a stable center. The path simplification provides is one that you will move off of on occasion, and will need to find your way back to. But because it's a path that defines and strengthens who you are together, it allows for bends and corrections. What your family can be without the centrifugal force of distractions and excess becomes internalized. It's a feeling you will come to recognize, treasure, and protect. A center that holds.

Is there a step in the process of simplification that seems absolutely doable, something you know is possible now, in your own home? This is your starting point, the trailhead of your path toward the larger changes you envision. Once you have a clear image of this task—what you need to do and what your daily life will look like when it is done—get started. Step into that picture. . . . Begin.

ACKNOWLEDGMENTS

I would like to warmly thank my colleagues at Antioch University New England and, in particular, Torin Finser and Peter Eppig for their unfailing support. To Lisa M. Ross for her inspiring talents and dedication to this book. To Marnie Cochran for her gentle but sure hand in editing.

Also to the many key members of the communities with whom I consult. It is because of their enthusiastic coordinating efforts that this work continues to reach out into the world.

Finally, to my family, and, in particular, Almuth and Harry Kretz, my parents-in-law, for their quiet and unfaltering support.

— K.J.P.

Kim John Payne was delightful to work with—gracious during the process and appreciative of the results. Our collaboration was made all the more enjoyable due to a mutual sense that this book was blessed from the beginning. Marnie Cochran's consistent editorial support only furthered that impression. Inspirational to me were Waldorf teachers William and Andree Ward and their view of childhood's rich promise. Thank you to my husband, Jamie, for always listening and offering moral support; to Janet Byrne and Nancy Wiley for their early encouragement; to my parents, Walt and Anita; and most of all to my children, Adair and Jack, who broaden my view of life's possibilities daily.

— L.M.R.

NOTES

Introduction

1. David Elkind, *The Power of Play: Learning What Comes Naturally* (New York: Da Capo, 2007), ix.

Chapter One: Why Simplify?

1. Fred J. Aun, "Study: Kids Latching On to Tech at Earlier Ages," *E-Commerce Times*, June 6, 2007.
2. Craig Lambert, "Deep into Sleep," *Harvard Magazine*, July–August 2005.
3. Ibid.
4. Kim John Payne, M.Ed., and Bonnie River, M.Ed., "From Attention Deficit to Attention Priority: A Study of Attention Related Disorders in Waldorf Schools," *The Waldorf Research Bulletin*, Spring 2002.
5. Richard DeGrandpre, *Ritalin Nation* (New York: Norton, 1999).
6. Sharon Begley, *Train Your Mind, Change Your Brain* (New York: Ballantine Books, 2007).

Chapter Three: Environment

1. Elkind, *The Power of Play*, 15.
2. Howard P. Chudacoff, *Children at Play* (New York: New York University Press, 2007).
3. Juliet B. Schor, *Born to Buy* (New York: Scribner, 2004).
4. "Kids: a Powerful Market Force," BNET Business Network, http://findarticles.com/p/articles/mi_hb4704/is_200107/ai_n17263171.
5. Schor, *Born to Buy*, 25; David Futrelle, "Are Your Kids Normal About Money," *Money*, December 2005.
6. Mary Pipher, *The Shelter of Each Other* (New York: Putnam, 1996), 93.
7. Michel Marriott, "Gadget or Plaything, Let a Child Decide," *New York Times*, February 17, 2005.
8. Schor, *Born to Buy*, 56.
9. Marriott, "Gadget or Plaything."
10. Victoria J. Rideout, Elizabeth A. Vandewater, and Ellen A. Wartella, *Zero to*

Six: Electronic Media in the Lives of Infants, Toddlers, and Preschoolers (Menlo Park, Calif.: Henry J. Kaiser Family Foundation, 2003).

11. Schor, *Born to Buy,* 62.
12. Alix Spiegel, "Old-Fashioned Play Builds Serious Skills," National Public Radio, *Morning Edition,* February 21, 2008.
13. Richard Louv, *Last Child in the Woods* (Chapel Hill, N.C.: Algonquin, 2005) 178.
14. Robin Marantz Henig, "Taking Play Seriously," *New York Times Magazine,* February 17, 2008.
15. Victoria J. Rideout and Elizabeth Hamel, *The Media Family: Electronic Media in the Lives of Infants, Toddlers, Preschoolers and Their Parents* (Menlo Park, Calif.: Henry J. Kaiser Family Foundation, 2006).

Chapter Four: Rhythm

1. Nancy Gibbs, "The Magic of the Family Meal," *Time,* June 4, 2006.
2. Alex Cohen, "Michael Pollan: If You Can't Say It, Don't Eat It," National Public Radio, April 24, 2008.
3. Eric Schlosser, *Fast Food Nation* (Boston: Houghton Mifflin, 2001), 54.
4. Ibid.
5. Gibbs, "The Magic of the Family Meal."
6. Po Bronson, "Snooze or Lose," *New York,* October 8, 2007.
7. Ibid.

Chapter Five: Schedules

1. David A. Kinney, Janet S. Dunn, and Sandra L. Hofferth, "Family Strategies for Managing the Time Crunch," Center for the Ethnography of Everyday Life, September 5, 2000.
2. Claudia Wallis, "The Myth About Homework," *Time,* August 29, 2006.
3. Elkind, *The Power of Play,* ix.
4. Walter Kirn and Wendy Cole, "What Ever Happened to Play?" *Time,* April 30, 2001.
5. Katharine Rosman, "BlackBerry Orphans," *Wall Street Journal,* December 8, 2006.
6. Tim Arango, "Social Site's New Friends Are Athletes," *New York Times,* March 26, 2008.
7. Jeannine Stein, "Kicking It Up a Notch," *Los Angeles Times,* May 22, 2007.
8. Laura Hilgers, "Youth Sports Drawing More Than Ever," CNN.com, July 5, 2006.
9. Bill Pennington, "Doctors See a Big Rise in Injuries for Young Athletes," *New York Times,* February 22, 2005.
10. Frank Brady, "Children's Organized Sports: a Developmental Perspective," *Journal of Physical Education, Recreation & Dance* 75 (February 2004).

11. Janice Butcher, Koenraad J. Lindner, and David P. Johns, “Withdrawal from Competitive Youth Sport: A Retrospective Ten-Year Study,” *Journal of Sport Behavior* 25 (2002).
12. Josephson Institute, *What Are Your Children Learning? The Impact of High School Sports on the Values and Ethics of High School Athletes,* 2006.

Chapter Six: Filtering Out the Adult World

1. Robert Putnam, *Bowling Alone: The Collapse and Revival of American Community* (New York: Simon & Schuster, 2000), 222.
2. Victoria J. Rideout, Donald F. Roberts, and Ulla G. Foehr, *Generation M: Media in the Lives of 8–18 Year-Olds* (Menlo Park, Calif.: Henry Kaiser Family Foundation, 2005), 46.
3. Marie Evans Schmidt, David S. Bickham, Brandy E. King, Ronald G. Slaby, Amy C. Branner, and Michael Rich, Center on Media and Child Health, *The Effects of Electronic Media on Children Ages Zero to Six: A History of Research* (Menlo Park, Calif.: The Henry J. Kaiser Family Foundation, 2005), 1.
4. American Academy of Pediatrics, “Media Education Policy Statement,” *Pediatrics* 104 (1999), 341–43.
5. Christine Ollivier, “France Bans Broadcast of TV Shows for Babies,” Associated Press, August 20, 2008.
6. Dade Hayes, *Anytime Playdate: Inside the Preschool Entertainment Boom* (New York: Free Press, 2008), 56.
7. Alissa Quart, “Extreme Parenting,” *Atlantic Monthly,* July/August 2006.
8. Alice Park, “Baby Einsteins: Not So Smart After All,” *Time,* August 6, 2007.
9. Schmidt et al., *The Effects of Electronic Media on Children Ages Zero to Six,* 1.
10. Elizabeth A. Vandewater, Victoria J. Rideout, Ellen A. Wartella, Xuan Huang, June H. Lee, and Mi-suk Shim, “Digital Childhood: Electronic Media and Technology Use Among Infants, Toddlers, and Preschoolers,” *Pediatrics* 118 (May 2007).
11. Rideout, Roberts, and Foehr, *Generation M,* 23.
12. American Academy of Pediatrics, “Children, Adolescents, and Television,” *Pediatrics* 107 (February 2001), 423.
13. Robert Kubey and Mihaly Csikzentmihalyi, “Television Addiction Is No Mere Metaphor,” *Scientific American,* February 2002.
14. Victoria Clayton, “What’s to Blame for the Rise in ADHD?,” MSNBC, September 8, 2004.
15. Michael Gurian and Kathy Stevens, *The Mind of Boys: Saving Our Sons from Falling Behind in School and Life* (New York: Jossey-Bass, 2005), 112.
16. American Association of Pediatrics, “Joint Statement on the Impact of Entertainment Violence on Children,” July 26, 2000.
17. Dave Grossman and Gloria Degaetano, *Stop Teaching Our Kids to Kill : A Call to Action Against TV, Movie and Video Game Violence* (New York: Crown, 1999).

18. Nicholas Carnagey, Craig Anderson, and Brad Bushman, "The Effect of Video Game Violence on Physiological Desensitization to Real-life Violence," *Journal of Experimental Social Psychology* 43, July 2007, 489–96.
19. Daniel G. McDonald and Hyeok Kim, "When I Die, I Feel Small: Electronic Game Characters and the Social Self," *Journal of Broadcasting and Electronic Media,* 45, Spring 2001, 241–58.
20. Jane Healy, *Failure to Connect: How Computers Affect Our Children's Minds—for Better and Worse* (New York: Simon & Schuster, 1998).
21. John Markoff, "Joseph Weizenbaum, Famed Programmer, Is Dead at 85," *New York Times,* March 13, 2008.
22. Rideout, Roberts, and Foehr, *Generation M,* 46.
23. Ibid., 16.
24. Ibid., 46.
25. Steve Farkas, Jean Johnson, and Ann Duffett, "A Lot Easier Said Than Done: Parents Talk About Raising Children in Today's America," Public Agenda, 2002.
26. Bob Livingstone, "The Media-Parent Connection: Overplaying Fear—How It Hurts and What We Can Do About It," www.boblivingstone.com.
27. J. Veitch, S. Bagley, K. Ball, and J. Salmon, "Where Do Children Usually Play?: A Qualitative Study of Parents' Perceptions of Influences on Children's Active Free Play," *Health & Place* 12:4, 2005, 383–93.
28. Maia Szalavitz, "*Today* Show Revises Number of Missing Kids Downwards," STATS Organization, George Mason University, March 9, 2006.
29. Kay Randall, "Mom Needs an A: Hovering, Hyper-Involved Parents the Subject of Landmark Study," www.utexas.edu, March 26–April 2, 2007.
30. Susan Gregory Thomas, *Buy, Buy Baby: How Consumer Culture Manipulates Parents and Harms Young Minds* (New York: Houghton Mifflin, 2007).

BIBLIOGRAPHY

Arnold, Johann Christoph. *Endangered: Your Child in a Hostile World.* Farmington, Pa.: Plough, 2000.

Begley, Sharon. *Train Your Mind, Change Your Brain: How a New Science Reveals Our Extraordinary Potential to Transform Ourselves.* New York: Ballantine, 2007.

Biddulph, Steve. *Raising Boys: Why Boys Are Different—And How to Help Them Become Happy and Well-Balanced Men.* Berkeley, Calif.: Celestial Arts, 1998.

Britz-Crecelius, Heidi. *Children at Play: Using Waldorf Principles to Foster Childhood Development.* South Paris, Maine: Park Street, 1996.

Brooks, Andrée Aelion. *Children of Fast-Track Parents: Raising Self-Sufficient and Confident Children in an Achievement-Oriented World.* New York: Viking, 1989.

Chudacoff, Howard. *Children at Play: An American History.* New York: New York University Press, 2007.

Conner, Bobbi. *Unplugged Play: No Batteries. No Plugs. Pure Fun.* New York: Workman, 2007.

Crain, William. *Reclaiming Childhood: Letting Children Be Children in Our Achievement-Oriented Society.* New York: Times Books, 2003.

DeGrandpre, Richard. *Ritalin Nation: Rapid-Fire Culture and the Transformation of Human Consciousness.* New York: Norton, 1999.

Doe, Mimi. *Busy but Balanced: Practical and Inspirational Ways to Create a Calmer, Closer Family.* New York: St. Martin's, 2001.

Drew, Naomi. *Peaceful Parents, Peaceful Kids: Practical Ways to Create a Calm and Happy Home.* New York: Kensington, 2000.

Elkind, David. *The Hurried Child.* 25th Anniversary Edition. New York: Da Capo, 2006.

——. *The Power of Play: Learning What Comes Naturally.* New York: Da Capo, 2007.

Goleman, Daniel. *Emotional Intelligence: Why It Can Matter More Than IQ.* New York: Bantam, 1995.

Grossman, Dave, and Gloria Degaetano. *Stop Teaching Our Kids to Kill: A Call to Action Against TV, Movie and Video Game Violence.* New York: Crown, 1999.

Gurian, Michael, and Kathy Stevens. *The Mind of Boys: Saving Our Sons from Falling Behind in School and Life.* New York: Jossey-Bass, 2005

Hayes, Dade. *Anytime Playdate: Inside the Preschool Entertainment Boom, or How Television Became My Baby's Best Friend.* New York: Free Press, 2008.

Healy, Jane. *Failure to Connect: How Computers Affect Our Children's Minds—and What We Can Do About It.* New York: Simon & Schuster, 1998.

——. *Your Child's Growing Mind: Brain Development and Learning from Birth to Adolescence.* New York: Broadway, 2004.

Honoré, Carl. *In Praise of Slowness: Challenging the Cult of Speed.* New York: HarperCollins, 2004.

James, Oliver. *Affluenza: When Too Much Is Never Enough.* London: Random House, 2006.

Kabat-Zinn, Jon, and Myla Kabat-Zinn. *Everyday Blessings: The Inner Work of Mindful Parenting.* New York: Hyperion, 1998.

Kenison, Katrinka. *Mitten Strings for God: Reflections for Mothers in a Hurry.* New York: Warner, 2002.

Levine, Mel. *A Mind at a Time.* New York: Simon & Schuster, 2002.

Louv, Richard. *Last Child in the Woods: Saving Our Children from Nature-Deficit Disorder.* Chapel Hill, N.C.: Algonquin, 2006.

Mellon, Nancy. *Storytelling with Children.* Gloucestershire, U.K.: Hawthorn, 2000.

Morrish, Ronald. *Secrets of Discipline: 12 Keys for Raising Responsible Children.* Ontario: Woodstream, 1998.

Patterson, Barbara, and Pamela Bradley. *Beyond the Rainbow Bridge: Nurturing Our Children from Birth to Seven.* Amesbury, Mass.: Michaelmas, 2000.

Payne, Kim, and Kate Hammond. *Games Children Play: How Games and Sport Help Children Develop.* Gloucestershire, U.K.: Hawthorn, 1997.

Petrash, Jack. *Navigating the Terrain of Childhood: A Guidebook for Meaningful Parenting and Heartfelt Discipline.* Kensington, Md.: Nova Institute, 2004.

——. *Understanding Waldorf Education: Teaching from the Inside Out.* Beltsville, Md.: Gryphon House, 2002.

Pipher, Mary. *The Shelter of Each Other: Rebuilding Our Families.* New York: Putnam's, 1996.

Putnam, Robert. *Bowling Alone: The Collapse and Revival of American Community.* New York: Simon & Schuster, 2001.

Rosenfeld, Alvin, and Nicole Wise. *The Over-Scheduled Child: Avoiding the Hyper-Parenting Trap.* New York: St. Martin's, 2001.

Sacks, Oliver. *The Man Who Mistook His Wife for a Hat and Other Clinical Tales.* New York: Summit, 1985.

Schlosser, Eric. *Fast Food Nation.* Boston: Houghton Mifflin, 2001.

Schor, Juliet B. *Born to Buy: The Commercialized Child and the New Consumer Culture.* New York: Scribner, 2004.

Sherlock, Marie. *Living Simply with Children: A Voluntary Simplicity Guide for*

Moms, Dads, and Kids Who Want to Reclaim the Bliss of Childhood and the Joy of Parenting. New York: Three Rivers, 2003.

Siegel, Daniel. *The Developing Mind.* New York: Guilford, 1999.

Siegel, Daniel, and Mary Hartzell. *Parenting from the Inside Out.* New York: Jeremy Tarcher, 2003.

Susanka, Sarah. *The Not So Big Life: Making Room for What Really Matters.* New York: Random House, 2007.

Thomas, Susan Gregory. *Buy, Buy Baby: How Consumer Culture Manipulates Parents and Harms Young Minds.* Boston: Houghton Mifflin, 2007.

Walsh, Peter. *It's All Too Much: An Easy Plan for Living a Richer Life with Less Stuff.* New York: Free Press, 2007.

INDEX

U

V

W

X

Y

About the Authors

A consultant and trainer to more than sixty U.S. independent and public schools, KIM JOHN PAYNE, M.Ed., has been a school counselor, adult educator, consultant, researcher, and educator for nearly thirty years and a private family counselor for more than fifteen years. He regularly gives keynote addresses at international conferences for educators, parents, and therapists and runs workshops and training sessions around the world. In each role, Payne has been helping children, adolescents, and families explore issues such as social difficulties with siblings and classmates, attention and behavioral issues at home and school, and emotional issues such as defiance, aggression, addiction, and low self-esteem. A partner of the Alliance for Childhood in Washington, D.C., he has also consulted for educational associations in South Africa, Hungary, Israel, Russia, Switzerland, Ireland, Canada, Australia, and the United Kingdom. Payne has worked extensively with the North American and U.K. Waldorf educational movements. He is currently project director of the Waldorf Collaborative Counseling Program at Antioch University New England and the Codirector of an extensive research program that is exploring and developing a drug-free approach to attention-related disorders. His Social Inclusion Approach, a program aimed at understanding and breaking the patterns of teasing and bullying, has been implemented in hundreds of schools. Australian born, he now lives with his wife, two children, and his in-laws in Harlemville, New York. For more information, visit his website at simplicityparenting.com.

Simplicity Parenting is one of several books LISA M. ROSS has written. She has been involved in publishing for twenty years, as an editor and literary agent, and now exclusively as a writer. She lives in Columbia County, New York, with her husband and her two children. More information about her work is available at lisamross.com.